Conversational English – Hindi Dictionary

Sri Garib Das Oriental Series No. 176

Conversational English – Hindi Dictionary

Compiled by

Anil Gupta

Sri Satguru Publications
A Division of
Indian Books Centre
Delhi-India

Published by:
Sri Satguru Publications
A Division of
Indian Books Centre
Oriental and Indological Publishers
40/5, Shakti Nagar,
Delhi - 110 007
INDIA

First Edition : Delhi, 1994.

ISBN - 81-7030-393-1.

Printed in India

A

A, B, C,	*Ka, kha, ga*
Abacus	*Gintara*
Abandon	*Tyagna, Tajna*
Abatement	*Ghatav*
Abdication	*Padtyag*
Abdomen	*Kokh*
Abducted	*Ahrit*
Ability	*Laykee*
Ablation	*Nahan*
Able	*Kabil*
Ablution	*Nitty-kriya*
Ably	*Yogyatapoorvak*
Abode	*Alay, Nivas*
Abode habitat	*Basa*
Aboriginal	*Adivasee*
Abortion	*Garbhpata*
Above	*Ooper*
Above all	*Sarvopari*
Abrasion	*Ghisaee*
Abridged form	*Sankshep*
Abridgement	*Sankshipti*
Absconder	*Farar, Bhagora*
Absence	*Gair maujoodgi*
Absent	*Anupasthit*
Absolute	*Nira,*
Absorbed	*Dhyanmagn*
Absorbent	*Avshoshak*
Abstaining from food	*Nirahar*
Abstemious	*Alpaharee*
Abstract	*Sar*
Abstruse	*Durooh*
Abstruseness	*Goorhta*
Absurd	*Ootpatang*

Abundance	*Bahutayat*
Abundant	*Vipul*
Abuse	*Gali*
Acacia tree	*Keekar, Babool*
Academic	*Gyanik*
Accept	*Sweekarna*
Acceptable	*Sweekary*
Acceptance	*Sweekar, Manzooree*
Access	*Abhigam*
Accessibility	*Gamyata*
Accessible	*Gammy*
Accident	*Durghatna, Vardat*
Accompaniment	*Sang-sath*
Accomplishment of object	*Karrysiddhi*
According (to)	*Mutabik*
According to class	*Darjavar*
According to rule	*Niyamanusar*
According to the situation	*Yathasthiti*
Accordingly	*Tadansuar*
Account	*Khata, Hisab*
Account-Book	*Bahee khata, Lakha bahee*
Accounts	*Hisab-kitab*
Accumulated	*Sancit*
Accuracy	*Parishudhta*
Accusation	*Arop, Ilzam*
Accused	*Abhiyukta*
Accuser	*Abhiyokta*
Accustomed	*Abbhyast, Adee*
Ache	*Pirana*
Achievement	*Kiya karaya, Siddhi*
Achromatic	*Avarnak*

Acid	*Amml, Tazab*
Acknowledgement of receipt	*Praptika*
Acquaintance	*Vakfeeyat, Ashna, Jan-pehcan, Milnavala*
Acquainted	*Paricit*
Acquiescence	*Maun-sehmati*
Acquired	*Abhigriheet*
Acquisition	*Abhiggrahan*
Acquittance	*Rinmukti*
Acquitted	*Baree*
Acrobat	*Kalabaz*
Across	*Arpar*
Act	*Karna*
Act of heating	*Tapan*
Act of hiding	*Gopan*
Act of lifting	*Uttolan*
Act of loading	*Ladaee*
Act of melting	*Galavat*
Act of mixing	*Milavat*
Act of peeling	*Chilan*
Act of pestling	*Ghotaee*
Act of piercing	*Bhadan*
Act of returning	*Vapsee*
Act of selection	*Cayan*
Act of separating	*Chanta*
Act of sewing	*Silvaee*
Act of showing	*Dikhlaee*
Act of singing	*Gan*
Act of stealing	*Chaury*
Act of sucking	*Chuoshan*
Act of swimming	*Tairaee*
Act of touching	*Choot*

Act of weaving	*Bunvaee*
Act of weighing	*Tulvaee, Tolan*
Actable	*Abhinay*
Acting	*Abhinay, Adakaree*
Acting upon	*Amal*
Action	*Kriya*
Active	*Kriya sheel, Sachasht*
Activities	*Kriyakalap*
Activity	*Sakkriyta*
Actor	*Abhineta*
Actress	*Abhinettree*
Actual	*Vastav*
Add	*Jorna*
Addicted to drinking	*Nashabaz*
Addiction	*Vyasan*
Addition and subtraction	*Jor-bakee*
Additional	*Atirikt*
Address	*Pata, Sambodhan*
Addressing one's ownself	*Swagat*
Adept	*Kritviddy*
Adherent	*Matanuyaee*
Adhesion	*Asanjan*
Adhesive	*Lesdar, Picpica, Asanjak*
Adhesive of flour	*Laee*
Adieu	*Vida*
Adjacent	*Nikatash, Asann, Nikatvartee*
Adjournment	*Karrysthagan*
Adjudication	*Faisla*
Adjusted	*Samayojit, Samanjit, Samayukt*
Adjuster	*Samayojak*
Administered	*Prashasit*

Administration	*Prashasan*
Administrative	*Prashasanik*
Administrator	*Prashasak*
Admirable	*Prashansneey*
Admiral	*Nausenapati*
Admiration	*Prashansa*
Admirer	*Prashansak*
Admission	*Pravesh, Dakhila*
Admission fee	*Pravesh shulk*
Admit	*Manna*
Admonition	*Ghurkee, Bhartsna*
Adolescence	*Navyauvan*
Adolescent	*Kamsin, Kishor*
Adopted	*Dattak*
Adopted son	*Palat, Mutbanna*
Adoption	*Dattak-grehan*
Adoptive father	*Dattak pita*
Adoptive mother	*Dattak-mata*
Adorable	*Araddy, Vandneey*
Adoration	*Vandana*
Adult	*Balig*
Adulterated	*Milavatee*
Adulterer	*Vyabhicaree*
Adulteress	*Pargamini*
Adultery	*Vyabhicar, Pargaman*
Adultress	*Vyabhicarinee*
Advance	*Saee, Aggrim, Peshgee*
Advancement	*Uruj*
Advent of luck	*Bhaggyadheen*
Adverb	*Kriya visheshan*
Adverse public opinion	*Lokapvad*
Adversity	*Vipta*
Advertised	*Viggyapit*

Advertisement	*Ishthar, Viggyapan*
Advertiser	*Viggyapak*
Advice	*Seekh, Paramarsh, Salah*
Adviser	*Paramarshdata, Salahkar*
Advisory council	*Mantrana-parishad*
Advocate	*Advokat*
Advocate General	*Mahadhivakta*
Aerial	*Havaee, Akashee*
Aerodrome	*Havaee-adda*
Aeronautical	*Vaimanik*
Aeroplane	*Vayuyan, Viman, Havaee jahaz*
Affectedness	*Coclabazee*
Affection	*Preeti, Sneh*
Affectionate	*Muhabatee, Dildar, Snahee*
Afferent	*Abhivahee*
Affidavit	*Shapath-pattr, Halafnama*
Affiliation	*Sambaddheekaran*
Affirmative	*Sweekaratmak*
Afflicted	*Dukhiya, Diljala*
Affliction	*Natsal*
Affluence	*Vibhav*
Afforestation	*Vanropan*
Affricate	*Sparsh sangharshee*
Aforesaid	*Poorvokt*
Afraid	*Bhaybheet*
After	*Bad*
After all	*Akhir*
After birth	*Janmotsav*
After noon	*Aprahn*
After one's heart	*Manbhaya*
After that	*Tadantar*
After wards	*Tatpashcat*
After-effect	*Uttar prabhav*

Again	*Punah*
Again and again	*Barambar*
Against	*Khilaf, Viruddh*
Age	*Ayu, Umr*
Age limit	*Ayuseema*
Aged	*Boorha*
Agency	*Arhat, Abhikaran*
Agenda	*Karrysoochi*
Agent	*Mutsaddee, Ajent*
Aggression	*Seemantikraman*
Aggressive	*Akkramankaree, Uggr*
Agile	*Furteela*
Agitated	*Andolit, Vyakul*
Agitation	*Andolan*
Agonisingly perturbed	*Vihval*
Agonizing pain	*Tarap*
Agony	*Vedana*
Agotism	*Hamahamee*
Agrarian	*krishkeey*
Agrarianism	*Gramyavad*
Agreable	*Gavar*
Agreed	*Rajamand, Razee*
Agreement	*Rajeenama, Karar*
Agriculture	*Krishik*
Agriculture science	*Krishi vigyan*
Agriculturist	*Kashtkar*
Ague	*Jooree*
Ailment	*Maraj, Vyadhi*
Aim	*Lakshya, Dhyey*
Aimless	*Nishoprayojan*
Air	*Hava*
Air mail	*Havaee dak*

Air pilot	*Havabaz*
Air-hostess	*Viman-paricarika*
Air-port	*Havai-adda*
Air-route	*Havai rasta*
Airconditioned	*Vatanukoolit*
Aircraft carrier	*Viman-vahak*
Airfield	*Vimankshettr*
Airy	*Havadar*
Airy palace	*Hava mahal*
Alarm	*Alarm*
Alarm clock	*Alarm gharee*
Album	*Elbam*
Alchemy	*Keemiya*
Alcohilism	*Nashabazee*
Alcohol	*Surasar, Maddysar, Sarab*
Alert	*Caukanna*
Alertness	*Custee, Mustaidee*
Aleximorphic	*Vishnashak*
Algebra	*Beejganit*
Alias	*Urf*
Alienation	*Manomalinny*
Alignment	*Sanrakhan*
Alive	*Zinda, Salamat*
Alkali	*Kshar*
All	*Akhil, Sarv*
All alone	*Akelee jan*
All entire	*Sab-kuch*
All of a sudden	*Sehsa, Acanak*
All out	*Jeetor*
All parts of body	*Sarvang*
All purpose	*Sarvarth*
All the time	*Uthtabaithta*
All-around discussion	*Pricarca*

All-conquering	*Sarvjit*
All-devouring	*Sarvgrasee*
All-in-all	*Sarva-sarva*
All-pervading	*Dig-vyapt, Sarvvyapak, Sarvgat*
All-round	*Sarvatah, Sarvangeen*
Allaying a doubt	*Shanka-samadhan*
Allegation	*Akshap, Abhikathan*
Alleged	*Abhikathit*
Allegiance	*Nishtha*
Allegory	*Prateek-katha*
Alliance	*Sanshray*
Allied	*Sanshrit*
Allies	*Mitrashtra*
Allocation	*Vinidhan*
Allopathy	*Ailopaithee*
Allotment	*Niyatan*
Allowance	*Bhatta*
Allure	*Rijhana, Lalcana*
Almighty	*Sarvshaktiman*
Almirah	*Almaree*
Almond	*Badam*
Almost	*Sham sabera, Takreeban*
Almost round	*Golmatol*
Alms	*Bhiksha, Bhikh*
Alms box	*Dan-patr*
Alone	*Nihang, Akela, Tanha*
Along with	*Sahit*
Along with wife	*Sapatneek*
Alphabet	*Varnmala*
Alphabetical glossary	*Varnanukramanika*
Alphabetical order	*Aksharkram, Akaradikram, Varnkarm*
Already counted	*Ginaginaya*

Also	*Bhee*
Altar of marriage	*Canvree*
Alterable	*Parivartansheel*
Alteration	*Raddobadal, Tabdeelee*
Altered	*Parivartit*
Although	*Yaddyapi*
Altruist	*Pararthi, Pararthvadee*
Altuism	*Pararthvad*
Alum	*Phitkaree*
Aluminium	*Alyoominiyam*
Always	*Hamesha*
Always lagging behind	*Phisaddee*
Amateur	*Shaukiya*
Amazed	*Acambhit, Dang*
Amazement	*Vismay, Achambha*
Ambassador	*Rajdoot*
Ambiguity	*Dwidharthakta*
Ambiguous	*Dhidharthah, Dufaslee, Ubhayarthak*
Ambition	*Mahattvakanksha*
Amen	*Ameen*
Amendment	*Tarmeem*
Amentia	*Balishshy*
Ammonium chloride	*Nausadar*
Ammunition	*Golabarood*
Amoke blue	*Abbasee*
Amomum sibulatum	*Baree Ilayacee*
Amorosity	*Shringarikta*
Amorous	*Rasik*
Amorous activity	*Raman*
Amount	*Dhanrashi, Rashi*
Amount drawn	*Aharan*
Amount realized	*Ugahee*

Amphitheatre	*Cakkrmandap*
Amputation	*Angacched*
Amulet	*Taveez, Jantar*
Amused	*Amodit*
Amusement	*Manovinod, Mahbhahlav, Manoranjan*
Anachronism	*Kaldosh*
Anaemia	*Rakt-ksenta*
Anaesthetic	*Nishcatak, Samvadanharee*
Analgetic	*Peeraharee*
Analysis	*Vishlashan*
Anarchist	*Arajaktavadee*
Anarchistic	*Arajak*
Anarchy	*Arajakta*
Ancestor	*Poorvaj*
Anchor	*Langar*
Ancient	*Praceen, Puratan,Purana*
And	*Tatha,Aur*
Angel	*Farishta*
Anger	*Gussa, Krodh*
Angle	*Kon*
Angry look	*Tyoree*
Anguish	*Vyatha*
Anhydrous	*Ajal*
Animal	*Janvar, Pashu*
Animal world	*Pashu Jagat*
Animate world	*Jeev-jagat*
Animosity	*Vaimanassy*
Ankle	*Gatta*
Ankle-joint	*Takhna*
Anklet	*Pazab, Noopur*
Annihilation	*Sanhar, Pralay, Nash*
Announced	*Akkhyapit*

Announcement	*Ailan*
Announcer	*Akkhyapak, Dhandhorcee*
Annual	*Varshik*
Annulment of treaty	*Sandhi-vicched*
Anointing	*Alapan, Uplapan*
Anonymous	*Gumnam*
Anonymous donation	*Guptdan*
Answer	*Javab*
Answerable	*Javabdeh*
Ant	*Ceentee*
Antagonistic	*Pratirodhee*
Anthem	*Udgeet*
Anthology	*Cayanika*
Antidote	*Vyadhihar, Marak, Tor*
Antiprogressive	*Pragativirodhee*
Antiquarian	*Puravid*
Anti-aircraft	*Havamar*
Anti-clockwise	*Vamavart*
Anti-national	*Arashtreey*
Anti-social	*Samaj-virodhee*
Antique	*Purakaleen*
Antonym	*Viparyay*
Anus	*Guda, Maldwar*
Anvit	*Nihaee*
Anxious	*Cintit*
Any	*Kisee*
Anyone	*Kahoo*
Anything crushed	*Kachumar*
Anything given in trust	*Amanat*
Apartheid	*Rangbhed*
Apartment	*Koshth*
Apathetic	*Arat*
Apex	*Shekhar, Çotee, Sheershbindu*

Aphelion	*Ravi-ucc*
Apparatus	*Upkaran*
Apparent	*Prateeyman, Zahir, Prakat*
Apparently	*Zahira, Prateeymanteh*
Apparition	*Chalava*
Appeal	*Apeel*
Appear	*Dikhna, Jhalakna, Prateet*
Appearance	*Avirbhav, Prateeti, Shakl soorat*
Appeasement	*Manuhar, Tushteekaran*
Appeasement of evil stars	*Grahshanti*
Appendix	*Parishisht*
Applause	*Vahvahee, Shabashee*
Apple	*Sab*
Applicability	*Prayojneeyta*
Applicable	*Lagoo, Prayojjy*
Applicant	*Avedak, Nivedak*
Application	*Prarthnapattr, Arzee*
Applied	*Avadit*
Apply butter, ghee etc.	*Cuparna*
Appointed	*Niyukt, Mukarar*
Appointment	*Niyukti*
Appraisal	*Koot*
Appreciation	*Gungrahan*
Appreciative fellow	*Gungrahak*
Apprehension	*Khutka, Ashanka*
Apprehensive	*Ashankit*
Apprentic	*Shikshu*
Approach	*Lag, Upgam, Rasaee*
Approach to shelter	*Sharnagati*
Approachable	*Gantavvy*
Appropriate	*Samuchit, Aucittypoorn*
Appropriateness	*Aucitty, Samucitta*

Appropriation	*Upyojan*
Approved	*Manzoor*
Approver	*Ikbaleegavah*
Approximately	*Lagbhag*
Apricot	*Khoobanee*
April	*Apprail*
Aquatic animal	*Jaljantu*
Aquatic creature	*Jalcar*
Aquatic dalliance	*Jalkali*
Aquatic festival	*Jalotsav*
Aquatic play	*Jalkreera*
Arabia	*Arab*
Arbiter	*Sakhee*
Arbitrary	*Manmana*
Arbitrary conduct	*Manmanee*
Arbitration	*Vivecan*
Arbitrator	*Vivecak*
Arborial	*Vrikshvasee*
Arbour	*Nikunj*
Arch	*Mehrab*
Archaeologist	*Puratattwaggy*
Archaeology	*Puratattw*
Archaeozoic era	*Adikalp*
Archer	*Teerandaz*
Archery	*Teerandazee*
Architect	*Vastukar*
Architecture	*Sthapatty, Vastu-kala*
Archpreceptor	*Jagadguru*
Archway	*Toran-path*
Ardent desire	*Spriha*
Arduous	*Dushvaree, Shramsaddhy*
Area	*Ilaka, Rakba*
Area Officer	*Kshetradhikaree*

Arguement	*Behas, Tark, Daleel*
Argument and counter-argument	*Vad prativad, Tark-vitark*
Argumentation	*Saval-jawab*
Arising from touch	*Sparshjanny*
Aristocracy	*Umra, kuleentantr*
Aristocrat	*Ameerzada*
Aristotle	*Arastoo*
Arithmetic	*Beeejaganit*
Arjuna	*Parth*
Arm	*Bhuja, Bahu,Bazoo*
Arm of bedstead	*Sura*
Armament	*Shastreekaran, Hathiyarbandee*
Armed	*Hathiyar band*
Armed soldier	*Shastrdharee*
Armistice	*Avhar, Sandhi-viram*
Armlet	*Bazooband, Bhujbandh*
Armour	*Baktar, Zirehbaktar*
Armoured	*Kavac dharee, Kavacit*
Armoury	*Shastragar*
Armpit	*Kankh*
Arms	*Shastr*
Army	*Fauj, Sena, Militaree*
Around	*Irdgird*
Arranged block of bricks, tiles etc.	*Catta*
Arranged in a chain	*Shrinkhalit*
Arrangement	*Intzam*
Arrayed in series	*Shrinkhlabaddh*
Arraying armies for a show-down	*Dharabandee*
Arrears	*Bakaya*
Arrest	*Giraftari, Dharpakar*

Arrival	*Agaman*
Arrive	*Pahucna*
Arrogance	*Darp*
Arrow	*Teer*
Arsenal	*Hathiyar-ghar*
Arson	*Agzanee*
Art	*Kala, Fan*
Art and craft	*Kalakaushal*
Art gallery	*Kalabhavan*
Art of dancing	*Nrittykala*
Art of giving sexual pleasure	*Kamkala*
Art of making, repairing, handling machine	*Yantr-vidya*
Art of wrestling	*Mallvidya*
Artful	*Kalapoorn*
Artificial	*Krittrim, Naklee, Banavatee*
Artificiality of manner	*Cocla*
Artillery	*Topkhana*
Artisan	*Dastkar, Mistree*
Artist	*Kalakar*
Artistic	*Kalatmak*
As	*Jaisa*
As before	*Yathapoorv, Yathavat*
As far as possible	*Yathasambhav, Yathashakti*
As if	*Goya, Mano*
As longed for	*Manvanchit*
As mentioned	*Yathakathit*
As much as	*Jitna*
As per	*Yatha*
As per leisure	*Yathavkash*
As per occasion	*Samayanusar*
As per order	*Aggyanusar*

As per order	*Adeshanusar*
As per statement	*Kathnanusar*
As soon as possible	*Yathasheeghr*
As, in the manner of	*Jyon*
Asafoetida	*Heeng*
Ascedance into Heaven	*Swargarohan*
Ascended	*Aroorh*
Ascent	*Carhaee, Aroh*
Ascetic	*Tapas*
Ascetical	*Tapomay*
Asexual	*Alaingik*
Ash	*Khauree*
Ashamed	*Lajjit, Sharminda*
Ashes	*Rakh*
Ashtray	*Rakhdan*
Asked for	*Munhmanga*
Asleep	*Supt*
Asparagus	*Satavar*
Aspirant	*Abhilashee*
Aspiration	*Abhilasha, Akanksha, Tamanna*
Aspired	*Akankshit*
Aspired after	*Manovanchit*
Ass	*Gadha*
Assailant	*Hamlavar*
Assembly	*Majlis, Sabha*
Assembly hall	*Sabha-bhavan*
Assembly of scholars	*Pandit sabha*
Assent	*Hamee*
Assertion of a claim	*Davedaree*
Assessment	*Nirdharan*
Assessor	*Nirdharak*
Assets and liabilities (in cash)	*Dena-pavna*

Assets and liabilities (in cash)	*Dena-lena*
Assiduous in performing duties	*Karmath*
Assigned	*Nirdisht*
Assimilated	*Atmsat*
Assistant	*Sahayak*
Associate	*Sahcar*
Associates and companions	*Havalee-mavalee*
Association	*Anjuman*
Assumption	*Abhikalpana*
Assurance	*Ashshwasan*
Assured	*Ashshwast*
Assuredly	*Zaroor*
Asthma	*Dama*
Astringency	*Kasailapan*
Astringent	*Kasaila*
Astrologer	*Jyotishee*
Astrology	*Jyotish*
Astronaut	*Antarikshyattree*
Astronomer	*Jyotirvid*
At a vital part	*Thaur-kuthaur*
At all odd hours	*Samay-kusamay*
At below market price	*Girta-parta*
At once	*Turant*
At some time	*Kabhee*
At that time	*Tabhee*
At that very place	*Vaheen*
At the proper place	*Yathasthan*
At this very place	*Yaheen*
Atheism	*Nastikta*
Atheist	*Nastik*

Athletic	*Kasratee*
Atlantic	*Atlantik*
Atlas	*Mancittravalee*
Atmosphere	*Vatavaran*
Atom	*Anu*
Atom bomb	*Anubomb*
Atonement	*Prayashcitt*
Atrium	*Prangan*
Atrocious	*Nrishans*
Attached	*kurk*
Attached to the fruit	*Phalasakt*
Attachment	*Moh-mamta*
Attachment of property	*Kurkee*
Attack	*Akkraman, Hamla*
Attacked and wounded	*Pratihat*
Attainable	*Saddhy*
Attained	*Sadhit, Labd*
Attainment	*Uplabdhi*
Attainment of one's goal	*Lakshyasiddhi*
Attempt	*Prayas*
Attendance and service	*Seva-tehal*
Attendant	*Teemardar, Anuchar*
Attention	*Tavajjah*
Attentive	*Avdhanee*
Attested	*Sakshyankit*
Attitude	*Cit-vritti*
Attitude of compassion	*Karuna-drishti*
Attitude of kindness	*Daya-drishti*
Attorney	*Nyayvadi*
Attorney General	*Mahanyayvadee*
Attorneyship	*Mukhtaree*
Attracted	*Akkrisht*

Attraction	*Khinchav, Kashish*
Attractive	*Manohar*
Attractivensss of features	*Manoharta*
Attributed	*Aropit*
Auction	*Neelam*
Audible	*Shravaneey*
Auditing	*Lekhapareekshan*
Auditor	*Janckarta*
Auditorium	*Prakshagrih*
Augmentation	*Alap*
Augur	*Shakunee*
August	*Agast*
Auspices	*Tattwadhan*
Auspicious	*Mangalkarak, Mangalik, Mubarak, Shubh*
Auspicious moment	*Lagn*
Auspicious pitcher of water	*Mangalghat*
Auspicious self	*Swastiman*
Auspicious sound	*Mangaldhwani*
Auspicious time	*Punnykal*
Auspiciousness for departure	*Cala*
Austere in food	*Mitaharee*
Austerity	*Tap*
Austerity in food	*Mitahar*
Austerity personified	*Tapomoorti*
Authentic	*Pramanik*
Authorised	*Pradhikrit*
Autobiography	*Atmkatha, Jeevani*
Autographed	*Swaksharit*
Automatic	*Swacalit*
Automatically	*Swatah*

Autonomous	*Khudmukhtar, Swayatt*
Autonomy	*Swayattta*
Autumn	*Patjhar, Sharat*
Autumn season	*Sharatkal*
Available	*Sulabh*
Avalanche	*Himanee*
Average	*Ausat*
Averment	*Drirhokti*
Averse	*Vimukh*
Aviation	*Vimancalan, Uddayan*
Aviator	*Urakoo*
Avocation	*Upvritti*
Awaited	*Prateekshy*
Awake	*Jagna*
Award	*Pancat*
Aware	*Avgat*
Awareness	*Sudh-budh*
Away	*Para*
Awe	*Rob-dab*
Awe-inspiring	*Robdar*
Awfulness	*Bheeshanta*
Awkward	*Bhadda*
Axe	*Kulhara, Gandasa*
Axiom	*Swayamtathy*
Axis	*Aksh, Dhuree*
Ayurved	*Ayurved*
Ayurvedic physician	*Vaidya*
Azimuth	*Digansh*
Azurian	*Cambaee*

B

Baby	*Chagan*
Baby's clout	*Potra*
Bachelor	*Kwara*
Back	*Pichla*
Back biter	*Cugalkhor*
Back bone	*Reerdar*
Back ground	*Prishthbhoomee*
Back part of the palm of hand	*karpristh*
Back-door	*Cor-darvaja*
Backbite	*Ninda*
Background singing	*Parshvgayan*
Backward	*Pichra*
Backyard	*Pichvara*
Bacteria	*Jeevanu*
Bad	*Kharab, Buri*
Bad colour	*Kurang*
Bad company	*Kusangati*
Bad conduct	*Kudachar*
Bad conductor	*Kucalak*
Bad custom	*Kupratha*
Bad days	*Durdin*
Bad habit	*Durvyasan*
Bad metal	*Kudhatu*
Bad motive	*Durashay*
Bad omen	*Ashakun*
Bad result	*Kuphal*
Bad shape	*Duravastha*
Bad smell	*Badboo*
Bad taste	*Kuruci*
Bad tendancy	*Kupravriti*
Bad times	*Kusamay*
Bad way	*Kumarg*

Badge	*Baij*
Badly written	*Durlekhy*
Baffling	*Ajeebogareeb*
Bag	*Thaila, Basta, Bag*
Bail	*Jamanat*
Bailee	*Ballee*
Bailiff	*Kurkameen, Ameen*
Baked in a tandoor	*Tandooree*
Baker	*Nanbaee*
Balance	*Santulan*
Balance of power	*Shakti-santulan*
Balance of trade	*Vyapar tula*
Balance-sheet	*Chittha*
Balcony	*Chajja*
Bald	*Ganja*
Ball	*Gaind*
Ball and bat	*Gaind-balla*
Balloon	*Gubbara*
Ballot	*Mata*
Ballot box	*Matdanpetika*
Bally-hoo	*Dhoom-dharakka*
Bamboo	*Bans*
Banana	*Kela*
Band	*Baja-gaja, Baind*
Banging sound	*Dharam*
Bangle of glass	*Curi, Cooree*
Bangle-seller	*Manihar*
Bank	*Kinara, Tat*
Bank of a river	*Pulin*
Bank of clouds	*Kadambinee*
Banker	*Bainkar*
Banking business	*Len-Den, Sahookara*
Banned	*Varjit*

Banner of victory	*Vijay pataka*
Banter	*Thatha*
Banyan tree	*Bargad, Vat*
Bar	*Madiralay, Maikhana*
Barber	*Naee, Hajjam*
Barber's shop	*Sailoon*
Barber's wife	*Nain*
Bard	*Caran, Bhat*
Bare	*Hurehra*
Bargainer	*Saudabaz*
Bargaining	*Saudabazee*
Bark	*Bhoonkna, Bhaunkna, Bakkal*
Barley	*Jau*
Barley seed	*Javar*
Barn	*Bhusaura*
Barometer	*Barometer*
Baron	*Nawab*
Barrack	*Bairak*
Barred by limitation	*Gatavadhi*
Barrel	*Peepa*
Barren	*Banjar*
Barren land	*Oosar*
Barrenness	*Banjhpan*
Barrister-at-law	*Bairistar, Vidhivakta*
Barter	*Vastuvinimay*
Base	*Adhar, Gadaee*
Based	*Adharit*
Baseless nonsense	*Vahee-tabahee*
Baselsss	*Niradhar*
Basement	*Tehkhana*
Bashful	*Lajeela, Lajaloo, Lajvant*
Bashfulness	*Lajeelapan*
Basic	*Buniyadee*

Basic Mantra	*Beejmantr*
Basic elements	*Mooltattw*
Basically	*Mooltah*
Basil	*Tulsee*
Basin	*Dronee*
Basket	*Tokree*
Bastard	*Haramzada*
Batch	*Jattha*
Batch of soldiers	*Garad*
Bath	*Nahana, Snan*
Bath room	*Snangrah, Gusalkhana*
Bathed in blood	*Lahoo-luhan*
Battalion	*Bataliyan*
Battery	*Marpeet, Baitree*
Battle-array	*Morcabandee*
Battle-axe	*Parashu*
Battle-field	*Yuddhkshattr, Rankshatr*
Bay	*Upsagar*
Bayonet	*Kirach*
Bead	*Guriya, Manka*
Beak	*Cancu, Conc*
Beam	*Shahteer, Beem, Kiran*
Bean	*Sem, Phalee*
Bear	*Bhaloo, Reech*
Bearable	*Sehneey, Sahhy*
Beard	*Darhee*
Bearer	*Dharankarta, Vahak*
Bearer in a hotel	*Baira*
Bearing fruit	*Phaldar*
Beast	*Haivan*
Beast of burden	*Laddoo*
Beastliness	*Pashuta, Haivaniyat*
Beastly	*Amanushik, Pashvik*

Beat	*Thonkna*
(to) beat down	*Pacharna*
Beaten	*Thukna*
Beating	*Pitant, Thukaee, Mar*
Beautiful	*Sundar, Roopvant, Khoobsoorat*
Beautiful handwiriting	*Sulekh*
Beautiful to look at	*Sudarshan*
Beautiful woman	*Roopasee, Sundaree*
Beauty	*Sundarta, Khoobsoortee*
Beauty of features	*Chavi*
Because	*Coonki*
Bed	*Palang, Shaiya, Masehree*
Bed bug	*Khatmal*
Bed of arrows	*Sharshaiya*
Bed of flowers	*Pushpshaiya*
Bed of flowers and vegetables	*Kyaree*
Bed side towards the feet	*Payanta*
Bed-chamber	*Shiynagar*
Bed-cover	*Cadar*
Bed-cushion	*Gadda*
Bed-fellow	*Hambistar*
Bed-ridden	*Shayyagrast*
Bed-room	*Shayan kaksh*
Bed-sheet	*Bichavan*
Bed-sore	*Shayyavran*
Bed-spread	*Khes, Takht-posh*
Bedding	*Bichona, Bistar*
Bedding and covering	*Orana bicchauna*
Bedstead	*Paryank*
Beef	*Gomans*

Befitting a human being	*Manavocit*
Befitting a munsif	*Munsifana*
Befitting remark	*Phabtee*
Before	*Samaksh*
Beg	*Mangna*
Beggar	*Bhikharee, Bhikhmanga, Mangta*
Beggar's bowl	*Khappar*
Beginning	*Arambh, Prarambh, Shurooat*
Begun	*Arabdh*
Behaviour	*Bartav, Vyavhar, Salook*
Behold	*Avlokna*
(to) behold	*Bilokna, Vilokna*
Beholden	*Kritarth*
Behoving women	*Striyocit*
Being	*Vujood*
Belch	*Dakarna*
Believing	*Vishwasan*
Bell	*Ghantee*
Belle	*Padmini, Naeenavalee*
Belleric myrobalam tree	*Bahara*
Bellicosity	*Akharabazee*
Belligerent	*Yuyutsu, Yuddhrat*
Bellow cow, buffalo	*Ranbhana*
Belly	*Pet*
Belonging to a city	*Shehree*
Belonging to a foreign country	*Pardeshee*
Belonging to a high family	*Khandani*
Belonging to a marriage party	*Baratee*

Belonging to previous time	*Poorvkalik*
Belonging to the middle class	*Maddhyvargeey*
Beloved	*Ladla, Mehboob, Praysee, Pranpyara*
Beloved one	*Premika, Prempatr*
Beloved woman	*Mehbooba*
Below	*Tala, Neeca*
Belt	*Mekhla*
Bemon	*Rona-kalpna*
Bench	*Banc*
Bend	*Jhukaw, Kham, Jhukna*
(to) bend	*Lacna, Lepna*
Beneath	*Adhah*
Benedictory auspicious	*Mangalprad*
Benedictory prologue	*Mangalacar*
Benedictory words	*Swastivacan*
Benefactor	*Upkarta*
Beneficence	*Upkar*
Beneficial	*Hitkar, Kalyankaree*
Beneficial to public	*Janopyogee*
Benevolence	*Parhit, Pararth*
Benevolent	*Paropkaree, Upkaree*
Benevolent to all	*Sarvopkaree*
Bengal	*Vang*
Bent	*Rujhan, Pranat, Nati, Tarha*
Bequest	*Rikth dan*
Bereaved	*Shokgrast, , Shoksantapt*
Bereft	*Rahit*
Beseech abjectively	*Ririyana*
Besides	*Alava, Siva*
Besmeared	*Lathpath*
Besotted	*Dhutt*

Best	*Shreshth, Uttam*
Best of all	*Sarvshreshth*
Bestowing	*Sampradan*
Bet	*Badna*
Betel seller	*Panvaree*
Betel-leaf	*Pan, Gilauree*
Betel-nut	*Suparee*
Betrayal	*Vishwasghat*
Betrothal	*Vardan*
Better	*Behtar*
Better condition	*Sadgati*
Betterment	*Bahtaree*
Bewildered	*Udbhrant, Badhavas*
Bicameral	*Dvisadnatmak*
Bicycle	*Bysikil*
Bid	*Bolee*
Biennial	*Dosala, Dvivarshik*
Bier	*Arthee, Janaja*
Big black ant	*Ceenta*
Big cooking pot	*Deg*
Big doll	*Gudda*
Big flat metallic dish	*Thal*
Big knife	*Chura*
Big needle	*Sua*
Big oven	*Bhatthee*
Big piece of stone	*Dheem*
Big pitcher	*Gagra*
Big reel	*Parata*
Big roundish water pot	*Kalash*
Big shallow pan	*Tasla*
Big trap	*Mahajal*
Bigamy	*Dvivivah*
Bigotted	*Kathmulla*

Bilateral	*Ubhaypaksheey, Dutarfa*
Bile	*Pitt*
Bilingual	*Dubhashiya*
Bill	*Prappyak*
Bill of exchange	*Hundee*
Billionaire	*Arabpati*
Billow	*Hilkora*
Binding	*Jild, Bandhan*
(to) bind tightly	*Jakarna*
Bio-chemistry	*Jeev-rasayan*
Bio-physics	*Jeev-phautikee*
Biographer	*Jeevaneekar*
Biography	*Jeevanee, Jeevan-carit*
Biologist	*Jeev-vaiggyanik*
Biology	*Jeev viggyan*
Bird	*Parinda, Pakshee, Khag, Panchee*
Bird droppings	*Beet*
Bird-catcher	*Cireemar*
Birth	*Paidaish, Janm*
Birth and death	*Marna jeena, Janm-maran*
Birth and rebirth	*Janm janmantar*
Birth anniversary	*Varshganth*
Birth day	*Janmdin, Salgireh*
Birth place	*Janm sthan*
Birth-rate	*Janm-dar*
Birthday of God Ram	*Ramnavmee*
Birthday of Lord Krishna	*Janmashtmee*
Biscuit	*Biskut*
Bisector	*Ardhak*
Bisexual	*Dvilingee*
Bit	*Khand, Khanp*
Bit of tough flesh	*Cheechra*

Bitch	*Kutiya*
Biting (beast)	*Katoo*
Bits gnawed by birds	*Kutran*
Bitter	*Karva*
Bitter and astringent	*Karva & kasaila*
Bitter enmity	*Katakatee*
Bitter gourd	*Toonba, Karala, Titlaukee*
Bitter remark	*Katookti*
Bitter taste	*Karvahat*
Bitterness	*Katuta, Karvapan*
Black	*Kala, Syah*
Black bee	*Madhukar, Bhramar, Bhring, Bhaunra*
Black colour	*Kajra*
Black gram	*Urad*
Black list	*Kalee soochi*
Black magic	*Yantr-mantr*
Black market	*Kalabazar, Corbazar*
Black money	*Kaladhan*
Black ointment	*Momiyaee*
Black salt	*Kala namak*
Black-board	*Shyampatt*
Black-out	*Jhanee, Cirag-gul*
Black-pepper	*Kalee mirc*
Blackened	*Kalushit*
Blackish cobra	*Kala nag*
Blackish deep red	*Karaundiya*
Blackish green	*Kahee*
Blackness	*Syahee, Kalikh*
Blacksmith	*Lohar*
Blacky	*Kaloota*
Bladder-stone	*Pathree*
Blade	*Blad*

Blank	*Nirank*
Blank verse	*Mukt chand, Atukantkavita*
Blanket	*Kambal*
Blast furnace	*Dhaman-bhatthee*
Blaze	*Lehak, Dahakna*
(to) blaze	*Dhadhakna, Lehakna*
Bleached	*Viranjit*
Bleat	*Mimiyana*
Blemish	*Khot, Lanchan*
Blended together	*Akjan*
Blessed	*Dhanny*
Blessed with a protector	*Sanath*
Blessedness	*Parmanand*
Blessing	*Dua, Ashish, Asheervad*
Blind	*Soor, Andha, Drishtiheen*
Blind devotee	*Andhbhakt*
Blind devotion	*Andhbhakti*
Blind tradition	*Andhparampara*
Blind valley	*Andhee ghatee*
Blindfolding	*Parcha*
Blink	*Mulmulana*
Blinking of an eye	*Nimish*
Blister	*Phaphola*
Blkackmail	*Bhayadohan*
Block	*Blak*
Block of wood	*Kunda*
Blockade	*Nakabandee*
Blockhead	*Ghamar*
Blood	*Lahoo, Khoon, Rakt*
Blood corpuscle	*Rakt-kanika*
Blood-pressure	*Raktcap*
Bloodshed	*Raktpat, Khoon-kharaba*
Bloody	*Raktranjit*

Bloody scuffle	*Mar-kat*
Bloom	*Bikasna*
Blossom	*Baur, Doda*
(to) blossom	*Khilna*
Blotless	*Akalush*
Blotting paper	*Sokhta*
Blouse	*Kurtee*
Blow	*Aghat, Prahar*
Blow at the vitals	*Marmprahar*
Blow given with the hand	*Thapara*
Blow the nose	*Sinakna*
Blow-pipe	*Dhaunknee, Funknee, Phunknee*
Blue	*Neela*
Blue lotus	*Neelophar, Indeevar, Neelkamal*
Blue-eyed	*Neelaksh*
Blueness	*Neelima, Neelapan*
Bluff	*Bhabhkee*
Bluffer	*Dhuppalbaz*
Blunt	*Kund, Khartal*
(to) blunt	*Gonthna*
Bluntness	*Rukhaee*
Boar	*Janglee suar*
Board	*Daftee, Bord*
Boast	*Garvokti*
Boastful	*Shakheebaz*
Boasting	*Shakhee*
Boat	*Nauka, Naw, Kashtee*
Boating	*Nauka vihar*
Boatman	*Manjhee, Mallah*
Bodge	*Dhuppal*
Bodice	*Colee*
Bodily	*Shareer, Jismanee*

Bodily infliction	*Yatna*
Body	*Deh, Badan, Tan, Jism, Kaya*
Body and soul	*Dehatm*
Body like a flower	*Gulbadan*
Bodyguard	*Ang rakshak, Shareer rakshak*
Boil	*Phunsee*
(to) boil	*Ubalana, Seejhna*
(to) boil and bubble	*Curna*
(to) boil in syrup	*Pagna*
(to) boil over	*Uphanana*
Boil caused by hair	*Baltor*
Boiled rice	*Bhat*
Boiled rice-water	*Manr*
Boiling	*Kwathan*
Boiling point	*Kwathanank*
Bold	*Diler*
Boldly	*Nihsankoc*
Boldness	*Dileree, Nirbheekta*
Bolt	*Baltoo, Citkanee, Citkanee*
Bomb	*Bam*
Bomb shell	*Bamgola*
Bomb-explosion	*Bamkand*
Bombing	*Bambaree, Golabaree*
Bond	*Baund, Rin patr*
Bondage of deed	*Karmbandhan*
Bone	*Har, Asthi, Haddee*
Bony	*Asthimay*
Book	*Pothee, Kitab, Pustak*
Book shop	*Pustaka ghar, Kitab-ghar*
Book-binder	*Zildsaz, Daftaree*
Book-binding	*Zild-bandee*
Book-post	*Pustak dak*
Book-series	*Granthmala*

Book-worm	*Kitabee keera*
Booking clerk	*Tikat baboo*
Booking office	*Tikat-ghar*
Bookish	*Kitabee*
Booklet	*Pustika*
Boorish	*Lanth, Jangloo*
Boot	*Boot*
Boquet	*Guldasta*
Borax	*Suhaga*
Border	*Sarhad*
Border-line	*Seema-rekha*
Bordered	*Kinaree dar*
Bore	*Beendhana*
Bored	*Chiddrit*
Boring gadget	*Sumba*
Born	*Janm*
Born blind	*Janmandh*
Born companions	*Hampyala hamnivala*
Born in a high family	*Kuleen*
Born of	*Janit*
Born of Imagination	*Kalpnaprasoot*
Born of that	*Tadbhav*
Born together	*Yamaj*
Born together of the same mother	*Sehjanma*
Borrow	*Dharna*
Botanist	*Vanaspatigya*
Botany	*Vanaspativigyan*
Both	*Dono*
Both ways	*Ubhaytah*
Bottle	*Botal*
Bottle guard	*Laukee, Ghiya*
Bottom	*Talee, Ganr, Tala*

Bottomless	*Bepanda*
Bought	*Kreet*
Bounce	*Tippa*
Bound	*Baddh*
Bound by one's word	*Vacanbaddh*
Boundary	*Seema, Catuseema, Cauhaddee*
Boundary of a field	*Para*
Boundary wall	*Cahardeevaree*
Boundless joy	*Ananda tirak*
Bounty	*Abhidan*
Bow	*Dhanush, Kaman*
Bow-string	*Jya, Prattyanca*
Bowed	*Namit*
Bowed low	*Vinat*
Bower of peace	*Shantikunj*
Bowery alcove	*Kunj-kuteer*
Bowl of stone	*Kundee*
Bowman	*Banait*
Box	*Baksa, Sandook*
Box for betel leaves	*Pandan*
Boxer	*Mukkebaz, Ghoonsebaz*
Boxing	*Mukkebazee*
Boy	*Lalla, Launda, Larka, Chokra, Balak*
Boy-child	*Babua*
Boycott	*Bahishkar*
Boyhood	*Balkal, Balakpan*
Bracelet	*Kangan*
Bracket	*Koshthak*
Brag	*Seetna*
Braggadocio	*Lantaranee*
Braggart	*Barbola*
Bragging	*Deeng*

Brahmanism	*Brahmmanvad*
Brahmin	*Pandit, Brahman*
Braid (of hair)	*Venee*
Braiding	*Marhee*
Brain	*Mastishk, Dimag, Bheja*
Brain racking	*Sirkhapaoo, Magajpaccee*
Brake	*Brek*
Bran	*Cokar*
Branch	*Dalee, Shakha, Dal*
Brass	*Peetal*
Bravado	*Zeet*
Brave	*Shoor, Veer, Mardana, Janbaz, Bahadur*
Bravery	*Veerta, Bahaduree, Mardangee*
Brawl	*Bamcakh*
Breach of law	*Vidhibhang*
Breach of peace	*Shantibhang*
Breach of promise	*Vacanbhang, Vada-khilafee*
Breach of treaty	*Sandhibhang*
Breach of trust	*Nyasbhang, Khayanat*
Breadth	*Cauraee*
Break	*Vicched*
(to) break	*Tootna, Torna*
Breakable	*Bhangy*
Breakage	*Toot, Tootphoot*
Breakfast	*Nashta, Kaleva*
Breaking	*Taraka, Bhanjan*
Breaking open	*Udbhedan*
Breast	*Stan, Vaksh*
Breast-sucking	*Stanpan*
Breath	*Sans, Dam*
Breathless	*Badam*
Breeze	*Sameer, Bayar*

Brevity *Laghav*
Bribe *Rishvat, Ghoos*
Bribee *Rishvatkhor*
Bribery *Rishvatkhoree*
Brick *Eeent*
Bride *Dulhan, Bannee*
Bridegroom *Var, Dulha, Banna*
Bridegroom's party *Varpaksh*
Bridegroom's shaplet *Sehara*
Bridge *Pul, Setu*
Bridle *Lagam*
Brief *Mukhtasar, Sankshipt*
Bright *Catakdar, Roshan, Ujjwal, Camkeela*
(to) brighten *Camkana*
Bright fortnight of the lunar month *Sudee*
Bright red *Sooha*
Brightened *Dhavlit*
Brightness *Ujjwalta, Camkeelapan*
Brilliant *Dadeepyman*
Brimming *Labalab, Akanth*
Bring *Lana*
(to) bring down *Utarana*
(to) bring out *Ubharna*
(to) bring to life *Jilana*
Bringing up *Lalan*
Brinjal *Baigan*
Bristle *Shook*
Brittle *Bhindur, Marmara*
Broach *Chavna*
Broad *Gherdar*
Broad shallow dish *Tabak*

Broad-minded	*Udarceta*
Broadcast	*Prasarit*
Brocade	*Kimkhab, Kamkhab*
Brochure	*Vivaranika*
Broken	*Tutha, Toota-phoota*
Broken and scattered	*Chinn-bhinn*
Broken fragments	*Tootan*
Broken into bits	*Caknacoor, Coor-coor*
Bronchital pipe	*Shwas-nalee*
Bronze	*Kansa*
Bronze age	*Kansy yug*
Broom	*Jharoo, Buharee*
Broom-seller	*Jharoovala*
Broth	*Jhol*
Brother	*Bhrata, Bhaee, Bhaiya, Bandhu*
Brother's daughter	*Bhateejee*
Brother's son	*Bhateeja*
Brother's wife	*Bhavaj, Bhabhee*
Brother-in-law	*Sarhoo, Behnoee*
Brotherhood	*Bandhuta, Bhaeecara*
Brothy	*Jholdar*
Brought near	*Upneet*
Brought under control	*Vasheebhoot*
Browbeat	*Jharapna*
Brown	*Bhoora*
Brownish red	*Kashay*
Brush	*Koocee, Burush*
Brutally frank	*Munh-phat*
Bubble	*Bulbula*
(to) bubble	*Khadbadana*
Bubbling with juice	*Cuhcuhata*
Bucket	*Dol, Balti*
Buckle	*Baksua*

Buckram	*Bakram*
Bud	*Mukal, Guncha*
Buddha temple	*Pagora*
Buddhist Monastery	*Sangharam*
Buddhist monk	*Shraman*
Buddhistic tale	*Jatak*
Budding (sharper)	*Fitna*
Budget	*Bajat, Ayvyayak*
Buffalo	*Bhains*
Buffer-State	*Antasth rajya*
Buffoonery	*Bhandaitee*
Bugbear	*Haua*
Bugle	*Bigul*
Build	*Banana*
Building	*Imarat, Vastu*
Built	*Nirmit*
Bulb	*Balb*
Bulging stomach	*Dheenrha*
Bulkiness	*Peenna*
Bulky	*Sthoolkay*
Bull	*Sand, Vrish, Baleevard*
Bull of Lord Shiva	*Nandee*
Bull-dog	*Buldag*
Bulletin	*Bulatin*
Bullion market	*Sarrafa*
Bullion merchant	*Sarraf*
Bullock	*Bail, Shand*
Bullock-cart	*Bailgaree*
Bunch	*Gumph, Guchccha*
Bunch of flowers	*Stabak*
Bundle	*Muttha, Bandal, Potlee, Gathree, Pulinda*
Bundle of papers	*Potha*

Bungling	*Golmal, Ghotala*
Bunk	*Shaynika*
Bunker	*Damdama, Targhar*
Buoy	*Taranda*
Burden of taxes	*Karbhar*
Bureaucracy	*Daftarshahee*
Burglar	*Sendhiya*
Burial	*Dafan*
Burner	*Barnar*
Burn	*Dahna, Jalna*
Burning	*Prajwalan, Dah, Dehan*
Burning sensation	*Jalan, Cuncunee*
Burning with rage	*Jalabhuna*
Burnisher	*Sikleegar*
Burnt	*Jwalit*
Bury	*Garna, Dafnana*
Bush	*Jhar*
Business	*Vyavsay, Karobar*
Business aptitude	*Vyapar-buddhi*
Businessman	*Saudagar, Vyavsayee*
Bust	*Avaksh*
Bust-up	*Gehmagehmee*
Bustle	*Daur dhoot, Khar khar*
Bustling with life	*Gulzar*
Busy	*Mashgool, Vyast, Rat*
But	*Kintu, Parantu, Magar, Lekin*
Butcher	*Boocar, Kasaee*
Butea frondosa	*Dhak*
Butter	*Makhan*
Butter-milk	*Chach, Matha*
Buttered and smooth	*Cikna-cupra*
Butterfly	*Titlee*
Buttocks	*Cootar*

Button	*Batan*
Buttressing	*Pushtabandee*
Buy	*Keenna*
Buyer	*Khareedar, Kreta*
Buying and selling	*Khareed-farokht, Liya-becee*
Buying capacity	*Kray shakti*
Buzz	*Bhanbhanahat*
(to) buzz	*Bhinakna, Bhinbhinana*
Buzzing sound	*Gunjan, Bhinbhin*
By Nature	*Prakritishah*
By chance	*Ittfakan*
By mere coincidence	*Sanyogvashat*
By or in instalments	*Kistvar*
By the grace of	*Badaulat*
By way of a gift	*Bhentswaroop*
By way of fun	*Mazakan*
By way of precaution	*Ehtiyatan*
Bye-law	*Upvidhi*
Bye-product	*Upotpad*
Bye-way	*Upmarg*
Byelection	*Up nirvacan*

C

Cabbage	*Patagobhee*
Cabinet	*Mantri-mandal*
Cable	*Sumudri tar, Kebal*
Cage	*Pinjra*
Cake	*Battee*
Calamitious	*Pralayankar*
Calamity	*Kehar, Apat*
Calcuation of Accounts	*Lekha-jokha*
Calculated	*Pariganit*
Calculating	*Hisabiya*
Calculation	*Pariganan*
Calculator	*Ganak*
Calculus	*Ashmaree, Kalan*
Calender	*Kalandar, Jantree*
Calf	*Bacha*
Calf of the leg	*Pindlee*
Call	*Pukarna, Bulava*
(to) call	*Bulana*
(to) call out loudly	*Gohrana*
Call loudly	*Tarna*
Called	*Amantrit*
Calling	*Amantran*
Calling of a farrier	*Nalbandee*
Calling of darner	*Rafoogaree*
Callus	*Ghattha*
Calm	*Shanti*
Calm by nature	*Shatancitt*
Calumny public censure	*Thuthkar*
Camel	*Oont*
Camera	*Kaimra*
Camp	*Shivir*
Camp-fire	*Alaw*
Campaign	*Abhiyan, Muhim*

Camphor	*Kapoor*
Canal	*Nahar*
Cancellation	*Nirasan*
Cancelled	*Nirast, Radd*
Candidate	*Ummedwar*
Candle	*Kandeel, Battee*
Candle-stick	*Mombattee*
Cane	*Baint*
Canister	*Kanastar*
Canker	*Ghun*
Cannibal	*Nar-bhakshee*
Cannon	*Top*
Canny	*Cust calak*
Canopy	*Shamiyana*
Canteen	*Kainteen*
Cantonment	*Chavnee*
Canvas	*Kirmic, Cittrphalak*
Cap	*Topee*
Capability	*Yoggyta*
Capable	*Samarth*
Capacity	*Bisat*
Capital	*Rajdhanee*
Capital punishment	*Prandand, Mrittyudand*
Capitalism	*Poonjeevad*
Capitalist	*Poonjeepati*
Capricious	*Maujee*
Capsule	*Samputika*
Captain	*Kaptan*
Caption of an article	*Sirnama*
Captive	*Bandhua*
Car	*Garee*
Carat	*Kairat*
Caravan	*Kafila, Karvan*

Carbon	*Karban*
Carbuncle	*Zeharvad*
Carcum copticum	*Ajvayan*
Card	*Dhunna*
Card cotton	*Peenjna, Toomna*
Cardamom	*Ilayachi*
Carder	*Dhuniya*
Cardinal number	*Gansankhya*
Care	*Dakhrakh, Dakhbhal, Parvah*
Carefree	*Bafikkr, Mast, Cintarahit*
Carefreeness	*Phakkarpan*
Careful	*Savdhan*
Carefulness	*Savdhanee*
Careless	*Laparvah*
Carelessness	*Asavdhanee, Beparvahee*
Caretaker government	*Kamcalaoo sarkar*
Cargo	*Potbhar*
Carnage	*Kata maree*
Carpenter	*Tarkhan, Barhaee*
Carpet	*Kaleen, Galeeca*
Carrot	*Gajar*
Carry	*Pahuncana*
(to) Carry on one's body	*Dhona*
Carrying away	*Haran*
Carrying of business	*Karobaree*
Cartilage	*Upasthi, Kurkuree*
Cartoon	*Kartoon, Vyang-cittr*
Cartridge	*Kartoos*
Carum	*Kalazeera*
Case	*Karak, Mamla*
Case-file	*Misil*
Cash	*Nagadnarayan, Nakad*

Cash in hand	*Rokar*
Cash-balance	*Rokar-bakee*
Cash-book	*Rokar-bahee*
Cash-box	*Galla*
Cash-memo	*Nakdee-purza*
Cashier	*Rokariya*
Casket	*Manjoosha*
Cassock	*Coga*
Caste	*Jati*
Casting	*Dhalaee*
Casting glances around	*Tak-jhank*
Castles in the air	*Kagzee mehal*
Castor	*Arand*
Castor oil	*Arandee*
Cat	*Bilaee*
Catalogue	*Sooceepattr*
Catalysing	*Utprarak*
Cataract	*Motiyabind*
Catarrh	*Nazla*
Catastrophe	*Kayamat, Mahavipatti*
Catch	*Pakar, Giraft*
(to) catch	*Grasna*
Catechism	*Prashnottaree*
Catechu tree resin	*Kattha*
Cattle	*Mavashee, Dhor-dangar, Dagcee*
Caught	*Grast*
Cauliflower	*Gobhee*
Causal	*Karanatmak*
Causative of grapple	*Bhirana*
Cause	*Karan*
Caustic	*Ksharak*
Cautioning	*Takeed*
Cautiously	*Satarktapoorvak*

Cave	*Khoh, Gufa*
Cave-man	*Gufa manav*
Cavity	*Vivar*
Ceasefire	*Yuddhviram*
Celebration	*Jalsa, Samaroh*
Celebrity	*Shohrat*
Celestial damsel	*Devbala, Surangna*
Celestial drink	*Surasav*
Celestial plane	*Devyan*
Celestial sphere	*Khagol, Akashmandal*
Celibacy	*Brahmcary*
Celibate	*Brahmcaree*
Cell	*Koshika*
Cement	*Seement*
Cenozoic era	*Navkalp*
Censor	*Sensar*
Censurable	*Nindneey*
Census	*Janganna*
Centenarian	*Shatayu, Shatpati*
Centenary	*Shatvarshikee*
Centeped	*Gojar*
Centipede	*Shatpad, Kankhajoora*
Central	*Kandreey, Maddhyvartee*
Centre	*Kendr*
Centre of gravity	*Guruttv*
Centre of noise and tumult	*Bhatiyarkhana*
Centrifugal	*Kandrabhimukhee*
Centrist	*Maddhymargee*
Century	*Sadee, Shatee*
Cereals used as pulse	*Dalhan*
Cerebrum	*Moordha*
Ceremonial	*Rasmee*

Ceremonial meet	*Milnee*
Ceremonial present	*Nag*
Ceremonial routine	*Nitty-karm*
Ceremonious tonsure	*Mundan*
Ceremony of flag hoisting	*Jhandottolan*
Ceremony of naming a child	*Namkaran*
Certain	*Nishcayatmak*
Certainly	*Yakeenan, Avashyamav*
Certificate	*Sanad, Pramanpatr*
Certificate of degree	*Upadhipattr*
Certificate-holder	*Sanadyafta*
Certification	*Pramanan*
Certitude	*Nishciti*
Cess	*Upkar*
Cessation of hostilities	*Laraeebandee, Yuddhsthagan*
Chaff	*Bhus*
Chain	*Sankal, Sikree, Laree, Tanta, Can, Zanjeer*
Chair	*Kursi*
Chairman	*Sabhapati*
Chalk	*Khariya*
Challan	*Calan*
Challenge	*Lalkar, Cunautee*
Chamber	*Prakoshth*
Chamelion	*Girgit*
Champion	*Caimpiyan*
Chance	*Daivyog, Ittafak*
Chancellor	*Kulpati*
Chandelier	*Fanoos*
Change	*Razgaree, Badal, Parivartan*
Change of climate	*Hava badal*

Change of name	*Namantaran*
Changeability	*Parivartansheelta*
Changed	*Tabdeel*
Changeless	*Nirvikar*
Changes	*Ulat phar*
Chaplain	*Kulguru*
Chapter	*Prakaran, Sarg, Addhyay, Paricched*
Character	*Caritr*
Character assassination	*Caritr-hatya*
Character-building	*Caritr-nirman*
Characteristic	*Vishsshak, Carittrik*
Characteristic of a caste	*Jati lakshan*
Characterization	*Caritr-citran*
Characterless	*Caritrheen*
Charge	*Dosharop, Karybhar*
Charge d'affairs	*Uprajdoot, Karrydoot*
Charge sheet	*Aroppatr*
Chariot	*Rath*
Charioteer	*Rathee, Rathvan, Sarathee*
Charitable	*Dharmarth, Danee*
Charitable endowment	*Dharmada*
Charity	*Khairat*
Charity account	*Dharmkhata*
Charm	*Lalitty, Caruta, Madhurima*
(to) charm	*Mohna*
Charm personified	*Manmohan*
Charming	*Lubhavna, Ramneey, Salona, Caru, Mohak*
Charming	*Manharan, Mohan*
Charming woman	*Kaminee*
Chase away	*Ragadna*
Chaste	*Satee, Sadhvee, Pak-daman*
Chastise	*Dhaunkna*

Chauvinism	*Atirashtreeyta*
Cheap	*Ghaslatee*
Cheap and third-rate	*Bajaroo*
Cheap as a farthing	*Takaiya*
Cheat	*Dagabaz, Thag, Dhokhebaz*
(to) cheat	*Thagna, Chalna*
Cheated	*Pravancit*
Cheating	*Dhokhabazee, Daga, Thagpana*
Check	*Kisht*
(to) check	*Sahajna*
Check in chess	*Sheh*
Check-post	*Naka*
Cheek	*Kapol, Gal*
Cheeky	*Mukhar*
Cheerfully	*Hansee-khushee*
Cheese	*Paneer*
Chemical	*Rasaynik*
Chemical laboratory	*Rasayanshala*
Chemist	*Rasayanaggy*
Cheque	*Cek*
Chequered cloth	*Carkhana*
Cherished	*Abheesht*
Cherished desire	*Lalsa, Arman, Manorath*
Cherished memory	*Pratahsmarneey*
Cheroot	*Curat*
Chess	*Shatranj*
Chest	*Chatee*
Chew	*Cabna*
(to) chew the cud	*Pagurana*
Chewing	*Carvan*
Chicken	*Chooza*
Chicken-pox	*Masoorika*
Chide	*Jhirkee*

(to) chide	*Tarjna*
Chief	*Sardar, Meer*
Chief Minister	*Rajya mantree*
Chief Queen	*Patranee*
Chief arbiter	*Sarpanc*
Chief of the army	*Sanadhyaksh*
Chiefly	*Mukhyatah*
Chieftain	*Aga*
Chieftain of a village	*Gop*
Chilblains	*Bivaee*
Child hood	*Chutpan, Ballykal, Larakpan, Bacpan, Balpan*
Child marriage	*Bal-vivah*
Childish	*Backana*
Childish frolics	*Balkreera*
Childish insistence	*Maclapan*
Childish mentality	*Larak-buddhi*
Childishly simple	*Allhar*
Childless	*Nipoota*
Childlike	*Balbhav, Balocit, Balsulabh*
Childlike intelligence	*Balbuddhi*
Children	*Balgopal*
Children's home	*Shishugreh*
Chilli	*Lalmirc, Mirc*
Chimney	*Cimnee, Dhuankash, Dhuvanra*
Chimpanzee	*Banmanush, Cimpanzee*
Chin	*Thoree, Cibuk, Thuddee*
Chirp	*Coon, Cehek*
(to) chirp	*Cehekna*
Chisel	*Chanee, Tankee*
(to) chisel	*Garhna*
Chit	*Parcee*
Chloroform	*Klorofarm*

Chocolate	*Caklat*
Choice	*Pasand, Varan*
Choice selection	*Samvaran*
Choked	*Ruddh*
Cholera	*Haiza*
Chopped fodder	*Kutee*
Chord	*Capkarn*
Chorus	*Sahgan*
Chosen	*Cunvan*
Christ	*Maseeh*
Christian	*Eesaee*
Christian church	*Kaleesa*
Christian community	*Kaleesiya*
Chronic diarrhoea	*Sangrahanee*
Chronicle	*Itivritt, Puravritt*
Chronological	*Kalkramik*
Chronologically	*Kalkramanusar*
Chronology	*Kalkram*
Chum	*Halee Malee, Hota Sota*
(to) churn	*Bilona, Mathna*
Chum girl	*Sakhee*
Chump of trees and bushes	*Jhurmut*
Church	*Charch*
Churn	*Rirakna*
Churned	*Mathit, Vilorit*
Churning	*Mathan*
Churning stick	*Mathanee, Raee*
Cigar	*Sigar*
Cigarette	*Sigrat*
Cinema	*Sinama*
Cinema hall	*Sinama ghar*
Cinnamon	*Darceenee*

Circle	*Halka, Gola, Vritt*
Circuit	*Paripath*
Circuitous	*Cakkardar, Cakpharee*
Circular	*Vrittakar, Mandalakar, Gol, Cakkreey*
Circular letter	*Gashtee chitthee*
Circular motion	*Cakkrgati*
Circumambulation	*Bhanvar*
Circumbulation	*Pradakshina*
Circumcision	*Sunnat*
Circumference	*Paridhi, Parima*
Circumference of the waist	*Phenta*
Circumlocution in talk	*Ghumaw-phiraw*
Circumstances	*Halat, Paristhiti*
Circumstantial	*Paristhitik*
Circus	*Sarkas*
Citadel	*Durg*
Citizen	*Nagrik, Nagarvasee*
Citizenship	*Nagrikta*
City	*Nagar, Puree*
Civics	*Nagric-shastr*
Civil	*Sivil, Deevanee*
Civil disobedience	*Savinay avaggya*
Civil war	*Grih yuddh*
Civilisation	*Tehzeeb*
Civilised	*Shisht*
Civility	*Shishtta*
Civilization	*Sabbhyta*
Civilized	*Sabbhy*
Claim	*Dava*
Claimant	*Davedar*

Clamour	*Cillpon*
Clamp	*Shikanja*
Clap	*Thap, Karkarahat*
Clapping	*Talee*
Clarified	*Spashteekrit*
Clarinet	*Nafeeree*
Clarion	*Turahee*
Clarity	*Spashtata*
Class	*Varg, Darja*
Class of celestial singers & musicians	*Gandharv*
Class-fellow	*Sehpathee*
Classical	*Shastreey*
Classical way of singing	*Ragdaree*
Classification	*Darajbandee*
Classification	*Vargeekaran*
Classified	*Vargeekrit*
Classless	*Vargheen*
Claw	*Cangul*
Claw	*Panja*
Clay	*Mittee*
Clay model	*Mrinmoorti*
Clay-tiled roof	*Khaprail*
Clean	*Nishkalush*
Clean	*Safa*
Clean	*Suthra*
Clean	*Swacch*
(to) clean	*Nikharna*
Clean sweep	*Safaya*
Clean-shaven	*Much-munda*
Cleaning the kitchens & utensils	*Cauka-bartan*

Cleanliness	*Safaee*
Cleanse	*Ponchna, Manjna*
Cleansing	*Marjan*
Cleansing the mouth after a meal	*Mukhshuddhi*
Cleansing the mouth with water	*Kulla*
Clear	*Saf*
Clear	*Spasht*
Clearly	*Spashttah*
Cleavage	*Phatan*
Clemency	*Kshamadan*
Clergyman	*Padree*
Clerical job	*Klarkee*
Clerk	*Klark*
Clerk	*Baboo*
Clerk	*Munshee*
Clerk	*Muneem*
Clerk	*Muhrir*
Clerk	*Lipik*
Clever	*Catur*
Clever	*Calak*
Clever	*Hoshiyar*
Cleverness	*Caturta*
Cleverness	*Sayanapan*
Client	*Asamee*
Client	*Muvakkil*
Cliff	*Ucchring*
Climate	*Jalvayu*
Climate	*Havapanee*
Climax	*Parakashtha*
Climb	*Carhna*
Cling	*Cimatna*

(to) cling to	*Lipatna*
Clinic	*Nidangrih*
Clinic	*Nidanshala*
Clinical	*Naidanik*
Clip	*Katarna*
Clipper	*Katarnee*
Clique	*Gut*
Clock-tower	*Ghantaghar*
Clock-wise	*Dakshinavart*
Close	*Jigree, Nazdeek*
(to) close	*Meencna*
Close associate	*Hamjolee*
Close association	*Uthna baithna*
Close combat	*Guttham-guttha*
Close consideration	*Gaur*
Close contact	*Ghispis*
Close friends	*Ishtmittr*
Close kinship	*Sagapan*
Close meeting	*Milap*
Close proximity	*Sannikarsh*
Closed	*Nimeelit*
Closed	*Meelit*
Closed	*Samvirt*
Closed palanquin	*Dola*
Closest	*Antartam*
Cloth	*Kapra*
Cloth	*Ceer*
Cloth	*Pat*
Cloth made of soft fine wool	*Pashmeena*
Cloth put round a dead body	*Kafan*
Cloth shop	*Vastragar*

Cloth used as a gambling board	*Phar*
Cloth woven with gold thread	*Zaree*
Cloth-market	*Bazaza*
Cloth-merchant	*Bazaz*
Clothes	*Vastr*
Clothes-line	*Arganee*
Clothes-line	*Alganee*
Clothes-moth	*Kaparkeera*
Clothing	*Vasan*
Cloud	*Badal*
Cloudiness	*Badlee*
Cloudless	*Nirabhr*
Clouds of dust	*Gard-gubar*
Clove	*Laung*
Cloven hoof	*Khur*
Club	*Klab*
Clue	*Atapata*
Clue	*Surag*
Clue of a story	*Kathasutr*
Clumsiness	*Bhondapan*
Clumsy	*Bhonda*
Clumsy whitewashing	*Leepa-potee*
Co-dweller	*Sehvasee*
Co-editor	*Sehsampadak*
Co-education	*Sehshiksha*
Co-existence	*Sah-astittw*
Co-operation	*Sehyog*
Co-option	*Sehyojan*
Co-partner	*Bhageedar*
Co-partner	*Sehbhagee*
Co-partner	*Sajhadar*

Co-professional	*Hampash*
Co-relation	*Sehsambandh*
Co-sharer	*Patteedar*
Co-traveller	*Sehyatree*
Co-wife	*Sapatnee*
Co-wife	*Saut*
Co-worker	*Sahkarmee*
Coach	*Koch*
(to) coach	*Sikhana-parhana*
Coachman	*Gareevan*
Coal	*Koyala*
Coal-tar	*Turkol*
Coalition government	*Sanyukt sarkar*
Coaltar	*Tarkol*
Coarse bed cushion	*Gadala*
Coarse cloth	*Gajee*
Coarse food	*Dal-daliya*
Coarse grain	*Kadann*
Coarse thick packing paper	*Malat*
Coastal	*Samuddratateey*
Coastguard	*Tatrakshan*
Coat	*Kot*
Coated	*Kalaeedar*
Coated with some oily substance	*Cupra*
Coating	*Lep*
Coating	*Lepan*
Cobbler	*Mocee*
Cobra	*Nag*
Cocaine	*Kokeen*
Cock	*Murga*
Cockroach	*Tilcata*

Cocktail party	*Pangoshthee*
Cocoa	*Koko*
Coconut	*Nariyal*
Coconut kernel	*Garee*
Coddle	*Puckarna*
Coddling	*Puckar*
Code	*Sanhita*
Code language	*Sanketikbhasha*
Code-script	*Kootlipi*
Code-writing	*Kootlekh*
Codification	*Sanhitakaran*
Codified	*Sanhitabaddh*
Coefficient	*Gunank*
Coercion	*Barjoree*
Coffee	*Kehva*
Coffee house	*Kafee ghar*
Coffin	*Taboot*
Cogent	*Susangat*
Cognisance	*Abhiggyta*
Cognisant	*Abhiggy*
Cognizable	*Pragyay*
Cognizance	*Avakshan*
Cohabit	*Codna*
Cohabitation	*Rati*
Cohabitation	*Ratikriya*
Cohesion	*Sansakti*
Cohesive	*Sansakt*
Coil	*Kundlee*
Coiling	*Valan*
Coin	*Sikka*
Coincidence	*Sampat*
Coincidence	*Sanyog*
Coincident	*Sampatik*

Coincident	*Sampatee*
Coiner of words	*Shabdkar*
Coitus	*Maithun*
Coitus	*Sambhog*
Cold	*Zukam*
Cold	*Thand*
Cold	*Sard*
Cold drink	*Thanda*
Cold storage	*Sheetagar*
Cold sweat	*Sitlee*
Cold war	*Sheetyuddh*
Cold wave	*Sheetlehree*
Cold-hearted	*Nirmohee*
Colic pain	*Petadard*
Collapse	*Bhehrana*
Collar	*Kalar*
Collar-bone	*Hansulee*
Collate	Malna
Collateral	*Sapind*
Collator	*Milan*
Colleague	*Joreedar*
Collect	*Ugahna*
(to) collect	*Jutana, Juhana*
(to) collect (dues)	*Tehseelna*
Collected	*Jama*
Collecting	*Samaharan*
Collection	*Sankalan*
Collection	*Sangrah*
Collection of Buddhistic tales	*Jatakmala*
Collection of articles	*Samaggree*
Collection of letters	*Pattravalee*

Collection of sundry articles	*Tant-ghant*
Collection of votes	*Matsangrah*
Collection of words	*Shabdsangrah*
Collective	*Samashtivacak*
Collective	*Samuccayarthak*
Collective	*Samoohvacak*
Collective	*Samoohik*
Collective feeding	*Brahmbhoj*
Collectivism	*Samashtivad*
Collector	*Kalaktar*
Collector	*Sangrahkarta*
Collectorate	*Kalaktaree*
College	*Kalaj*
College	*Mahavidyalaya*
Collide	*Bhirna*
Collision	*Takkar*
Collision	*Bhirant*
Colloquial parlance	*Bol-cal*
Collusion	*Milee-bhagat*
Collyrium	*Surma*
Colonial	*Aupnivashik*
Colophon	*Pushpika*
Colour	*Rang*
Colour blind	*Varnandh*
Colour distinction	*Varn-bhed*
Colour made from lac	*Lakha*
Colour of Ganga and Jamuna	*Ganga jamunee*
Colour of a snake	*Sanpiya*
Colour of catechu	*Katthaee*
Colour of catechu	*Khaira*
Colour of copper	*Tanbaee*

Colour of copper	*Tamra*
Colour of husk	*Toosee*
Colour of lac	*Lakhee*
Colour of myrtle	*Manhdiya*
Colour of myrtle	*Hinaee*
Colour of narcissus	*Nargisee*
Colour of pearl	*Motiya*
Colour of poppy seed	*Khaskhasee*
Colour of water-melon	*Tarboozaee*
Colour-blindness	*Rangaudhee*
Colour-blindness	*Varn-andhta*
Coloured	*Rangeen*
Coloured, shining thin paper	*Pannee*
Colourer over-cloth	*Cunree*
Colourful	*Rangeela*
Colourfullness	*Rangeenee*
Colourfulness	*Rangeelapan*
Colouring of hair	*Keshranjan*
Colourless	*Avarn*
Colt	*Bachara*
Column	*Kalam*
Column	*Stambh*
Columnist	*Stambhlakhak*
Comb	*Kangha*
Combat	*Joojhna*
Combinable	*Sanyojjy*
Combination	*Sanyojan*
Combined	*Sanyojit*
Combing and dressing of hair	*Kashkarm*
Combining	*Sammilan*
Combustible	*Jwalansheel*

Combustible	*Dahhy*
Come back	*Lautna*
(to) come near	*Niarana*
(to) come out	*Ubharna*
Comeliness	*Kamneeyta*
Comely	*Kamneey*
Comely figure	*Kancan kaya*
Comet	*Dhoomketu*
Comet	*Pucchaltara*
Comfortability	*Saukkhy*
Coming	*Anevala*
Coming again	*Punaragaman*
Coming and going	*Ana jana*
Coming from a far	*Dooragat*
Comma	*Alpviram*
Comma	*Kama*
Command	*Farman*
Command	*Samadash*
Commander	*Kamandar*
Commander	*Seenapati*
Commander-in-chief	*Senadhipati*
Commanding officer	*Senanee*
Commencement	*Samarambh*
Commencement	*Soottrpat*
Commencement of some work	*Shreeganesh*
Commencement of work	*Lagga*
Commendable	*Sprihneey*
Commendation	*Sanstavan*
Comment	*Tippanee*
Commentary	*Tippan*
Commentary	*Bhashshy*

Commentator	*Teekakar*
Commentator	*Bhashshyakar*
Comments	*Teeka-tippanee*
Commerce	*Vanijjy*
Commercial	*Vyaparik*
Commission	*Ayog*
Commission	*Kameeshan*
Commission agent	*Arhatiya*
Commission of a broker	*Dalalee*
Commissioner	*Ayukt*
Commissioner	*Kamishnar*
Commitment to save (someone's) life	*Jeevandan*
Committed to memory	*Kanthasth*
Committee	*Kamatee*
Committee	*Samiti*
Committee room	*Samiti kaksh*
Commode	*Kamod*
Commodity	*Jins*
Commodity	*Pannyvastu*
Common	*Sajhee*
Common dinner	*Sambhojan*
Common factor	*Samapavartak*
Common good	*Janhit*
Common good	*Sarvhit*
Common multiple	*Samapavarty*
Common noun	*Jativacaksangya*
Common people	*Logbag*
Common to both	*Ubhaynishth*
Commonwealth	*Rashtrmandal*
Commotion	*Halla-gulla*
Communal	*Jatigat*

Communal	*Sampradayik*
Communal	*Samudayik*
Communal enmity	*Jativair*
Communalism	*Sampradayvad*
Communalism	*Sampradayikta*
Communication	*Sancar*
Communism	*Sammyvad*
Communist	*Kamyunist*
Community	*Kaum*
Community	*Jansamuday*
Community	*Biradaree*
Community	*Sampraday*
Community dinner	*Sehbhoj*
Community feast esp.of holy mendicants	*Bhandara*
Compact	*Sanhat*
Compact	*Susanhat*
Compactness	*Susanhati*
Companion	*Sangee*
Companion	*Sathee*
Company	*kampdni*
Company	*Sath*
Company	*Sohbat*
Company of the good	*Satsang*
Comparable	*Tulneey*
Comparison	*Tulna*
Comparison	*Milan*
Compartment	*Khana*
Compass	*Kampas*
Compass	*Digsoocak*
Compasses	*Parkar*
Compassion	*Karuna*

Compassionate	*Dayavan*
Compatible	*Sangat*
Compatriot	*Hamvatan*
Compelled	*Baddhy*
Compensation	*Kshatipoorti*
Compensation	*Muavaja*
Competent	*Saksham*
Competition	*Pratiyogita*
Competition	*Hor*
Compiled	*Sankalit*
Compiler	*Sankalankarta*
Complainant	*Parivadee*
Complaint	*Upalambh*
Complaint	*Gila*
Complaint	*Parivad*
Complaint	*Fariyad*
Complaint	*Shikayat*
Complementary	*Sampoorak*
Complete	*Poorn*
(to) complete	*Pugana*
Complete and perfect	*Mukammal*
Complete in all respects	*Sarvangpoorn*
Complete ruination	*Sarvnash*
Complete silence	*Cupkee*
Completed	*Nishpann*
Completely	*Jarmool*
Completely	*Sarvatha*
Completely fatigued and exhausted	*Past*
Completely full	*Bharpoor*
Completely ruined	*Matiyamat*
Completely ruinous	*Sarvnashee*

Completely unified *Akakar*
Completeness *Sampoornta*
Completion of sixty years of age *Shastipoorti*
Complexity *Peceedapan*
Complicated *Jatil*
Complicated *Peceeda*
Complicated situation *Jhanjhat*
Complication *Jatilta*
Complication *Peceedgee*
Component *Sanghatak*
Compose *Viracna*
Composed *Praneet*
Composed *Viracit*
Composed and mentally sound *Swasth-citt*
Composer *Racaita*
Composer of songs *Geetkar*
Composer of the Vedas *Vadkarta*
Composing *Kampoz*
Composing a verse with a line given *Samassya-poorti*
Compositor *Kampozitor*
Compound *Ahata*
Compound *Mishshrit*
Compound *Yaugik*
Compound *Samas*
Compound *Hata*
Compound consonant *Sanyukt vyanjan*
Compound interest *Cakkrvriddhi*
Compound sentence *Sanyukt vakky*
Compounder *Kampaundar*
Comprehend *Pratibodhak*

Comprehension	*Pratibodh*
Comprehensiveness	*Vyapakta*
Compressed	*Sampeerit*
Compromise	*Samjhauta*
Compromise	*Suleh*
Compromise	*Suleh-safaee*
Compulsory	*Lazim*
Compunction	*Glani*
Computation	*Abhikalan*
Computation	*Sanganan*
Computer	*Sanganak*
Comrade	*Kamrad*
Comradeship	*Sahcarry*
Concave	*Natodar*
Concealment	*Duraw*
Conceit	*Akar*
Conceit	*Ainth*
Conceit	*Ghamand*
Concentrated	*Akcitt*
Concentrated	*Akaggr*
Concentrated	*Dattcitt*
Concentrated	*Sankandrit*
Concentration	*Akagrata*
Concentration	*Sankandran*
Concept	*Ardharna*
Concept	*Sankalpana*
Conception	*Garbhdharan*
Conceptual	*Sankalpvacee*
Concern	*Sarokar*
Concert	*Sangeetika*
Concession	*Choot*
Concession	*Riayat*
Conch	*Shankh*

Conch of Lord Krishna	*Pancjanny*
Conciliation	*Sanradhan*
Concise	*Mitakshar*
Concluding	*Upsanharatmak*
Conclusion	*Nivartan*
Concord	*Mal*
Concourse	*Jamghat*
Concourse	*Samvay*
Concrete	*Kankreet*
Concrete	*Moort*
Concubine	*Uppatni*
Concubine	*Dharalee*
Concubine	*Surait*
Concurred	*Sehmat*
Concurrence	*Aikmatty*
Concurrence	*Sehmati*
Condensed	*Ghanit*
Condiment	*Masala*
Condition	*Dasha*
Condition	*Hal*
Condition of being in distress	*Sankatavastha*
Condition of the mind	*Manodasha*
Conditional	*Sopadhi*
Condolence	*Samvedna*
Condolence meeting	*Shoksabha*
Condom	*Nirodh*
Conducive to good health	*Swasthykar*
Conduct	*Acharan*
Conduct	*Achar*
Conduct	*Calcalan*
Conduct	*Taur-tareeka*

Conduct	*Paricalan*
Conduct	*Rangdhang*
Conduction	*Sanvehan*
Conduction	*Samvahan*
Conductivity	*Sancalakta*
Conductor	*Kandaktar*
Conductor	*Paricalak*
Conductor of conducting heat	*Tapcalak*
Cone	*Shanku*
Confectioner	*Halvaee*
Confederation	*Rajjysangh*
Conference	*Sammelan*
Conferring a boon	*Varad*
Confess	*Kaboolna*
Confession	*Kabool*
Confession	*Sweekarokti*
Confident	*Pragalbh*
Confidential	*Gopneey*
Confirmation	*Abhipushti*
Confirmation	*Pushti*
Confirmation	*Sampushti*
Confirmation	*Sthaeekaran*
Confirmatory	*Pushtikaree*
Confirmed	*Abhipusht*
Confirmed	*Shatir*
Confiscated	*Zabt*
Conflagration	*Agnikand*
Conflict	*Kheenchtan*
Conflict	*Pratidwandw*
Conflict	*Lagee*
Confluence	*Sangaman*
Confluence (of rivers)	*Sangam*

Confluence of the good and the great	*Satsamagam*
Conformity of temperaments	*Meeja*
Confounded	*Cakrana*
Confounded	*Hatbuddhit*
Confrontation	*Samna*
Confused	*Vibhrant*
Confusing	*Bhrantijanak*
Confusing	*Bhrantimoolak*
Confusing	*Bhramak*
Confusion	*Bhranti*
Confusion	*Labar-dhondhon*
Confusion	*Vibhranti*
Confusion	*Sambhram*
Congenital	*Janmgat*
Congestion	*Sankulta*
Congratulations	*Mubarakbad*
Congregation	*Vrind*
Congregational singing	*Keertan*
Congregational singing	*Sankeertan*
Congress	*Kangras*
Congress	*Mahasabha*
Conjecture	*Andaza*
Conjecturing	*Atkalbazee*
Conjunct	*Sanyut*
Conjurer	*Abhicharee*
Connection	*Sambaddhta*
Connoisseur	*Gunaggy*
Connoisseur of art	*Kalavid*
Conquerable	*Jay*

Conquerable	*Vijay*
Conquerer	*Vijata*
Conqueror of the world	*Vishshwavijayee*
Conscience	*Zameer*
Conscious	*Caitanny*
Conscious	*Sacetan*
Consciousness	*Cet*
Consciousness	*Cetna*
Consciousness	*Bhan*
Consecration	*Abhishek*
Consecration	*Pavitreekaran*
Consecutive	*Kramagat*
Consequence	*Parinam*
Consequently	*Phalswaroop*
Conservatism	*Roorhivad*
Conservative	*Dakiyanoos*
Conservative (custom, practice etc.)	*Dakiyanoosee*
Conserve prepared of rose petals	*Gulgula*
Consideration	*Soc*
Consisting of a thousand	*Hazara*
Consolation	*Dilasa*
Consolidation of holdings	*Cakbandee*
Consoling factor	*Ganimat*
Consonant	*Vyanjan*
Conspiracy	*Sharyantr*
Conspiracy	*Sazish*
Conspirator	*Sharyantrkaree*
Conspiring	*Sazishee,*

Constable	*Pulismain, Sipahee*
Constellation	*Taramandal*
Constellation (of stars)	*Nakshatr*
Constipation	*Kabz*
Constituency	*Cunaw-kshetra*
Constituted	*Samvihit*
Constitution	*Samvidhan*
Constrict	*Simatna*
Constructed	*Racit*
Construction	*Nirman*
Constructive	*Racnatmak*
Constructor	*Nirmata*
Consulation	*Vimarsh*
Consultation fee	*Paramarsh shulk*
Consumable	*Upbhoggy*
Consume	*Khapat*
Consumer	*Upbhokta*
Consumption	*Upbhog*
Contact	*Sampark*
Contagious	*Chutaha*
Container	*Pateelee*
Contamination	*Pooti*
Contemplate	*Dhyana*
Contemplation	*Vicarna*
Contemporary	*Tatkaleen*
Contemptible	*Mardood*
Content of a story	*Kathavastu*
Contented	*Santoshee*
Contents	*Antarvastu*
Contest	*Pratidwandwita*
Context	*Sandarbh*
Contiguity	*Samvartita*
Continent	*Mahadweep*

Continental	*Mahadweepeey*
Continual repetition	*Rat*
Continually	*Jharajhar*
Continued	*Jaree*
Continuous	*Aviral*
Continuous	*Nirantar*
Continuous	*Niravacchinn*
Continuous (in space)	*Santat*
Continuously	*Lagatar*
Continuously as the falling of rain	*Jhamajham*
Contraband	*Vinishiddh*
Contract	*Anubandh*
Contract	*Theka*
Contraction	*Sankoc*
Contractor	*Thekadar*
Contradicted	*Nirakrit*
Contradiction	*Khandan*
Contradiction	*Nirakriti*
Contrary	*Vipreet*
Contrastive	*Vyatirakee*
Contribution	*Anshdan*
Contribution of labour	*Shramdan*
Contributor	*Anshdata*
Control	*kantrol*
Control	*Niyantran*
Controller of destiny	*Bhaggyvidhata*
Controversial	*Vivadgrast*
Convalesce	*Aroggylabh*
Convenant	*Prasamvida*
Convenience	*Suvidhanusar*
Convention	*Roorhi*
Conventional	*Roorhigat*

Conventional meaning	*Roorharth*
Conversant well-informed	*Jankar*
Conversation	*Guftgoo*
Conversation	*Varta*
Converse	*Bolna-calna*
Conversely	*Vilomtah*
Conversion	*Dharmparivartan*
Convetable	*Sprihy*
Convex	*Uttal*
Convex	*Unnatodar*
Convicted	*Saza yafta*
Conviction	*Abhishansa*
Conviction	*Abhishasti*
Conviction	*Diljamaee*
Coo	*Kukna*
(to) coo and fondle	*Cumkarana*
Cooing of a cuckoo	*Kook*
Cooing of a pigeon	*Gutargoon*
Cook	*Bavarcee, Rasoiya*
(to) cook	*Pakana*
(to) cook by boiling	*Ubalana*
Cooked	*Pakkw*
Cooked or fried in one lot	*Ghan*
Cooking	*Rasoee*
Cool	*Sheetal*
Coolie	*Kulee*
Coolness	*Sheetalta*
Cooperation	*Sahkar*
Cooperative	*Sahkar-samiti*
Cooperative	*Sahakaree*

Coordinated	*Samannvit*
Coordinating	*Samannvaykaree*
Coordination	*Tal-mel*
Coordination	*Samannvay*
Coordination	*Samanjassy*
Coordinator	*Samannvayee*
Copper	*Tamba*
Copper Sulphate	*Neela thotha*
Copper coin	*Taka*
Copper horn	*Narsinha*
Copper-coloured	*Tamrvarn*
Copy	*Nakal*
Copy book	*Kapee*
Copyist	*Nakal-navees*
Copyright	*Kapeerait*
Coquet	*Nakshabaz*
Coral	*Moonga*
Coral tree	*Parijat*
Corase grain given to birds	*Cugga*
Cord used for churning	*Natee.*
Cord, chain, noose, etc.for tying	*Pash*
Coriander seed	*Dhaniya*
Corinda	*Karaunda*
Cork	*Datta*
Corn	*Bhutta*
Corner	*Kona*
Corner	*Nukkar*
Cornice	*Karnis*
Corollary	*Arthapatti*
Corollary	*Uppramay*

Coronation	*Rajtilak*
Corporation	*Nagarmahapalika*
Corporation	*Nigam*
Corpse	*Loth*
Corpulent	*Peen*
Correct	*Durust*
Corrected	*Sanshodhit*
Correction of an error	*Bhoolsudhar*
Corrective	*Sanshodhak*
Correspondence	*Cittheepatree*
Correspondence	*Pattrvyavhar*
Correspondence (of letters)	*Likha-parhee*
Correspondent	*Sanvaddata*
Corresponding	*Sanvadee*
Corridor	*Galiyara*
Corroboration	*Mandan*
Corrupt	*Bhrasht*
Corundum	*Kurand*
Cosmic	*Brahmmandeey*
Cosmology	*Brahmvidya*
Cosmopolitan	*Sarvdeshik*
Cost	*Lagat*
Costliness	*Mahengee*
Costly	*Keemtee*
Costume	*Paridhan*
Cosy boat	*Shikara*
Cot	*Khat*
Cot	*Carpaee*
Cot which is bent	*Tarpat*
Cottage Industry	*Grih-uddyog*
Cotton	*Ruee*

Cotton	*Sootee*
Cotton plant	*Kapas*
Cotton yarn	*Soot*
Cotton-roll for spinning	*Poonee*
Cotton-seed	*Binaula*
Cough	*Khansee*
(to) cough	*Khansna, Dhansna*
(to) cough like a horse	*Dhansna*
Council	*Kaunsil*
Council	*Jamaiyat*
Council	*Parishad*
Councillor	*Kaunsilar*
Counsel	*Mantrana*
Counsellor	*Mantranakar*
Count	*Ginna*
Count	*Shumar*
Countable	*Gananeey*
Countenance	*Mukhmandal*
Counter	*Kauntar*
Counter-argument	*Vitark*
Counter-attack	*Prattyakkraman*
Counter-attack	*Prattyaghat*
Counter-charge	*Prattyarop*
Counter-example	*Prattyudaharan*
Counter-reply	*Punaruttar*
Counter-revolution	*Pratikranti*
Counter-signature	*Pratihastakshar*
Counterfeit	*Koot*
Counterfoil	*Adhpanna*
Counterpart	*Pratiroop*
Counting	*Gintee*

Counting of votes	*Matganna*
Countless	*Aganneey*
Countless	*Anginat*
Country	*Desh*
Country	*Mulk*
Couple	*Jugal*
Couple	*Jora*
Couplet	*Doha*
Couplet	*Shlok*
Coupon	*Koopan*
Courage	*Jigra*
Courage	*Himmat*
Courageous	*Dilavar*
Courageous	*Sahasik*
Course	*Kors*
Course	*Kramak*
Court	*Adalat*
Court	*Kort*
Court of justice	*Kacehree*
Court official	*Nazir*
Court-yard	*Sehan*
Courteous welcome	*Satkar*
Courteousness	*Susheelta*
Courtesy	*Saujanny*
Courtier	*Darbaree*
Courtyard	*Angna*
Courtyard	*Cauk*
Cover	*Avaran, Khol*
(to) cover	*Dhakna, Jhanpna*
(to) cover (vessel, plate etc.)	*Topna*
(to) cover with a sheet	*Urhana*

(to) cover with cloth	*Orhana*
Covered	*Acchadit*
Covered by veil	*Burkaposh*
Covered inner terrace	*Dalan*
Covered pit used for storing grain	*Khatta*
Covering	*Kholee*
Covering	*Patna*
Covertability	*Kammyta*
Covetous	*Lolup*
Covetousness	*Lolupta*
Cow	*Gaoo, Gay*
Cow milk	*Godoodh*
Cow pea	*Lobiya*
Cow-killer	*Goghatee*
Cow-killing	*Gohattya*
Cow-owner	*Gopal*
Cow-pan	*Pinjrapol*
Cow-protection	*Goraksha*
Cowardice	*Kayarta*
Cowardly	*Buzdil*
Cowardly timid person	*Kapurush*
Cowrie	*Kauree*
Crack	*Tarar, Darar*
(to) crack	*Catkana, Tarakna*
(to) crack down	*Murmurana*
Cracker	*Pataka*
Crackle	*Karkarana*
Crackling sound	*Catak*
Craft	*Shilp*

Craft of a blacksmith	*Luharee*
Craft school	*Shilpshala*
Craftiness	*Calbazee, Tikrambazee*
Craftsman	*Shilpkar*
Craftsmanship	*Kareegaree*
Craftsmanship	*Shilpkaushal*
Crafty	*Khurrat*
Crafty	*Calbaz*
Crafty	*Tikramee*
Crafty	*Dhoort*
Crafty fellow	*Gurughantal*
Cram	*Ratna*
Cramming	*Ratant*
Crane (bird)	*Saras*
Crank	*Sir-fira*
Crankishness	*Sir*
Cranky	*Siree*
Crash	*Khataka, Dharaka*
(to) crash	*Bharbharana*
(to) crash down	*Dhehna*
Craving	*Murad*
Craving	*Vasna*
Crawled	*Sarpit*
Craze	*Khabt*
Craze	*Janoon*
Craze	*Jhak*
Craziness	*Jhakkipan, Sankeepan*
Crazy	*Khabtee, Deevana*
Creak	*Carmarana, Citakna*
Creaking	*Carmara*
Cream	*Sarhee*
Crease	*Shikan*
Creation	*Prabhav, Sarjan*

Creative	*Sarjanatmak*
Creator	*Karta, Vidhata*
Creator of the unwise	*Jagat-pita*
Creature	*Jantu*
Credentials	*Pratyay-pattr*
Credit	*Sakh*
Credit (in the market)	*Bharam-bhav*
Credit Account	*Jama-khata*
Credit and debit	*Jama-kharc*
Credit balance	*Jama-bakee*
Creditor	*Lendar*
Creeper	*Lata*
Creeper bearing fragrant flowers	*Madhvee*
Creeper yielding sweet-smelling flower	*Maltee*
Creeping	*Sarpan*
Cremation	*Shavdah*
Cremation ground	*Marghat*
Crescent	*Candrkala*
Crest	*Mukut*
Crest on the head of a bird	*Coora*
Cricket (insect)	*Jheengur*
Cricket bat	*Balla*
Criminal	*Apradhee*
Criminal	*Faujdaree*
Criminal law	*Dand-vidhi*
Crimson	*Kirmij*
Cripple	*Lunj*
Crippled	*Apahij, Vikalang*
Crisis	*Visthiti*
Crisp	*karara, Kurkura*

Crisp sweetmeat	*Ravree*
Crispness	*Kurkurapan*
Criterion	*Mandand*
Critic	*Alochak*
Critical	*Alochnatmak*
Critical	*Shocneey*
Croak	*Tarrtarr*
(to) croak	*Tarrana*
Crocodile	*Ghariyal, Magarmacch*
Croesus	*Karoon*
Crooked	*Kaj*
Crookedness	*Kutilta*
Croon	*Miskee*
Crop	*Fasal*
Crore	*Karor*
Cross	*Kroos*
Cross	*Saleeb*
Cross-breed	*Sankaraj*
Cross-examination	*Jireh*
Cross-examination	*Pratipareekshan*
Cross-reference	*Pratinirdesh*
Cross-reference	*Prattyabhidesh*
Crossbred among humans	*Varnsankar*
Crossed over	*Nisteern*
Crossing	*Cauraha*
Crossing over	*Taran*
Crossing the Rubicon	*Santaran*
Crossword puzzle	*Varg-pahelee*
Crow	*Kaua*
Crowbar	*Sabbal*
Crowd	*Bheer-bhar, Jansamooh, Hujoom*
Crowded	*Sankul, Janakeern*

Crowded	*Sankul*
Crowing	*Kanw-kanw*
Crown	*Maur*
Crown	*Mukat, Sirtaj*
Crown made of peacock feathers	*Mormukut*
Crowning	*Tajposhee*
Crucible	*Ghariya*
Cruel	*Zalim*
Cruel	*Nirmam*
Cruel use of power	*Zor-zulm*
Cruel virago	*Candalinee*
Cruelty	*Kroorta*
Crusade religious war	*Jihad*
Crush	*Masalna, Kuchalna*
Crushed	*Pilna*
Crusher	*Kolhoo*
Crushing	*Dalan*
Crust	*Papree*
Crutches	*Baisakhee*
Cry	*Hoonk*
(to) cry	*Cillana*
(to) cry aloud	*Ciciyana*
(to) cry and wail loudly	*Rona-peetna*
Cry for help	*Gohar*
Cry of distress	*Hahakar*
Cry of joy	*Harshdhwani*
Cry out	*Dakarna*
Crystal	*Sphatik, Kalas*
Crystal clear	*Hastamalak*
Crystal sugar	*Dana-ceenee*
Cuberoot	*Ghanmool*

Cubic	*Ghanatmak*
Cubic measure	*Ghanman*
Cuckoo	*Kadambaree*
Cuckoo	*Sarika*
Cucumber	*Kakree, Kheera, Cittra*
Cuff of shirt	*Kaf*
Culmination	*Pratiphalan*
Cultivable	*Krishiyoggy*
Cultural	*Sanskritik*
Culvert	*Puliya*
Cummin seed	*Zeera*
Cuneiform	*Keelakshar*
Cunning	*Cant, Makkar*
Cunning	*Dhongee*
Cunning fellow	*Ghagh*
Cunning tactics	*Chakka-panja*
Cunningness	*Cantaee*
Cup	*Pyala*
Cup made of leaves	*Patokha*
Cup of wine	*Sagar*
Cupid	*Madan*
Cupola	*Golambar*
Curable	*Cikitsy*
Curb of a well	*Panghat*
Curd	*Dahee*
Curd deverage	*Lassee*
Curd-pot	*Daharee*
Cure	*Arogan*
Curiosity	*Jiggyasa*
Curious	*Kutuhalpoorn*
Curl	*Alak*
Curling lock	*Kakul*
Curly	*Ghunghrala, Challadar*

Currant	*Munakka*
Currency	*Karensee*
Current	*Caloo*
Current	*Samayik*
Current account	*Calta khana*
Curriculum	*Patthykram*
Curry comb	*Kharrehra*
Curse	*Abhishap, Baddua*
(to) curse	*Sharapna*
Cursed	*Shapgrast*
Cursory	*Sarsaree*
Curtain	*Parda*
Curtain made of bamboo strips	*Cilman*
Curtained	*Pardadar*
Curve	*Tarh*
Curved	*Kutil*
Curved	*Bank*
Curved	*Vakkr*
Cushion	*Gaddee*
Custard apple	*Shareefa*
Custody	*Parirakshan*
Custody	*Supurdgee*
Custody	*Hajat*
Custom	*Pratha, Rivaj, Reeti*
Customer	*Grahak*
Customs and manners	*Reeti-rivaj*
Customs duty	*Seemakar*
Cut	*Katna*
(to) cut and separate	*Chantna*
Cut-off	*Alagthalag*

Cut-piece	*Katpees*
Cutter	*Katar*
Cutting	*Katran*
Cutting to measurement	*Katarbyont*
Cuttings	*Chant*
Cuttings	*Chantan*
Cycle	*Saikil*
Cycle of events	*Ghatna-chakkr*
Cyclic	*Cakkrakar*
Cyclone	*Bavandar*
Cymbal	*Manjeer*
Cynic	*Jandwashee*
Cyst	*Guthla*

D

Dacoity	*Daka*
Dagger	*Kripan, Khanjar*
Daily	*Dainik, Rozana, Pratidin, Rozmarra*
Daily routine	*Dincarya*
Dairy	*Daree, Dugdhshala*
Dais	*Sabha-manc*
Dak bungalow	*Dak bangla*
Dam	*Bandh*
Damages	*Nuksan, Harjana*
Damnation	*Lanat*
Damned	*Narakvasee, Munhjala*
Damp	*Nam*
Dampness	*Seelan, Namee*
Dance	*Nritty, Nac*
(to) dance	*Nacna*
(to) dance about	*Humakna*
(to) dance lightly	*Thirakna*
(to) dance with	*Humasna*
Dancer	*Nartak, Dansar*
Dancing	*Nartan*
Dancing and merry-making	*Nac-rang*
Dancing and singing	*Nac-gana*
Dancing girl	*Nacnavalee*
Dancing hall	*Nrittyshala*
Danger	*Khatra*
Dangerous	*Khatarnak*
Dark	*Tamas*
Dark Ages	*Andhkaryug*
Dark blue	*Jamunee*
Dark cell	*Andheree kotharee*
Dark half of a lunar month	*Krishnpaksh*

Dark horse	*Chiparustam*
Dark red	*Kashay*
Dark well	*Andh koop*
Dark-complexioned	*Shyam, Shyamal*
Darkness	*Andhkar, Shyamalta*
Darling	*Balam, Dulara*
Darner	*Rafoogar*
Darning	*Rafoo*
Dash	*Rakhika, Put, Daish*
Dashehra	*Dashehra*
Dashing	*Dhakar*
Date	*Tithi, Dinank, Tareekh*
Date of birth	*Janmtithi*
Date-palm	*Chuhara*
Daub	*Pathna*
Daughter	*Betee, Bitiya, Kanaya, Puttree*
Daughter's daughter	*Natinee*
Daughter's son	*Natee, Navasa, Dauhittr*
Daughter-inlaw	*Kulvadhu*
Dauntless	*Sharbacca*
Dauntless fighter for a religious cause	*Dharmveer*
Dawn	*Usha*
Day	*Roz, Din, Divas*
Day after tomorrow	*Parson*
Day and night	*Din rat*
Day-blind	*Dinandh*
Day-break	*Vihan, Usha kal*
Day-dream	*Divasvapn*
Days of affluence	*Subhiksh*
Dazed	*Stambhit*
Dazzle of reflected light	*Camkara*

Dead	*Mrit, Nirjeev, Murda*
Dead body	*Lash, Shav*
Dead drunk	*Madhosh*
Dead past	*Gaya-beeta*
Dead set	*Utaroo*
Deadlock	*Gattyavrodh*
Deadly poison	*Halahal*
Deaf	*Behra*
Deafness	*Behrapan*
Deal	*Arthbandh*
Dean of a faculty	*Sankayadhyaksh*
Dear	*Priyjan, Priy*
Dear child	*Munna*
Dear loved	*Dilbar*
Dear to all	*Sarvpriy*
Dearest	*Priytam*
Dearest lady	*Priyatama*
Dearness	*Mehangaee*
Dearness allowance	*Mahengaee bhatta*
Death	*Maut, Dehant, Mrittyu, Svargvas*
Death certificate	*Mrittyupramanak*
Debased	*Acharbhrasht*
Debate	*Shastrarth, Vad-vivad*
Debit balance	*Nama-bakee*
Debit side	*Rinpaksh*
Debris	*Malba*
Debt	*Udhar, Karz*
Debt owed to the ancestors	*Pitririn*
Debtor	*Dandar, Karzdar*
Decade	*Dashak*
Decantation	*Nithar*
Decanter	*Kattar*

Decay	*Kshay, Cheej*
(to) decay	*Chaina*
Decaying	*Kshayee*
Deceit	*Chadm, Jul, Dhokha-dharee*
Deceitful	*Vancak, Kaptee, Prapancee*
Deceitful conduct	*Kat-Kapat, Mitthyacar*
Deceitful talk	*Cakar-makar*
Deceitfulness	*Dagabazee, Vancakta*
Deceiver	*Julbaz*
December	*Disambar*
Decentralisation	*Vikendrikaran*
Decentralised	*Vikendrit*
Deception	*Vancan*
Deceptive	*Indrjalee*
Decided	*Tai, Nirneet*
Decimal	*Dashamlav*
Decision	*Nirnay, Vinishcay*
Decisive	*Nirnayak, Nishcayak*
Declaration	*Ghoshna*
Declinable	*Vikaree*
Decline	*Utrav, Abhibhav*
(to) decline	*Dhurna*
Decoction	*Kwath, Joshanda*
Decompose	*Sarana*
Decomposed	*Sara, Vighatit*
Decomposition	*Vighatan*
Decorated	*Sajjit, Alankrit*
Decoration	*Saj-Sajja, Sajavat, Sajja*
Decrease	*Hras, Ghattee*
(to) decrease	*Ghatana*
Decreasing	*Hrasonmukh*
Decree	*Decree*
Decrepit	*Jarjar*

Deduction	*Nigamit, Nigaman*
Deed	*Pralekh, Karnama*
Deed of agreement	*Ikrareenama*
Deed of compromise	*Sulehnama*
Deed of gift	*Dan-patr*
Deed of treaty	*Sandhipatr*
Deep	*Gahen, Gehra*
Deep anguish	*Marmvedna*
Deep pit	*Khadd*
Deep-rooted	*Baddhmool*
Deer	*Mrig, Hiran*
Deer-eyed	*Mrignaynee*
Defamation	*Manhani*
Defame	*Badnamee*
Defamed	*Badnam*
Defaulting	*Nadihand*
Defeat	*Har, Parajay*
(to) defeat	*Harana*
Defeat and victory	*Har jeet*
Defeated	*Harna, Parast*
Defect	*Dosh, Kharabe, Truti, Nuks*
Defect in sight	*Drishtidosh*
Defection	*Dalbadal*
Defective	*Nakis, Doshyukt*
Defence	*Raksha*
Defence side	*Safaee paksh*
Defendant	*Muddaleh, Prativadee*
Defensive	*Surakshatmak*
Deferentially modest (woman)	*Sheelvatee*
Deferentially modest	*Sheelvan*
Deferment	*Asthagan*
Deficiency	*Kor-kasar, Nyoonta*

Definite	*Sunishcit*
Definitely	*Avashshy*
Definition	*Paribhasha*
Deflated	*Avaspheet*
Deforestation	*Bankataee*
Deformation	*Viroopan*
Deformed	*Vikkrit, Viroopee*
Deformity	*Vikkriti, Viroopta*
Deft	*Siddhhast*
Degraded	*Padcyut, Patit*
Degraded (woman)	*Patita*
Degree	*Upadhee*
Degree (education)	*Decree*
Dehydrated sugarcane	*Khoee*
Deification of an idol	*Pranpratishtha*
Deity	*Devta*
Delay	*Deree*
Delegate	*Deligat*
Delegate	*Prattyayukt*
Deliberation	*Vicar-vimarsh*
Delicacy	*Sukumarta*
Delicacy or tenderness (of body)	*Nazakat*
Delicate	*Nazuk*
Delicious	*Zayakedar, Mazedar*
Delighted	*Anandit*
Delightful coolness	*Taree*
Delighting	*Harshkarak*
Delimitation	*Pariseeman*
Delirium	*Sarsam*
Deliverance	*Najat, Mocan*
Delivered	*Prasoot*
Delivery	*Nistaran*

Delivery of a child	*Japa*
Delta	*Delta*
Delude	*Bharmana*
Deluge	*Jalpralay*
Deluxe edition	*Raj-sanskaran*
Demarcation	*Seemankan*
Demented	*Vikshipt*
Dementia	*Buddhibhransh*
Dementia	*Vikshiptta*
Demerit	*Avgun*
Demiliarisation	*Asainikikaran*
Demise	*Parlokagaman*
Democracy	*Jamhooriyat, Prajatantr*
Demolish	*Dhana*
Demon	*Rakshas, Asur*
Demon king of Lanka	*Ravan*
Demonical	*Paishacee*
Demonstrative	*Pradarshanik*
Demy	*Dimaee*
Den	*Mand*
Denary	*Dashmik*
Dengue fever	*Langra-bukhar*
Denial	*Oon hoon*
Denominative verb	*Nam-dhatu*
Denoting	*Upari*
Denoting 'holder'	*Geer*
Denoting 'above'	*Ut*
Denoting 'accepter'	*Grahee*
Denoting 'aversion'	*Dur*
Denoting 'fulness'	*May*
Denoting 'manifoldness'	*Guna*
Denoting 'negation'	*Nih*

Denoting 'period' of time	*Kaleen*
Denoting 'weight' in seers	*Saree*
Dense	*Kalil*
Denseness	*Saghanta*
Density	*Ghanata*
Dental	*Danty*
Dentist	*Dant-cikitsak*
Dento-labial	*Dantoshthy*
Departed	*Ravana*
Departed soul	*Gatatma*
Department	*Mehkama*
Department of education	*Shiksha-vibhag*
Department of revenue	*Mal-mehkama*
Departmental	*Vibhageey*
Departure	*Ravangee, Kooch*
Departure and arrival	*Gamn agaman*
Dependence	*Paradheenta*
Dependent	*Ashshrit, Nirbhar*
Depiction of character	*Carittrankan*
Depilatory	*Bal-safa*
Deposited	*Nyast*
Depot	*Dipo*
Depressed	*Paddalit*
Deprived	*Mehroom, Vancit*
Depth	*Gambheerry, Gehraee*
Depth (of water)	*Dubav*
Deputation	*Pratinidhan*
Deputy	*Nayab*
Deputy Minister	*Upmantree*

Deputy Commissioner	*Upayukt*
Deputy Leader	*Upneta*
Deputy-Director	*Upsanchalak*
Derision	*Khillee*
Derivation	*Nirukti, Vyutpatti*
Derivative	*Vyutpattik*
Descent	*Avroh, Utraee*
Description	*Byora, Vivran*
Description of a journey	*Safarnama*
Descriptive	*Varnanatmak*
Desert	*Maru, Registan*
Desert land	*Marusthal*
Deserted place	*Veerana*
Deserving be killed	*Vaddhy*
Deserving of being abandoned	*Parityajjy*
Deserving person	*Satpattr*
Design	*Dizain, Banat*
Design of a mattress	*Cataeedar*
Designated	*Padnamit*
Designation	*Padnam*
Desirability	*Vanchneeyta*
Desirable	*Vanchneey*
Desire	*Chah, Cahat*
(to) desire	*Cahna*
Desire to die	*Mumoorsha*
Desired	*Icchit*
Desirelessness	*Nishkambhav*
Despair	*Hatasha*
Despairing	*Hatash*
Despatched	*Prashit*
Despatcher	*Pariprakshak*

Despatching	*Paripreshan*
Desperation	*Nirashonmad*
Despicable	*Kutsit*
Despotic rule	*Nirankush shasan*
Destined	*Niyat*
Destined fated	*Bhavitavvy*
Destined to happen	*Hotavy*
Destiny	*Naseeb, Honee, Niyati*
Destitute	*Akincan, Deen-heen*
Destitution	*Akincanta*
Destroy	*Ghalna*
Destroyed	*Tehas-nehas*
Destructible	*Nashshwar*
Destruction	*Dhwans*
Destruction all round	*Vinash*
Destructive	*Vinashak*
Detached	*Virakt, Vairagee*
Detachment	*Vairag*
Details	*Tafseel*
Detained	*Nazarband*
Detective	*Jasoos*
Detention	*Nazarbandee*
Detenue	*Havalatee*
Determination	*Abhinivash, Kasd, Avdharan*
Determine	*Thanna*
Determined	*Katibaddh, Kritsankalp*
Detestable	*Garhaneey*
Detestation	*Garhan*
Dethroned	*Nichatr*
Devaluation	*Avmoollyan*
Devastation	*Pamalee*
Developability	*Vikassheelta*
Developed	*Viksit*

Development	*Vikas*
Deviate	*Digna*
Deviated	*Vicalit*
Deviated from the right path	*Pathbhrasht*
Deviation	*Vicalan*
Device	*Sippa*
Devil	*Pishac*
Devil-may-care	*Mastram*
Devilish	*Paishacik*
Devilish deed	*Shaitanee*
Devnagri script	*Nagaree*
Devoid of air	*Vayuheen*
Devoid of mobility	*Lunj-punj*
Devoid of thought	*Vicarheen*
Devoid of zest	*Murdadil*
Devoted	*Nishthavan*
Devoted to Truth	*Sattyaparayan*
Devoted to the father	*Pitribhakt*
Devotee	*Upasak*
Devotee of Lord Vishnu	*Bhakt, Vaishnav*
Devotion	*Bhaktee, Lagan*
Devotional acclaim	*Jay-jaykar*
Devotional song	*Bhajan*
Devour	*Bhakosna*
Devout	*Deendar*
Dew	*Shabnam, Os*
Dewy	*Oseela*
Dexterity	*Kushalta*
Diabetes	*Prameh*
Diadem	*Taj*
Diagnosis	*Nidan*

Diagonal (geom.)	*Vikarn*
Diagram	*Arakh*
Dialect	*Vibhasha*
Dialect of Bundalkhand	*Bundalee*
Dialectical	*Vaibhashik*
Diameter	*Vyas*
Diamond	*Heera*
Diamond jubilee	*Heerak-jayantee*
Diarchy	*Dwitantr*
Diarrhoea	*Atisar*
Diary	*Dayree, Roznamca*
Dice	*Pasa*
Dictation	*Imla*
Dictator	*Tanashah*
Dictatorship	*Tanashahee*
Dictionary	*Kosh*
Didactic	*Updeshatmak*
Die	*Thappa*
Diehard	*Kattarpanthee*
Diesel	*Deezal*
Diet	*Khurak*
Diety	*Ishtdev*
Difference	*Antar, Fark, Bhinnta*
Difference in version	*Pathbhed*
Different	*Alag, Bhinn*
Different countries	*Desh-videsh*
Different version	*Pathantar*
Differentiation	*Vibhadan*
Difficult	*Kathin, Mushkil*
Difficult to execute	*Dushkar*
Difficult to hold	*Gilgila*
Difficult to penetrate	*Durbhaddy*
Difficulty	*Kathinta, Dikkat, Museebat*

Dig	*Khodna*
(to) dig and upturn soil	*Gorna*
Digest	*Sarsangrah*
(to) digest	*Pacana*
Digested	*Hazam*
Digestion	*Pacan*
Digestive	*Pacak*
Digestive powder	*Cooran*
Digging	*Khudaee*
Digit of finger	*Por*
Dignified	*Garimapoorn*
Dignity	*Garima, Abroo*
Dilapidated	*Uddhwast, Ucchinn*
Dilapitated	*Gira-para*
Dilatory	*Deerghsoottri*
Dilemma	*Dharmsankat*
Diligence	*Uddyam*
Dilution	*Tanookaran*
Dimensional	*Ayamik*
Diminutive	*Alparthak*
Dine (sp. at ease)	*Jeemna*
Dining cloth	*Dastarkhan*
Dinner	*Byaloo*
Dip	*Dubkee*
Diplomacy	*Kootneeti*
Diplomat	*Kootneetiggy*
Diplomatic	*Rajnayik*
Direct	*Sulta*
Direct perception	*Prattyaksheekaran*
Directed	*Sancalit*
Direction	*Disha, Sancalan, Nirdeshan*
Directional	*Nideshatmak*

Directly	*Seedha*
Director	*Nirdeshak*
Directorate	*Nideshalay*
Directory	*Nideshika*
Dirt	*Mail*
Dirtiness	*Mailapan*
Dirty	*Ganda, Maila*
Dirty and pugnacious	*Maila-kucaila*
Disagreeing	*Asehmat*
Disagreement	*Asehmati*
Disappear	*Choo-mantar*
Disappearance	*Antardhan*
Disappeared	*Gayab*
Disappointed	*Mayoos*
Disappointing	*Nirashajanak*
Disarmed	*Nirastr*
Disarrayed	*Vishrinkhalit*
Disc	*Rakabee*
Disc of the moon	*Candrmandal*
Discharge	*Nirvahan, Sraw*
Discharge of semen	*Veerypat*
Disciple	*Shagird, Cela*
Discipleship	*Shagirdee*
Discipline	*Anushasan*
Disconnection	*Vicchedan*
Disconsolate	*Bakarar*
Discord	*Bigar*
Discordance	*Vaimatty*
Discordant	*Vivadee*
Discordant note	*Viswar*
Discount	*Mitikata*
Discourse	*Pravacan*
Discourteous laughter	*Theethee*

Discovery	*Upaggya*
Discreet	*Vivekee*
Discretionary	*Vivakadheen*
Discrimination	*Bhedbhav*
Discriminative	*Bhedak*
Discussed	*Vivecit*
Discussion	*Mubahisa*
Disease	*Beemaree, Rog*
Diseased	*Roggrast*
Disenchantment	*Mohbhang*
Disgrace	*Ayash*
Disgrace to family	*Kul-kalank*
Disguise	*Kapat vash, Chadmvash*
Disgust	*Nirvad*
Dish of cereal flour	*Phulauree*
Dish of fried or roasted meat	*Korma*
Dish of rice and pulse	*Khichree*
Disharmony	*Viswarta*
Disheartened	*Nirutsahit, Hatotsah*
Dishonest	*Baeeman*
Dishonour	*Baizzattee*
Dishonoured	*Baizzat*
Disinfection	*Visankraman*
Disintegrable	*Vightansheel*
Disintegration	*Viggrah*
Disjoined	*Ashlisht*
Disjointed	*Vilag*
Dislike	*Aruchi*
Disloyal	*Bevafa*
Disloyalty	*Bevafaee*
Dismal	*Muharamee*
Dismissal	*Barkhastgee*

Dismissed	*Kharij*
Disobedience	*Avaggya*
Disorder	*Avvyavastha*
Disorder of the three humours	*Sannipat*
Disorderliness	*Astvyastta*
Disorderly	*Basilsila*
Disorderly crowd	*Bharbhar*
Disparate	*Asam*
Dispensary	*Davakhana*
Dispenser of law	*Muftee*
Dispiritedness	*Avsannta*
Displace	*Hatana*
Displaced	*Visthapit*
Displacement	*Visthapan*
Displeased	*Naraj, Rusht, Nakhush*
Displeasure	*Rushta*
Disposal	*Hala-bhala*
Disposed	*Visarjit*
Disposed to forgive	*Kshamasheel*
Disposition	*Manovritti, Sheel*
Disposition of spending all one earns	*Kapot-vritti*
Disposition to forgive	*Kshamasheelta*
Dispossessed	*Bedakhal*
Disproportionate	*Bedaul*
Disputable	*Vivaddy*
Disputed	*Vivadit*
Disquiet	*Bekararee*
Disregard	*Tiraskar*
Disregarded	*Tiraskrit*
Disrepute	*Rusvaee*
Disreputed	*Kukhyat*

Disrespect	*Anadar, Tauheen, Niradar*
Disruptive	*Vightankaree*
Dissatisfaction	*Asantosh*
Dissatisfied	*Asantusht*
Dissection	*Vyavcchadan*
Dissection hall	*Ceer-phar ghar*
Dissent	*Vimati*
Dissolution	*Vilay*
Dissolve (in the mouth)	*Ghulana*
Distaff	*Takua*
Distance	*Dooree*
Distance of two miles	*Kos*
Distant	*Doorvartee*
Distilled extract	*Arak*
Distillery	*Sharab-khana*
Distinction of caste and community	*Jat-pant*
Distinctive	*Prabhadee*
Distinguishable	*Vibhaddy*
Distinguished	*Ganmanny, Sanbhrant*
Distortion	*Tor-maror*
Distress	*Sankat*
Distressed	*Dukhee*
Distribute	*Bantna*
Distribution	*Vitran*
Distributor	*Vitrak*
District	*Zila*
Disturbed	*Ashant*
Ditch	*Khandak*
Dive	*Gota*
Diver	*Gotakhor*
Diversion	*Dhyan-bhang*
Divided	*Vibhajit*

Divided by maths	*Bata*
Divided into parts	*Vikhand*
Dividend	*Labhansh*
Dividing	*Vibhajak*
Dividing into two equal parts	*Dvibhajan*
Divine	*Eeshshvareey*
Divine being	*Divvy-purush*
Divine figure	*Divvy-moorti*
Divine form of life	*Devyoni*
Divine insight	*Divvy-drishti*
Divine messenger	*Paigambar*
Divine radiance	*Brahmtaj*
Diviner	*Daivaggy*
Divinity	*Davattw*
Divisible	*Vibhajjy*
Division	*Kand, Vibhag*
Division (maths)	*Batana*
Division of labour	*Shramvibhajan*
Divisional	*Mandalik*
Divisional officer	*Pramandaladhikaree*
Divisor	*Bhajak*
Divorce	*Vivah-vicched*
Divorced	*Talakshuda*
Do	*Karna*
Do's and dont's	*Vidhi-nishedh*
Doctor	*Daktar*
Doctrine of re-incarnation	*Punarjanmvad*
Documentary film	*Vritt-cittr*
Documents	*Kagazpatr*
Dodge	*Bhulava, Butta*
Dodger	*Tareebaz*

Dodgery	*Julbazee*
Doer	*Karvaiya*
Dogged pertenacity	*Hameer hath*
Dogmatism	*Mataggreh*
Dogmatist	*Mataggrahee*
Doing a thing over again	*Pishtpashan*
Doings	*Karnee*
Doll	*Guriya*
Dollar	*Dalar*
Dome	*Dumbad*
Dome of the sky	*Gagan mandal*
Domestic	*Ghareloo*
Domiciled	*Avasit*
Domineering	*Havee*
Donation	*Dan*
Donation of land as a religious act	*Bhoodan-yaggy*
Done	*Krit*
Done away with	*Rafa-dafa*
Done with the two hands	*Duhatee*
Donkey	*Gadha*
Donor	*Data*
Donor of blood	*Raktdata*
Door	*Darvaza, Kivar*
Door-chain	*Kundee*
Door-frame	*Caukhat*
Doorkeeper	*Darban*
Doorsill	*Dehree*
Doorway	*Pravashdwar*
Dormancy	*Prasuptavastha*
Dormant	*Prasupt*

Dot	*Bindu*
Dotage	*Sathiyaw*
Double	*Dugna*
Double deck boat	*Bajra*
Double haver-sack	*Khurjee*
Double vision	*Dwidrishti*
Double-barrelled	*Donalee*
Double-storeyed	*Dumanzila*
Doubt	*Shanka*
Doubtful	*Shankaneey*
Doubtfulness	*Sandigdhta*
Doubting	*Sanshyalu*
Doubting nature	*Shakkeepan*
Doubtless	*Asandigdh*
Doubtlessness	*Nirbhrantata*
Dove	*Paraee, Pandukee*
Dow and out	*Phatehal*
Downfall	*Adhahpatan*
Downtrodder	*Dalit*
Downward slope	*Dhal*
Dowry	*Jahez, Dahej*
Doze	*Jhapkee*
Dozen	*Darjan*
Draft	*Pralekh*
Draftsman	*Naksha-navees*
Drain	*Nala*
Drama	*Natak, Drama*
Dramatic art	*Nattykala*
Dramatic paly of the Ramayana	*Ramleela*
Dramaturgist	*Nattyashastree*
Dramaturgy	*Nattyshastr*
Draw	*Urahana*

(to) draw out	*Karhna*
Drawbar	*Argal*
Drawer	*Daraz*
Drawer of wire	*Tarkashee*
Drawing	*Aggrahan*
Drawing of graphs	*Alekhan*
Drawing room	*Deevankhana*
Dreadful	*Bheeshm, Ruddr, Karal*
Dreadfulness	*Ruddrata, Bhayanakta*
Dream	*Sapna*
Dreamer	*Swapndrashta, Swapndarshee*
Dreamland	*Swapnlok*
Dreamvision	*Swapn-darshan*
Dregs	*Seethee*
Drenched	*Tarabor, Sharabor*
Dress	*Libas, Poshak, Dres, Pehnava*
Dressing bandaging	*Malhampatti*
Dried cow-dung used as fuel	*Upala, Kanda*
Dried ginger	*Sonth*
Dried plum	*Aloo bukhara*
Drill	*Kavayad*
(to) drill	*Chedna*
Drill (for making holes)	*Barma*
Drink	*Peena*
Drinker and meat-eating	*Sharabee-kababee*
Drinking of wine	*Maddypan, Surapan*
Drive	*Hankna*
(to) drive a nail	*Keelna*
(to) drive away	*Khadna*
Driver	*Calak, Draivar*

Drizzle	*Phuhar, Tapakna, Jheensee*
Dromedarian	*Sanrnee-savar*
Dromedary	*Sanrnee*
Drop	*Katra, Boond*
Dropsy	*Jalodar*
Dross	*Dhatu-mail*
Drought	*Avarshan, Jhoora*
Drown	*Dubona*
Drowsiness	*Khumaree*
Drug	*Bhashaj*
Drum	*Pakhavaj, Bharee, Dram, Daundee*
Drummer	*Nakkarcee*
Drunk	*Matvala*
Drunkard	*Sharabee, Nashakhor, Piyakkar*
Drunkenness	*Nashakhoree, Madonmattta*
Dry	*Sookha, Shushk, Khushk, Nirjal*
(to) dry up	*Jharna, Sukhana*
Dry and prosaic	*Arasik*
Dry cleaning	*Sookhee-dhulaee*
Dry cough	*Dhaska*
Dry crust over an wound	*Khurand*
Dry flour used to help	*Palathan*
Dry fruit	*Mava*
Dry itch	*Sookhee khujlee*
Dryad	*Vandavee*
Dryness	*Khushkee*
Dualism	*Dwaitvad*
Duality	*Dwait*
Dubitative	*Sandahsheel*
Duck and plunge out (again and again)	*Cubhakna*

Due	*Day, Praptavvy*
Due Respect	*Adarsamman*
Due to cause	*Karanvash*
Due to relation	*Nata*
Due to shyness	*Sankocvash*
Duel	*Dwandw*
Dues	*Pavna, Lehna*
Duet	*Jugal-bandee, Dugana*
Duffer	*Capargattu*
Dug off	*Khudna*
Dull	*Mandbuddhi*
Dull and toilsome	*Pittamar*
Dullard	*Bhondoo*
Dullardness	*Bhondoopan*
Dumb	*Goonga*
Dumbness	*Goongapan*
Dump	*Parna*
Dumping	*Pataee*
Dun	*Takaza*
Dunce	*Koorhmagz*
Dune	*Teeba*
Dung	*Gobar*
Dunghill	*Ghoor*
Duplicate	*Dwitteeyak, Pratilipi*
Duplication	*Dvittw*
Durability	*Tikaoopan*
Durable	*Paydar, Tikaoo*
Duration	*Muddat, Kalavadhi*
Duress	*Hirasat*
Dust	*Dhool, Garad*
Dust absorbing	*Mailkhora*
Dust and din	*Dhool-dhakkar*
Dust of the feet	*Carandhoolee*

Dust-absorbing	*Gardkhor*
Dust-coloured	*Matmaila*
Dustbin	*Kuradan*
Duster	*Jharan*
Dusting and cleaning	*Jhar-buhar*
Dusty	*Mateela*
Dutch	*Dac*
Dutiful	*Kartavyanishth*
Dutiful son	*Supattr*
Dutifulness	*Kartavyata*
Duty	*Kartavya, Farz*
Duty of a Patwari	*Patvareegeeree*
Duty of a woman	*Naree-dharm*
Duty of an envoy	*Doot-karm*
Dwarf	*Vaman*
Dwarfish	*Nata, Bauna*
Dweller	*Bashinda*
Dwelling	*Dera, Besara*
Dwelling in Heaven	*Swargasth*
Dwelling in the forest	*Banvas, Vanvasee*
Dye-stuff	*Ranjak*
Dyed	*Rangna*
Dyer	*Rangraj*
Dying	*Rangaee*
Dying together	*Sehmaran*
Dynamic	*Gatik*
Dynasty	*Gharana, Rajvansh*
Dysentry	*Pacis*
Dyspepsia	*Mandagni*

E

Each	*Fee, Prattyek*
Eager	*Utsuk, Lalayit*
Eagerness	*Aturta, Utsukta*
Eagle	*Ukab, Garur, Baz*
Ear	*Karn, Kan*
Ear-top	*Kanphool, Kundal, Jhumka*
Early in the evening	*Sarasham*
Early morning	*Tarka, Prabhat, Pratahkal*
Earn	*Kamana*
(to) earn one's livelihood	*Khana-kamana*
Earned	*Arjit*
Earnest insistence	*Aggrah*
Earnest money	*Bayana*
Earning	*Kamaee*
Earth	*Dhartee, Prithvee*
Earth bed	*Bhooshayya*
Earthen ball	*Gulta*
Earthen bowl	*Kasora, Sakora*
Earthen firepot	*Borsee*
Earthen funnel	*Cilam*
Earthen lamp	*Deeya*
Earthern pitcher	*Matka*
Earthen pot with a hole	*karva*
Earthen roofing tile	*Khapra*
Earthen water pot	*Gagar, Ghara*
Earthly existence	*Ihleela*
Earthquake	*Bhookamp, Zalzala*
Earthworm	*Kanchua*
Earty	*Kshiti*
Easement	*Abhog, Paribhog*
Easily	*Sugamtapoorvak*

Easily digestible	*Supaccy*
Easily intelligible	*Subodh*
Easiness	*Asanee, Sugamta*
East	*Poorab*
East wind	*Purvaee*
Eastern	*Poorvee, Poorbeey*
Easy	*Asan, Sahaj, Sugam*
Easy availability	*Sulabhta*
Easy life	*Mauj-panee*
Easy-loving	*Suvidhajeevee*
Eat	*Khana*
(to) eat just a little for taste	*Jutharna*
(to) eat slowly and bit by bit	*Toongna*
(to) eat something in a small quantity	*Colna*
(to) eat to the full	*Thoorna*
Eatable	*Khady*
Eater	*Bhojee*
Eaves dropping	*Kansuee*
Ebony	*Abnoos*
Ebullience	*Uphan*
Eccentric	*Jhalla*
Echo	*Goonj*
(to) echo	*Gunjna*
Ecliptic	*Ravi marg, Krantivritt*
Ecology	*Paryavarna*
Economic	*Arthik*
Economic crisis	*Arthsankat*
Economic policy	*Arthneeti*
Economics	*Arthshastr*
Economist	*Arthshastree*

Economy	*Arthvyavastha*
Ecstasy	*Harshonmad*
Ecstatic	*Samadhimagn*
Eczema	*Pama, Chajan*
Edge	*Kor*
Edge of a kite	*Kannee*
Edible	*Bhojy*
Edible and inedible	*Bhakshya-bhakshy*
Edible part of a nut	*Giree*
Edited	*Sampadit*
Editing	*Sampadan*
Edition	*Sanskaran*
Editor	*Sampadak*
Editorial	*Sampadakeey*
Editorial board	*Sampadak-mandal*
Editorship	*Sampadakattw*
Educated	*Shikshit*
Educated man	*Baboo sahab*
Education	*Shiksha, Taleem*
Educative	*Shikshaprd*
Effect	*Asar, Taseer*
Effect of dazzling light on the eyes	*Cakacaundh*
Effective	*Gunkaree, Prabhavee*
Effects	*Mal-mata*
Effeminacy	*Strainta*
Effeminate man	*Shikhandee*
Effervescence	*Budbudahat*
Efficacious	*Akseer*
Efficiency	*Dakshta, Karyakushalta*
Efficient	*Daksh, Karyakushal*
Effigy	*Putla, Pratipurush*
Effort	*Prayatn, Koshish*

Effulgence	*Samujjwalta*
Effulgent	*Samujjwal*
Egg	*And*
Egg shaped	*Andakar*
Ego	*Aham*
Egoism	*Ahambhav*
Egotism	*Asmita, Ahammannyta*
Egotistic	*Ahammanny*
Egypt	*Missr*
Eight	*Ath*
Eight-faced	*Athpehla*
Eight-times	*Athguna*
Eighth	*Athva*
Eighty	*Assee*
Eighty-five	*Pacasee*
Eighty-four	*Caurasee*
Eighty-nine	*Navasee*
Eighty-one	*Ikkyasee*
Eighty-seven	*Sattasee*
Eighty-six	*Chiyasee*
Eighty-three	*Tirasee*
Eighty-two	*Bayasee*
Ejected	*Utkshipt*
Ejection	*Utkshapan*
Ejectment	*Badakhlee*
Elaborate	*Vishad*
Elaborately	*Vistarpoorvak*
Elastic	*Laceela, Lacakdar, Tanny*
Elasticity	*Tannyta, Lap, Loc*
Elbow	*Kohnee*
Elder	*Gurujan, Jatha*
Elder brother	*Daoo, Aggraj*
Elder person	*Buzurg*

Elder sister	*Jeejee, Deedee*
Elderliness	*Barappan, Buzurgee*
Eldest	*Jyashth*
Elected	*Nirvacit*
Election	*Nirvacan*
Election campaign	*Cunaw-ahbiyan*
Election petition	*Cunaw-yacika*
Election propaganda	*Cunaw-pracar*
Elector	*Nirvacak*
Electorate	*Cunav-mandal*
Electricity	*Viddyut*
Elegance	*Anban*
Elegance of words	*Shabdsaushthav*
Elegy	*Marsiya, Shokgeet*
Element	*Tattw*
Elementary	*Arambhik*
Elephant	*Hathee, Gaz*
Elephant driver	*Mahavat, Hatheevan*
Elephant-shed	*Hatheekhana*
Elephantiasis	*Shleepad, Feelpanw*
Elevated	*Unnat*
Eleventh month of the Ḥindu Calendar	*Magh*
Eligibility	*Pattrta*
Eligible person	*Pattr*
Eliminated	*Vilopit*
Elimination	*Vilopan*
Elixir	*Sanjeevnee, Somras*
Elongation	*Tabalat, Deergheekaran*
Emancipated	*Vimocit*
Emancipation	*Mukit, Vimocan*
Embankment	*Pushta, Tatbandh*
Embarassment	*Sakucahat*

Embarrassed	*Dik*
Embarrassed to end	*Khwar*
Embassy	*Dootavas*
Embedded	*Khachit*
Embellish	*Mandna*
(to) embellish and decorate	*Sajana-sanvarna*
Embellished	*Shobhit, Vimandit*
Embezzlement	*Gaban*
Embrace	*Alingan, Parirambhan*
(to) embrace	*Cipatna*
(to) embrace tightly	*Bheencna*
Embrace of love	*Pramalingan*
Embroidered	*Patwa, Bootadar*
Embroidered cloth	*Cikan*
Embroidery	*Nakshee, Bel-Boota*
Emcumbrance	*Rinbhar*
Emerald	*Panna*
Emergency	*Apatkal, Apat kaleen*
Emergent	*Apatik*
Emigration	*Pravas*
Eminence	*Prakarsh*
Emissary	*Alcee*
Emit foul smell	*Gandhana*
Emotion	*Jazba*
Emotion of love	*Prambhav*
Emotional	*Bhavpravan*
Emotive	*Bhavottajak*
Emperor	*Samrat, Maharaj, Raja*
Emphasis	*Balaghat*
Empire	*Raj-pat, Samrajjy*
Empiric	*Anubhavik*
Empirical	*Prayogvadee*

Employable	*Niyojjy*
Employee	*Mulazim, Karmchari*
Employment	*Mulazmat*
Empress	*Maharanee, Sammraggyee*
Emptiness	*Reetapan*
Empty	*Rikt, Khalee*
Enacted	*Abhineet*
Enamel	*Tamceenee*
Enameller	*Meenakar*
Enamoured	*Fida*
Enchanted dust	*Burkee*
Enchanting	*Dilruba*
Enchantment	*Mohnee*
Encircled	*Avrit, Parivashtit*
Encirclement	*Ghar-ghar*
Enclose	*Gharna*
Enclosed	*Samavrit, Sannivisht*
Enclosing	*Pariveshtan*
Enclosure	*Bara, Ghar*
Encomium	*Yashogan*
Encounter	*Mukabla, Amnasamna*
Encouraged	*Utsahit, Protsahit*
Encouragement	*Protsahan, Utsahvardhan*
Encyclopaedia	*Vishshwakosh*
End	*Sira, Ant*
Endeavour	*Uddyog*
Endeavouring	*Prayatnvan, Prayatnsheel*
Ending	*Samapan*
Endless	*Antheen, Baintiha*
Endorsed	*Prishthankit*
Endorsement	*Bacan, Prishthankan*
Endowment	*Nyas*
Endure	*Saharna*

Endurance	*Sahhyta, Titiksha*
Enduring spirit	*Sthaee bhav*
Enemy	*Shatru, Vairee, Bairee, Ari, Dushman*
Energetic	*Uddyamee, Oorjasswee*
Energy	*Urja*
Energygiving	*Shaktivardhak*
Enervated	*Avsann*
Engaged	*Vagdatta*
Engagement	*Sagaee*
Engime pectoris	*Urshool*
Engine	*Injan*
Engine-driver	*Injan draivar*
Engineer	*Ingeeniyar*
English	*Angrazee*
Engrave	*Ukarna*
(to) engrave	*Nakashna*
Engraved	*Utkeern, Nakkasheedar*
Engraver	*Nakkash*
Engraving	*Nakkashee*
Engrossed	*Lipt, Magn, Nirat, Talleen*
Engrossment	*Talleenta*
Enigma	*Bujhauwal*
Enjoy	*Khelna khana*
(to) enjoy life	*Khana-peena*
Enjoyment	*Sukhbhog, Bhog*
Enlarged	*Parivardhit, Sanvardhit*
Enlargement of the scrotum	*Koshvriddhi*
Enlightened	*Sambuddh, Udbuddh, Prabuddh*
Enlightening	*Prabodhan*
Enlightenment	*Sambuddhi, Atmbodh*
Enmity	*Shatruta, Bair, Adavat*

Enough	*Bas, Kafee, Paryapt*
Enquiries	*Poochtach, Khojkhabar*
Enraged	*Kupit*
Enrolment	*Namlikhaee*
Ensign	*Potdhwaj*
Entangle	*Uljhana*
Entanglement	*Uljhav, Janjal*
Entangling	*Bajhaoo*
Enter	*Paithna*
(to) enter in the proper register	*Khatiyana*
Entered	*Dakhil, Pravisht*
Enternal spirit	*Brahm*
Entertainment	*Manoranjan, Pramod*
Enthroned	*Gaddeenasheen, Rajjybhishikt*
Enthusiasm	*Utsah, Umang*
Enthusiastic	*Utsahee, Utsahvardhak*
Enthusiastically	*Utsahpoorvak*
Entice	*Lubhana*
Entire	*Salim, Samast, Sampoorn, Kul, Tamam*
Entire assets	*Laee-poonjee*
Entirely	*Poorntah, Sampoorntah*
Entity	*Bhav, Astittv*
Entomology	*Keetvigyan, Krimivigyan*
Entrance	*Intrains*
Entrap	*Phansana*
Entrapment	*Phansav*
Entreat	*Girgirana*
Entreated	*Abbhyarthit*
Entreaty	*Abbhyarthana, Girgirahat, Vintee*
Entrust	*Saunpna*
Entrusted	*Supurd*

Entry	*Nivishti, Pravishti*
Envelope	*Lifafa*
Enviable	*Eershy*
Envious	*Dehee*
Environment	*Parivesh, Paryavaran*
Environmental	*Paryavarik*
Envoy	*Doot*
Envy	*Dah, Keena, Kurhan*
Eon	*Kalp*
Ephemeral	*Kshanbhangur*
Epic	*Mahakavvy*
Epidemic	*Marak, Vaba*
Epigram	*Cutkula*
Epigrammatism	*Cutkulebazee*
Epigrammatist	*Cutkulabaz*
Epigraph	*Puralakh*
Epilepsy	*Mirgee*
Epilogue	*Bharatvakky*
Episode	*Antarkatha*
Episode of one's life	*Ramkahanee*
Epitaph	*Samadhi-lakh*
Epitome of qualities	*Gunakar*
Epochmaker	*Yug-pravartak*
Equal	*Saman, Sam, Tully, Pattar*
Equalising	*Samkaree*
Equality	*Samanta, Samta, Barabaree*
Equanimity	*Samdarishti*
Equanimous	*Sambuddhi*
Equator	*Vishuvat vritt, Bhoomaddhyrakha*
Equatorial	*Vishvat*
Equilateral	*Sambahuj, Sambahu*
Equilibrium	*Samtolan, Sammyavastha*
Equinox	*Vishuv*

Equipage	*Saj*
Equipped	*Sannaddh*
Equipped with a quiver	*Tarkashband*
Equipped with parachute	*Chatreedharee*
Equitable	*Nyayvan, Nyaysangat*
Equity	*Suneeti*
Equivalence	*Tullyta, Samanarthakta*
Equivalent	*Pratishabd, Samanarth*
Era	*Samvat*
Erase	*Mitna*
(to) erase	*Mitana*
Erotic	*Shringaree*
Errata	*Shuddhipatr*
Error	*Digbhram, Bhool, Cook*
Errors and omissions	*Bhool-chok*
Eruption	*Sphotan*
Escaped	*Palayit*
Escort	*Margrakshak*
Esoteric	*Deekshaneey*
Espionage	*Guptcharrya*
Essay	*Nibandh*
Essence	*Satt, Nicor, Lubba-lubab*
Essential	*Sarbhoot*
Essential portion	*Sarbhag*
Essetial element	*Madda*
Established	*Kayam, Pratishthapit*
Establishment	*Sansthapan, Pratishthan*
Estate	*Riyasat, Bhoosampatti, Jageer, Tallukadaree*
Estate holder	*Ilakedar*
Esteemed	*Sammanit*

Estimate — *Ankna*
(to) estimate — *Kootna*
(to) estimate the depth — *Thahna*
Estimated — *Akalit*
Estimation — *Prakkalan, Aganan*
Estrangement — *Manmutav*
Estuary — *Muhana*
Etcetera — *Vagairah*
Eternal — *Sanatan, Shashshwat*
Eternal sleep — *Cir-samadhi, Cir-niddra*
Eternity — *Shashshwatta*
Ether — *Eethar*
Ethics — *Neetishastr*
Etiquette — *Saleeka*
Etteminate — *Strain*
Etymological derivaion — *Vyutpadan*
Etymology — *Nirukt*
Eulogy — *Sadhuvad, Yashgan, Virud*
Eulogy of hero — *Veergatha*
Eunuch — *Khoja*
Euphemism — *Mangalbhashan*
Euphemistic — *Mangalbhashit*
Euphorbia species plant — *Thoohar*
European — *Yooropiyan, Firangee*
Evacuation — *Shauc, Niptan, Nishkraman*
Evacuee — *Nishkrant*
Even — *Taham*
Even then — *Tadapi, Punrapi*
Evening — *Sanjh, Sham, Sandhya*
Evening meet — *Sandhya goshthee*
Evening of life — *Jeevan-sandhya*

Evening time	*Sayankal, Sandhykal*
Evening worship	*Sandhya opasna, Sandhya vandan*
Eventful	*Ghatnapoorn*
Eventide	*Sandhyabala*
Ever	*Sarvada*
Ever ready	*Mustaid*
Ever-green	*Sadabahar*
Ever-memorable	*Cirasmarneey*
Everlasting	*Akshay*
Everpestering enemies	*Rahu-ketu*
Everyone	*Harak*
Everywhere	*Sarvattr*
Evidently	*Prattyakshtaya*
Evil	*Pap, Badee*
Evil conjunction of stars	*Bhaddra*
Evil day	*Kudin*
Evil deed	*Kukarm*
Evil effect	*Kuprabhav*
Evil practice	*Kureeti*
Evil result	*Kuparinam*
Evil spirit	*Bhootprat*
Evil tradition	*Kusanskar*
Evil-faced	*Kalmunha*
Evil-minded	*Durmati*
Evil-tongued	*Badzaban*
Evolutionary	*Vikasvadee*
Ex-communication	*Jatibahishkar*
Exact	*Avitath*
Exact half	*Adho adh*
Exactly	*Yatharthtah*
Exactly in the midway	*Beeconbeec*

Exactly like	*Hoobahoo*
Exaggerated	*Atishayoktipoorn*
Exaggerated description	*Panvara*
Exaggeration	*Atishayokti*
Exaltation of emotion	*Bhavotkarsh*
Examination	*Imtahan, Pareeksha*
Examine	*Nirakhna*
(to) examine critically	*Parakhna*
Examined	*Jancna, Pareekshit*
Examinee	*Pareeksharthee*
Examiner	*Pareekshak*
Example	*Misal, Udaharan*
Exceeding	*Samadhik, Ateev*
Excellence	*Uttama*
Excellent idea	*Suvicar*
Excellent result	*Satphal*
Excess	*Atirek, Attyadhikta*
Excessive	*Bahad, Attyadhik*
Excessive rain	*Ativrishti*
Excessively eager	*Utavala*
Exchange	*Badlaul, Vinimay*
(to) exchange pleasantries	*Hansna-bolna*
Exchange of blows	*Mukka-mukkee*
Exchange of ideas	*Vicar-vinimay*
Exchangeability	*Vinimayta*
Exchangeable	*Vinimay*
Excise	*Abkaree*
Excite	*Ukasna*
(to) excite	*Lehkarna*
Excitement	*Josh, Uttajana*

Excitement of sex-urge	*Kamoddeepan*
Exclusive	*Akantik*
Excrement	*Vishtha, Chiya, Pureesh*
Excusable	*Kshammy*
Executed	*Nishpadit, Karyanvit*
Execution	*Tameel, Karryanviyan*
Executioner	*Vadhik*
Executive	*Nishpadak, Karrypalika*
Executive power	*Kartrittw shakti*
Exercise	*Dand*
Exggeration	*Mubalga*
Exhalation	*Nishwas*
Exhausted	*Nidhal, Parishshrant*
Exhaustion	*Thakavat*
Exhibit	*Darshana*
Exhibited	*Pradarship*
Exhibition	*Numaish, Pradarshanee*
Exhibition of news	*Samacar-darshan*
Exhibitive	*Pradarshak*
Exhilirating	*Ullasjanak*
Exile	*Vanvas, Nirvasan, Desh-nikala*
Exiled	*Nirvasit*
Existence	*Satta, Asti, Bhav*
Exit	*Nikas*
Expanded	*Spheet, Prasarit*
Expanse	*Pasar*
Expansible	*Prasaransheel*
Expansion	*Vistar, Phailaw, Prasaran*
Expansionism	*Vistarvad*
Expansive	*Prashast*
Expatiation	*Vivecana*
Expectant	*Prattyashee*

Expectation *Prattyasha*
Expected *Prattyashit*
Expectorate *Khakharana*
Expedition *Abhidhavan*
Expelled *Nishkasit*
Expenditure *Vyay*
Expense *Kharch*
Expensive *Mehanga*
Experience *Anubhav, Tajarba*
Experienced *Tajarbekar*
Experimentalism *Prayogvad*
Experimenter *Prayogee*
Expert *Mahir, Parkhee, Praveen*
Expiatory *Prayashtitatmak*
Expiration *Nihshvas*
Explanation *Vyakhya*
Explanatory *Vyakhyatmak*
Explicit protest *Cee-capar*
Exploded *Sphotit*
Exploitation *Shoshan*
Exploiter *Shoshak*
Explosion *Visphot*
Explosive *Visphotak*
Exponent *Pratipadak, Vyakhyata, Meemansak*
Export *Niryat*
Exporter *Niryatak*
Expose *Fash, Ugharna*
Exposition *Pratipatti*
Exposure *Ughara, Bhandaphor*
Expounded *Paratipann, Pratipadit*
Express *Akspres*
(to) express umbrage *Pirakna*
Expressed *Abhivyakt, Vyajit*

Expression	*Abhivyakti*
Expression of gratitude	*Abharpradarshan*
Expression of sentiment	*Bhavvyanjan*
Expressive	*Vyanjak, Bhavvyanjak*
Expressiveness	*Abhivyanjakta*
Expulsion	*Nikala*
Extended	*Vitat*
Extending over a fixed period	*Miyadee*
Extension	*Vistriti, Vistran, Prasar, Vitati*
Extent	*Vistar*
Extermination of a family	*Vanshnash*
External	*Bahirang, Bahhy, Bahree*
Externally	*Bahhyta*
Extinction	*Nirvapan, Vilop*
Extinguished	*Shamit*
Extirpated	*Utpatit*
Extirpation	*Utpatan*
Extra-ordinary	*Gairmamooli*
Extract	*Ark*
Extracted	*Nissrit*
Extraction	*Ucched*
Extravagance	*Fajoolkharcee*
Extravagant	*Uraoo, Kharceela, Fajoolkharc*
Extreme	*Nitant, Curant, Dhur*
Extreme cruelty	*Kasaeepan*
Extremely cunning	*Chatteesa*
Extremely niggardly	*Makkheecoos*
Extremely pleased	*Lahalot*
Extremely sour	*Cukk*

Extremely unlucky	*Karmjalee*
Extremism	*Ativad, Uggrvad*
Extremist	*Ativadee, Uggrvadee*
Extremist party	*Garam dal*
Extrovert	*Bahirmukhee*
Exuberance of emotion	*Bhavatirak*
Exuberant	*Cakacak*
Eye	*Nain, Netr, Nayan, Deeda, Ankh*
Eye ball	*Koya, Dala*
Eye brow	*Bhroo, Tavar, Bhrikutee*
Eye lashes	*Parbal, Baraunee*
Eye of a needle	*Nakka*
Eye sight	*Drishti, Nazar*
Eyelid	*Palak*

F

Fabricated	*Jalee*
Fabrication	*Jalsazee*
Fabulous	*Akkhyanik*
Face	*Cehra, Mukhra*
Face to face	*Amna Samna, Hoobahoo*
Facet	*Pehal, Pehloo*
Facial expression	*Mukhakriti*
Facility	*Suvidha, Sahooliyat*
Facing	*Abhimukh*
Facing east	*Poorvabhimukh*
Fact	*Tatthy*
Factor	*Ghatak*
Factory	*Faiktree, Karkhana, Nirmanshala*
Factual	*Tatthyak, Satatthy*
Faculty	*Sankay, Kriya-shakti*
Faculty of discrimination	*Bhedbuddhi*
Faculty of reasoning	*Vivak*
Fade	*Kumhlana, Murjhana*
Faded	*Vivarn*
Faded colour	*Badrang*
Faeces	*Goo*
Fagged	*Last*
Failed	*Viphalta, Nakam, Anutteern, Fel*
Fainting	*Gash, Moorcha*
Fair-complexion	*Gora*
Fairly Good	*Acchakhasa*
Fairly well off	*Khata-peeta*
Fairness	*Gorapan*
Fairy	*Hoor*
Fairy land	*Pareelok, Paristan*
Faith	*Astha, Itbar*
Faithful	*Asthavan*

Faithful friend	*Damsaz*
Faithful to husband	*Pativrata*
Faithfulness	*Patneevrat*
Faithless	*Totacashm*
Faithlessness	*Totacashmee*
Fake	*Kritak*
Falcon	*Sacan*
Fall	*Bhransh, Patan, Giravat, Nipat*
(to) fall	*Girna*
(to) fall off	*Jharna*
Fallacy logic	*Hattwabhas*
Fallen flat	*Dharashayee*
Fallen from duty	*Kartavyacyut*
Falling	*Patanonmukh*
Falling down	*Skhalan*
Fallow	*Partee*
False	*Jhootha, Mitthya*
False accusation	*Tohmat*
False excuse	*Heela-havala*
False hope	*Durasha*
False notion	*Vaham*
False pride	*Mitthyabhiman*
False show	*Dhaddha*
False-hope	*Dam-pattee*
Falsehood	*Jhooth*
Falsify	*Jhuthlana*
Falt-finding	*Nuktaceenee*
Falter	*Bicakna, Larkharana*
Fame	*Mashhooree, Prasiddhi, Khyati, Namvaree*
Family	*Khandan, Pariwar*
Family custom	*Kulachar*
Family deity	*Kuldevta*

Family feeling	*Parivarikta*
Family history	*Vanshcarit*
Family relationship	*Natagota*
Family set-up	*Ghargrihasthee*
Family succession	*Vanshanukram*
Family tradition	*Kulparampara, Vansh-parampara*
Famine	*Bhukhmaree, Akal, Kehat*
Famine stricken	*Akalpeerit*
Famished	*Bhukhar, Bhukhmara*
Famous	*Mashhoor, Prasiddh*
Fan	*Pankha*
(to) fan	*Jhalna*
Fanatical	*Tassubee, Dharmandh*
Fanciful imagination	*Kapol kalpna*
Fancy	*Fainsee*
Fancy fair	*Meenabazar*
Fang of a snake	*Sarpdant*
Far East	*Sudoorpoorw*
Far away	*Door*
Far off	*Sudoor*
Far-sighted	*Doorandash*
Far-sightedness	*Doorandashee*
Fare	*Bardana*
Farewell	*Vidaee, Bida*
Faring	*Vyomcaree*
Farrier	*Nalband*
Farsight	*Doordrishti*
Farsightedness	*Doordarshita*
Fascimile	*Pratikriti*
Fascinated	*Mohee, Mugdh, Mohit*
Fascinating	*Hridaygrahee, Sammohak, Sammohan*
Fascination	*Sammoh, Moh, Mugdhta*

Fascination of dress	*Catak-matak*
Fascism	*Fasizm*
Fashion	*Faishan*
Fashionable	*Shaukeen*
Fast	*Vrat, Upvas*
Fast-moving	*Drutgati, Kshipprgamee*
Fasting	*Anahar*
Fat	*Vasa, Mota, Sthool*
Fat person	*Mutka*
Fat-bellied	*Lambodar*
Fatal	*Pranghatak*
Fatalistic	*Bhaggyvadee*
Fate	*Takdeer, Kismat*
Fated	*Bada*
Father	*Babul, Bapoo, Pita, Bap*
Father hood	*Pittrittv*
Father land	*Pittri desh*
Father's elder brother	*Taoo, Taya*
Father's sister	*Bua, Phoophee*
Father-in-law of son/daughter	*Samdhi, Samdhee*
Father-in-law's father	*Dadiyasasur*
Father-in-law's mother	*Dadiya sas*
Father-inlaw	*Sasur*
Fatigue	*Thakan*
Fatigued	*Klant, Sashshram*
Fatness	*Mutapa, Sthoolta, Motapan*
Fatten	*Mutana*
Fattiness	*Mutaee*
Fatty	*Vaseey*

Fatty part of milk	*Malaee*
Fault	*Kasoor*
Fault-finder	*Nuktacee*
Faultless	*Beab*
Faulty	*Aibee, Dooshit*
Favour	*Inayat, Kripa*
Favourable	*Anukool*
Favourableness	*Abhimukhta*
Favourably inclined	*Mafik*
Favourite disciple	*Pattshishy*
Fawn	*Mrigchauna*
Fear	*Dar, Bhay*
(to) fear	*Darna*
Fearless	*Nirbhay, Nidar*
Fearlessness	*Dabangpan, Nidarpan, Nirbhayta*
Feast	*Jevnar, Davat, Jyonar*
Feat	*Kamal, Kartab, Karamat*
Feat of wisdom	*Buddhikaushal*
Feather of a peacock	*Koorch*
Feathers cut off	*Parkata*
February	*Farvaree*
Fed up	*Uktana*
Federal	*Sangheey*
Federated	*Sanghbaddh*
Fee	*Fees, Shulk*
Feed (with respect)	*Jimana*
Feeding bottle	*Bharan, Doodh-pilaee*
Feel	*Anubhav karna, Mahsoos karna*
(to) feel a scaratchy sensation	*Culculana*
(to) feel agonizing pain	*Tarapna*
(to) feel bored	*Oobna*

(to) feel drowsy	*Alsana*
(to) feel embarassed	*Sakucana*
(to) feel half-hearted	*Kachiyana*
(to) feel irritated	*Kheejna*
(to) feel itching sensation	*Salsalana*
(to) feel like wriggling	*Kasmasana*
(to) feel with the hands	*Tatolna*
Feel restless	*Akulana*
Feel shy	*Jhanpna, Sharmana*
Feeling	*Anubhooti*
Feeling of vomitting	*Ubkaee*
Fees paid for serving summons	*Talbana*
Fefresher course	*Punashcarya*
Felicitation Volume	*Abhinandan granth*
Fellow countryman	*Dashvasee*
Fellow student	*Gurubhaee*
Fellow-traveller	*Hamsafar*
Felt	*Mehsoos*
Female	*Agammya*
Female Blackbee	*Bhaunree*
Female Pigeon	*Kabootree*
Female animal	*Mada*
Female ascetic	*Tapsee*
Female beggar	*Bhikharin*
Female calf of a buffalo	*Katiya*
Female child	*Baccee*
Female companion	*Sanginee, Sahalee*
Female dancer	*Nartakee*

Female elephant	*Hastinee*
Female genital organ	*Bur*
Female ghost	*Bhutnee*
Female green grocer	*Kunjrin*
Female guest	*Pahunee*
Female messenger	*Dootee*
Female monkey	*Bandariya*
Female mouse	*Cuhiya*
Female of frog	*Mandhakee*
Female scorpion	*Beechee*
Female serpent	*Nagin*
Female servant	*Caree*
Female snake	*Sanpin, Sarpinee*
Female spider	*Makree*
Female successor	*Uttaradhi karinee*
Female swan	*Hansinee*
Female tailor	*Darjen*
Female volunteer	*Svayamsevika*
Female water-carrier	*Paniharin*
Female worshipper	*Upasika*
Feminine	*Zanana*
Fence	*Ghara*
Fennel	*Saunf*
Fenugreek	*Mathee*
Ferriage	*Ghat shulk*
Fertile	*Urvar, Upjaoo*
Fertile soil	*Urvara*
Fertility	*Urvarkta*
Fertilization	*Urvareekaran*
Fertilizer	*Urvarak*
Festival	*Tyohar, Parv*
Festival of illumination	*Deepotsav*

Festival of triumph	*Vijayotsav*
Festivity	*Mangalotsav, Jashan, Anandotsav*
Festoon	*Toran*
Festoon of flowers	*Bandanvar*
Fete	*Anandmala*
Fetters	*Nigar, Baree*
Feudal chieftain	*Samant*
Feudalism	*Samantvad*
Feudalistic	*Samantvadee*
Fever	*Bukkhar, Jwar, Tap*
Few	*Cand, Inagina*
Fiancee	*Mangetar*
Fibre	*Rasha, Tantu, Faibar*
Fibrous	*Rashadar*
Fickle minded	*Cancal*
Fictional	*Aupannyasik*
Fictitious	*Mangarhant*
Fictitious stories	*Kissa kahanee*
Fidelity to truth	*Sattyanishtha*
Field	*Kary-kshetr*
Field and its granary	*Khet khalihan*
Field of action	*Karmbhoomi*
Field where the game is played	*Caugan*
Field with records	*Dakhil-daftar*
Fielf	*Khat*
Fierce	*Ghamasan*
Fiery	*Agnay*
Fifteen	*Pandreh*
Fifteenth	*Pandrahvan*
Fifth	*Pancam*
Fifth column	*Pancamang*
Fifth columnist	*Pancamangee*

Fifth month of Hindu Calender	*Savan*
Fifty	*Pacas*
Fifty-five	*Pacpan*
Fifty-four	*Cauvan*
Fifty-nine	*Unsath*
Fifty-seven	*Sattavan*
Fifty-six	*Chappan*
Fifty-two	*Bavan*
Fig	*Anjeer*
Fight	*Larna*
Fighter	*Jujhar*
Fightine with shoes	*Jootpazar*
Fighting and killing	*Mardhar*
Fighting terms	*Lagee-badee*
Figurative	*Alankarik*
Figurative meaning	*Lakshyarth*
Figure	*Akkriti*
Filaria	*Failariya*
File	*Pattrpanjee, Natthee*
(to) file	*Ratna*
Filing	*Nattheekaran*
Fill in	*Bharna*
Fill to the brim	*Poorna*
Filled	*Poorit*
Filled with attachment	*Ragee*
Filled with kindness	*Saday*
Filling	*Bharav*
Filling in blanks	*Padpooran*
Filling the gaps	*Pooran*
Film version	*Filmantar*
Film	*Cal-citrit*
(to) film	*Filmana*

Filming	*Cal-citran*
Filter	*Punna*
Filth	*Mal*
Filthiness	*Gandgee*
Filthy	*Galeez*
Filthy desire	*Kuvasna*
Filthy thought	*Kuvichar*
Finale	*Parayan*
Finally	*Anttah*
Finance	*Vitt*
Finance minister	*Arthmantree*
Financial	*Malee, Vitteey*
Find fault	*Khuchar*
Finding no words to say	*Shabdheen*
Fine	*Jurmana*
Fine carpet	*Gilam*
Fine cloth	*Dukool*
Fine-flour	*Maida*
Fineness	*Uttamta*
Finger (Thumb)	*Angusht*
Finger	*Ungli*
Finger print	*Unglee cchap*
Finger ring	*Angoothee*
Finish	*Finish*
Finished	*Khatm, Samapt*
Finished off	*Nipatna*
Finishing touch	*Poornahuti*
Fire	*Aag, Agni*
(to) fire	*Dagna*
Fire Extinguisher	*Agnishamak*
Fire arms	*Agnayastr*
Fire ball	*Agnipind*

Fire in a jungle	*Davagni*
Fire of holi ceremonially	*Holika-dahan*
Fire pot	*Angeethee*
Fire proof	*Agniseh*
Fire test	*Agnipareeksha*
Fire work	*Agnikreera*
Fire worship	*Agnipooja*
Fire-brigade	*Damnkal*
Fire-pot	*Agnikund*
Fired	*Dagna*
Firefly	*Jugnoon*
Fireman	*Fayarmain*
Fireworks	*Atishbazi*
Firing	*Bandookbazee*
Firm	*Atal, Drirh*
Firm determination	*Sunishcay*
Firm grip	*Jakar*
Firm-bodied	*Drirhang*
Firmament	*Nabh*
Firmness	*Drirhta*
First	*Pehla*
First cash sale of the day	*Bohnee*
First day of a lunar fortnight	*Pratipada*
First death anniversary	*Barsee*
First delivery	*Pehlautee*
First half	*Poorvardh*
First month of the Hindu calender	*Caitr*
First of all	*Pehla*

First person *Uttam purush*
First priority *Prathamta*
First ray of sunlight *Pau*
First-born *Pehlauta*
Firstly *Prathamtah*
Fiscal *Rajvitteey*
Fish *Machlee*
Fish hook *Kantiya*
Fish-line *Dheevree*
Fish-plate *Jorpattee*
Fisherman *Machua*
Fishing Industry *Matsy uddyog*
Fishing rod *Laggee*
Fist *Mutthee*
Fist-blow *Ghoonsa*
Fistula *Bhagandar*
Fit *Tican, Fit*
Fit for coitus *Sanbhoggy*
Fit for dwelling *Nivassy*
Fit for tat *Vair-shuddhi*
Fit to be chosen *Varaneey*
Fit to be described *Varny*
Fit to be explained *Vyakhyay*
Fit to be given up *Tyajjy*
Fit to be murdered *Hanneey*
Fit to be sucked *Cooshaneey*
Fit to be supported *Poshshy*
Fitted *Yukt*
Fitted *Lais*
Fitter *Fitar*
Five *Panc, Panj*
Five and a half times *Paunca*
Five sacred jewels *Pancratn*

Five strings	*Panclara*
Five tenets	*Pancsheel*
Five times	*Pancguna*
Five-coloured	*Pancranga*
Five-storeyed	*Panckhana*
Fix	*Buddhivibhram*
Fixation of instalment	*Kistbandee*
Fixed	*Sthir*
Fixedness	*Sthirta*
Flabbergasted	*Bhaucakka*
Flabby	*Thulthul*
Flabby with hollow inside	*Phapphas*
Flag	*Jhanda, Dhwaj*
Flag day	*Jhanda-divas*
Flag-hoisting	*Dhwajarohan*
Flag-pole	*Dhwajdand*
Flag-ship	*Dhwaj-pot*
Flame	*Jyoti*
Flame of fire	*Shola*
Flame of the lamp	*Deepshikha*
Flannel	*Falalain*
Flare up	*Bharakna*
Flash	*Kaundh*
Flashing on the mind	*Sphurit*
Flat	*Capta*
Flat boat	*Patala*
Flat metallic dish	*Thalee*
Flat stone used for grinding purpose	*Sil*
Flatterer	*Khushamadee tattoo, Caploos*
Flattery	*Khushamad, Caploosee*
Flatulent	*Badee*

Flavour	*Ramak*
Flaw	*Dosh*
Flea	*Pissoo*
Fleet	*Bara*
Flesh	*Amish*
Flesh-eating	*Darinda*
Fleshiness	*Mansalta*
Fleshy	*Gijgija, Mansal*
Fleshy and plump	*Motataza*
Flexibility	*Lacak*
Flexible	*Locdar*
Flier	*Urankoo*
Flight	*Uran*
Flint	*Cakmak*
Flirtatious	*Mancala*
Flirtatious pretension (with an emphasis	*Nakhra-tilla*
Flit	*Catkara*
Float	*Tiraunda*
(to) float	*Utrana*
Floating	*Plavan*
Flock	*Jhund*
Flock of pack beasts	*Tanra*
Flood	*Sailav*
Flooded	*Plavit*
Flooded with light	*Jyotit*
Flooding	*Jalplavan*
Floor	*Farsh*
Flooring	*Patkan*
Flour	*Ata*
Flour-cake	*Pua*
Flourish	*Lehlahana*
Flourishing	*Tehtaha*

Flow	*Bahaw*
Flower	*Pushp, Phool*
Flower garden	*Pushpvatika, Phulvaree*
Flower of a pomegranate	*Gulnar*
Flower pot	*Phooldan*
Flower which blooms in the night	*Ratkeeranee*
Flower-garland	*Phool-mala*
Flower-pot	*Gamla, Guldan*
Flowered	*Pushpit*
Flowery	*Phooldar*
Fluctuating	*Ghatta barhta*
Fluctuation	*Ghat-barh*
Fluency	*Pharrata, Ravanee*
Fluent	*Dhara-pravah*
Fluffy piece of cotton	*Phoha*
Flurry of excitement	*Avash*
Flute	*Bansuree, Murlee*
Flute	*Vanshee*
Flute player	*Bansureevadak*
Flute-seller	*Murlee-vala*
Flutter	*Pharpharahat, Phur*
(to) flutter	*Tinakna, Phatphatana*
(to) flutter in the air	*Pheharna*
Fly	*Urna*
(to) fly	*Urana*
Fly-flapper	*Makkheemar*
Flying	*Uraka*
Flying cot	*Urankhatola*
Flying dish	*Uranthal*
Flying insect	*Phatinga*
Flying saucer	*Urantashtaree*

Flying squad	*Urandasta*
Foam	*Phen*
Fodder	*Cara*
Foeticide	*Bhroonhatya*
Foetus	*Bhroon, Dimb*
Fog	*Dhundh, Kohra*
Fold	*Tahee, Parat, Teh*
(to) fold	*Bhanjna*
(to) fold (up)	*Tehana*
Folding	*Tootdar*
Folk Song	*Lokgeet*
Folk dance	*Loknritty*
Folk play	*Loknatty*
Folk song of separation	*Birha*
Folk tale	*Lokkatha*
Folk-ethics	*Lokneeti*
Follower	*Anugamee*
Follower of Moses	*Moosaee*
Follower of avowed to religious tenets	*Dharmvrati*
Follower of Sikhism	*Sikh*
Following	*Nimnlikhit*
Following one's own wish	*Swaicchik*
Foment	*Sankna*
(to) foment lightly	*Takorna*
Fomentation	*Sank*
Fond of talking	*Batakkar*
Fondle	*Dularna*
Fondling	*Dular*
Fondly affectionate towards devotees	*Bhaktvatsal*

Fondness	*Caska*
Fondness for talk	*Batras*
Font	*Thuskee*
Food	*Bhojan, Ahar*
Food and clothing	*Bhojan-vastr*
Food and fodder	*Dana-panee*
Food material for a specified period	*Khurakee*
Food provided by others	*Parann*
Foodgrains	*Khaddyann*
Foolery	*Ulloopan*
Foolish	*Bevakoof, Moorkh*
Foolish person	*Shakhcillee*
Foolishness	*Bevakoofee, Moorkhta*
Foot	*Caran, Pag, Panw, Pad*
Foot-disease of animals	*Khurat*
Foot-disease of hoofed animals	*Khurpaka*
Foot-print	*Padcihn*
Foot-rest	*Panyca*
Foot-rest in a latrine	*Kadmaca*
Foot-rug	*Panwra*
Foot-rule	*Futa*
Foot-soldier	*Padati*
Foot-step sound	*Ahat*
Football	*Futball*
Footboard	*Paydan, Pavdan*
Footfall	*Padcap*
Footman	*Pyada*
Footnote	*Talteep*
Footpath	*Pagdandee*

Footstep	*Kadam*
Footwear	*Paduka, Padtran*
Foppery	*Chabeelapan*
Foppish	*Chail-chabeela,*
Foppish woman	*Camakko*
Foppishness	*Bankapan*
For	*Vasta, Lie*
For ages after ages	*Yugyugantar*
For example	*Udaharantah*
For instance	*Maslan*
For no reason	*Khwahma khwah*
For one's own happiness	*Swantahsukhay*
For perusal	*Avloknarth*
For sale	*Bikaoo*
For the present	*Filhal*
For the sake of	*Baray*
For this purpose	*Atadarth*
Forbearance	*Sehansheelta, Rastee*
Forbearing	*Sehansheel*
Forbid	*Hatakna*
Forbidance	*Mumaniyat*
Forbiddance	*Manaee*
Forbidden	*Mana*
Force	*Zabardastee, Bal*
Force of attraction	*Akarshanshakti*
Force of character	*Catitr-bal*
Forced labourer	*Bagaree*
Forced or involuntary labour	*Begar*
Forceful	*Jordar*
Forcefully	*Jabran*
Forcefulness	*Sashaktata*

Forceps	*Sarsee*
Forcibly	*Balat*
Forecast	*Poorvanuman*
Forecasting about future	*Phalaphal*
Forefinger	*Tarjnee*
Forehead	*Mastak, Matha*
Foreign	*Vaideshik*
Foreign Country	*Pardash, Vilayat*
Foreigner	*Videsiya*
Foremost	*Aggranee, Agr*
Forenoon	*Poorvahn*
Forest	*Jungle, Van*
Forest of bushes	*Jharkhand*
Forest sanctified by austerities	*Tapovan*
Forest-dweller	*Banvasee*
Forester	*Vanpal*
Foreword	*Prakkathan*
Forg	*Mandook*
Forgerer	*Jalsaz*
Forget	*Bhulana*
Forgetfulness	*Bhulakkarpan, Vismaransheelta*
Forgetting	*Vismaran*
Forgetful	*Bhulakkar*
Forgiveable	*Kshamayoggy*
Forgive	*Bakhshana*
Forgiven	*Maf*
Forgiveness	*Kshama*
Forgiving	*Kshamavan, Titikshu*
Forgotten	*Bhoola-Bisra, Vismrit*
Forhead	*Bhal*
Form	*Vidha*

Form (of application etc.)	*Prapatr*
Form of Classical Indian Music	*Dhrupad*
Formal	*Aupcarik, Reetik*
Formal address	*Abhibhashan*
Formal proceedings	*Amaldaramad*
Formality	*Rasm, Takalluf*
Formation	*Sanghatan*
Formation of cliques	*Tarbandee*
Forme	*Farma*
Former	*Bhootpoorv, Poorvvartee*
Formless	*Nirakar*
Formula	*Soottr, Farmoola*
Formwise	*Juzbandee*
Forsaken	*Tyakt*
Fort	*Kila, Garh*
Fort-guard	*Durgpal*
Forth day of the lunar month	*Caturthee*
Forthcoming	*Agamee*
Forthwith	*Saddyah*
Fortieth	*Caleesvan*
Fortification	*Kilabandee*
Fortnight	*Pakhvara*
Fortnightly	*Pakshik*
Fortunate	*Khushkismat*
Fortune teller	*Bhavishshyvakta*
Forty	*Calees*
Forty-five	*Paintalees*
Forty-four	*Cauvalees*
Forty-nine	*Unchas*
Forty-one	*Iktalees*

Forty-seven	*Saintalees*
Forty-six	*Chiyalis*
Forty-three	*Tantalees*
Forty-two	*Bayalees*
Forward	*Aggrgamee*
Forwarding	*Aggrsaran*
Fossil	*Jeevashm*
Fostered	*Pala-posa*
Foul play	*Kapat vyavhar*
Foul smell	*Bhabhak, Durgandh, Boo*
Foundation	*Adharshila, Buniyad*
Foundation stone	*Shilanyas*
Founded	*Sthapit*
Founder	*Sansthapak*
Fount of nectar	*Sudhanidhi*
Fountain	*Phuhara*
Fountain of energy	*Samidhanee*
Fountain pen	*Fauntanpen*
Four	*Car*
Four cornered frame	*Caukha*
Four months of the rainy season	*Caturmas*
Four times	*Cauguna*
Four wheeled	*Caupehiya*
Four-faced	*Caturmukh*
Four-horse carriage	*Bagghee*
Fourteen	*Cauda*
Fourteenth day of the lunar fortnight	*Caudas*
Fourth	*Cautha*
Fourth stage	*Tureey*
Fowler	*Baheliya*
Fox	*Lomree*

Fractional	*Bhinnatmak*
Fracture	*Asthibhang*
Fragile	*Curmura, Bhangur*
Fragment	*Kutka, Cindee*
Fragrance	*Sugandh, Khushboo*
Fragrant	*Khushbudar*
Fragrant flower pandanus	*Kavra*
Frame	*Dhanca*
(to) frame	*Marhna*
Frame (of picture, painting etc.)	*Fram*
Franchise	*Matadhikar*
Frank	*Balag*
Fraternal	*Bhrattreey*
Fraternal relation	*Bandhav*
Fratricide	*Bhatrihattya*
Fraud	*Kapat, Chal, Dhokha*
Fraudulent	*Kapat poorn, Dhokhebaz*
Fraudulent deception	*Chal-kapat*
Free	*Muft*
Free from all desires	*Nisprih*
Free from debt	*Rinmuktta*
Free from desire	*Akam*
Free from doubts	*Nirbhrant*
Free trade	*Muktvyapar*
Free translation	*Bhavanuvad*
Freed	*Mukt*
Freedom	*Swacchandta*
Freedom from worry	*Nishcintta*
Freedom of thought	*Vicar-swatantry*
Freedom of vote	*Matswatantry*
Freeholder	*Mafeedar*

Freeze	*Zamna*
Freight	*Bhara*
French	*Franseesee*
Frequency	*Barambarta, Varamvarta*
Frequently	*Varamvar*
Fresh	*Taza*
Fresh (plant)	*Dehdaha*
Fresh and trepid	*Dharoshn*
Freshness	*Tazapan*
Fret	*Cirhana*
(to) fret and fume	*Bhunbhunana, Bhakbhakana*
Fretful	*Circira*
Friability	*Bhurbhurapan*
Fricative	*Sangharshee*
Friction	*Ragar, Gharshan, Ghissa*
Friday	*Shukkrvar*
Friend	*Dost, Mitr, Yar*
Friend since childhood	*Langotiya*
Friendly	*Dostana*
Friendly approach	*Sam*
Friendly association	*Malmulakat*
Friendly attitude	*Mittrbhav*
Friends and companions	*Sangee-sathee*
Friendship	*Mittrta, Yarana, Dosti*
Fright	*Dehal*
Fright (as on the stage)	*Dharak*
Frighten	*Darana*
Frightened	*Bhaytrast*
Frightening	*Traskarak*
Frill	*Jhalar*
Frill of a helmet	*Jhilam*

Frilled	*Jhalardar*
Frisk	*Kudakka*
Frog	*Maindhak*
Frog of the well	*Koop-mandook*
Frolic	*Athkhalee, Kalol*
Frolicsome	*Cuhalbaz*
Frolicsome gaiety	*Cuhalbazee*
From	*Sa*
From head to foot	*Nakhshikh*
Front of the tongue	*Jihhvagr*
Front part	*Agaree*
Frontier	*Seemant*
Frontispiece	*Mukhcittr*
Frost	*Pala, Tushar*
Frost-bite	*Tushardansh*
Frost-fall	*Tusharpat*
Fructified	*Phaleebhoot*
Fruit	*Phal*
Fruit cordia myxa	*Lisora*
Fruit diet	*Phalahar*
Fruit of righteous act	*Punnyphal*
Fruit of the citrus family	*Cakotra*
Fruit seed	*Gutthal*
Fruit sugar	*Phal-sharkara*
Fruitarian	*Phalaharee*
Fruitful	*Phaldayak, Suphal, Phalyukt*
Fruitless	*Befayda, Phalheen*
Frustrated	*Nirash, Kunthit*
Frustration	*Kuntha, Nirasha*
Fry	*Talna*
(to) fry	*Talna*

Frying pan	*Karahee*
Fuel	*Eendhan*
Fulfil responsibility	*Nibhana*
Fulfilling	*Parayan*
Fulfilling of all purposes	*Sarvarth-Sadhan*
Full grown	*Kaddavar*
Full load	*Bharat*
Full marks	*Poornank*
Full of amours	*Ashikana*
Full of compassion	*Karunamay*
Full of compound words	*Samas-bahul*
Full of darkness	*Timirmay*
Full of desires	*Sarvkam*
Full of doubt	*Shankit*
Full of good taste	*Surucipoorn*
Full of joy	*Anand may*
Full of juice	*Rasbhara*
Full of knowledge	*Gyanmay*
Full of nectar	*Sudhamay*
Full of power	*Shakti-sampann*
Full of sentiment	*Bhavnamay*
Full of struggle	*Sangharshmay*
Full of troubles	*Kashtmay*
Full of turnings	*Terha-merha*
Full powers	*Sarvadhikar*
Full speed	*Bagchut*
Full stop	*Poornviram, Viram cinh*
Full-moon	*Poorncandr*
Full-moon day	*Poornima*
Full-throated cry	*Dhar*
Fully convinced	*Kayal*
Fully covered	*Paricchann*

Fully harnessed and ready	*Kasa-kasaya*
Fully paid up	*Babak*
Fully soaked	*Sarabor*
Fumble	*Bhakuana*
Fumbler	*Bhakua*
Fumigation	*Dhoopan*
Fun	*Lutf*
Fun and frolic	*Hansee-khal*
Fun and laughter	*Has parihas*
Function of a caste	*Jatidharm*
Functioning body	*Kriya nikay*
Fund	*Fund, Nidhi*
Fundamental	*Moolbhoot*
Funeral pyre	*Cita*
Funeral rites	*Dahsanskar, Kriyakarm*
Fungus	*Khumbee, Kukurmutta*
Fungus mould	*Phaphoondee*
Funnel	*Conga, Keep*
Fur	*Lom*
Furlong	*Farlang*
Furore	*Tehalka, Bavela, Harkamp, Vavaila*
Furore in time of disress	*Kuhram*
Further more	*Punashc*
Fury	*Prakop*
Fuse	*Paleeta*
Fusible	*Samakaneey*
Fusion	*Samakan*
Fuss	*Vabal, Pacra*
Future	*Bhavishshy*
Future tense	*Bhavishshykal*
Fuzz	*Ruan*

G

Gabble	*Barrana*
Gadget	*Parkhee*
Gaf	*Densely woven*
Gaiety	*Cehal-pehal, Amodpramod, Madhurta*
Gain	*Fayda, Hasil*
Gainful	*Labhdayak*
Gala festival	*Mahotsav*
Galaxy	*Chayapath, Mandakinee*
Gale	*Pravat, Vattya, Jhanjha*
Gall bladder	*Pittashay*
Gallant	*Parakkramee*
Gallantry	*Javanmardee*
Gallery	*Gailaree, Deergha*
Galley	*Galee*
Gallon	*Gailan*
Gallopping	*Sarpat*
Gallows	*Tikthee*
Gambler	*Juaree*
Gambling	*Jua*
Gambling den	*Juaghar*
Gambol	*Uchal-kood, Kood phand*
(to) gambol about	*Kudakna*
Game	*Khel*
Game of tip-cat	*Gillee danda*
Gamut music	*Sargam*
Gandhism	*Gandhivadi*
Gang	*Giroh*
Gang of idlers	*Candal-caukree*
Ganga	*Ganga river*
Gangsterism	*Dadageeree*
Gap	*Gurra*
Garage	*Gairij*

Garden	*Bag, Uddyan, Vatika, Bageeca, Bagiya*
Garden party	*Uddyan goshthee*
Gardener	*Bagban*
Gardening	*Bagbanee*
Gargle	*Garara*
Garland	*Mala*
Garland of victory	*Jaymala*
Garlic	*Lehsun*
Garment of babies	*Jhabla*
Garment worn round the neck	*Gareban*
Garments	*Veshbhoosha*
Garrage	*Garaj*
Gasconade	*Seet-Patang*
Gastropod	*Udarpad*
Gate	*Darwaja, Phatak*
Gate-keeper	*Pratiharee, Dyorheedar*
Gateway	*Mukhdwar*
Gather	*Batorna*
Gathered	*Ikattha*
Gaudiness	*Catkeelapan*
Gaudy	*Catkeela*
Gay-tempered	*Khushmizaj*
Gaze	*Takna*
Gazette	*Rajpattr, Gazat*
Gazetted	*Rajpatrit*
Gazetteer	*Gazatiyar, Bhaugolikee*
Gelatine	*Saras*
Genealogical table	*Vanshtalika*
Genealogy	*Vanshavalee*
General	*Sananayak, Janral, Sarvik*
General Merchant	*Bisatee*

General controller	*Dhoree*
General merchandise	*Bisatkhana*
Generalisation	*Sadharaneekaran, Samanyeekaran*
Generally	*Samantaya*
Generated by separation	*Viyogjanny*
Generation	*Peerhee*
Generous	*Udar, Hatim*
Genetic	*Jananik*
Genetics	*Anuvanshikee*
Genocide	*Janvadh, Jansanhar*
Genorrhoea	*Soozak*
Gentleman	*Bhalmanas, Bhaddrpurush, Sajjan*
Gentlemanliness	*Sajjanta*
Gentlemanly	*Sajjanocit*
Genuine	*Aslee, Khara*
Genuineness	*Sadashayta*
Geographical	*Bhaugolik*
Geography	*Bhoogol*
Geological	*Bhaumik*
Geology	*Bhooviggyan*
Geometry	*Jyamiti, Rekhaganit*
Germ	*Keetanu, Jaraseem*
Germany	*Jarman*
Germicide	*Keetanunashak*
Gestation period	*Garbhkal*
Gesticulation	*Angvikshap*
Gesture	*Angbhangee*
Gestures and postures	*Hav-bhav*
Get	*Pana*
(to) get angry	*Risana*

(to) get damp	*Seelna*
(to) get dissolved	*Ghulna*
(to) get down or come down	*Utarna*
(to) get embroidered	*Karhana*
(to) get engaged	*Jutna*
(to) get fat	*Mutiyana*
(to) get going	*Sidharna*
(to) get into temper	*Tunakna*
(to) get old	*Burhana*
(to) get printed	*Chapvana*
(to) get proficient	*Manjna*
(to) get released	*Churana*
(to) get rid of	*Mocna*
(to) get scared	*Sehamna*
(to) get scratched	*Nucvana*
(to) get shaven	*Mundana*
(to) get sired	*Dhanana*
(to) get something exorcized	*Jharvana*
(to) get something framed	*Jarana*
(to) get sour	*Khatana*
(to) get spoiled by wrong handling	*Ginjna*
(to) get stitched	*Silvana, Gathvana*
(to) get thrust	*Dhansna*
(to) get tightened	*Kasvana*
(to) get washed	*Dhulana*
Ghee	*Ghee, Ghrit*
Ghee used in kneading flour	*Moyan*

Ghost	*Jinn, Prat*
Giantess	*Danavee*
Giddiness	*Ghumta, Ghumaree*
Gift	*Uphar*
Gift from a deity	*Prasad*
Gigantic	*Bheem, Daittyakar*
Gilder	*Mulammasaz*
Gill	*Galphara*
Gilt	*Mulamma*
Gimlet	*Girmit*
Ginger	*Adrak*
Giraffe	*Ziraf*
Girder	*Gatar*
Girdle	*Kamarband, Makhal*
Girl	*Kannya, Larhkee*
Girl student	*Chattra*
Girt up	*Baddhparikar*
Gist	*Saransh, Labab*
Give	*Dana*
(to) give a kicking	*Latiyana*
(to) give a shake up	*Jhakjhorna*
(to) give a shaking	*Jhorna*
(to) give a violent jerk	*Jhatkarna*
(to) give a violent shaking	*Jhanjhorna*
(to) give back	*Lautana*
(to) give birth to	*Janna*
(to) give or make a small jerk	*Thumkarna*
(to) give out fragrance	*Gamakna*
(to) give the slip	*Satakna*

(to) give way	*Masakna*
Given	*Datt, Pradatt*
Giver	*Dival, Daee, Pradayak*
Giving a shape	*Roopayan*
Giving away a daughter in marriage	*Kanyadan*
Giving milk	*Dudhar*
Glacier	*Himnadee*
Gladdening	*Ahhladkaree*
Gladness	*Ahhlad*
Glance	*Jhalak, Drishtipat*
Glass	*Kanch, Sisa*
Glass bead	*Maniya*
Glass jar	*Kunda*
Glazing	*Camacam*
Gliding dance	*Thirak*
Glimmering	*Jagmagahat*
Glimpse	*Jhankee*
Glitter	*Damak*
(to) glitter	*Camcamana, Jagmagana*
(to) glitter off and on	*Jhamakna*
Glittering	*Jagmag*
Global	*Golkeey*
Globe	*Golak, Bhoomandal*
Gloom	*Mayoosee, Vishad, Avsad*
Gloominess	*Nahoosat, Vishannta*
Gloomy	*Vishann, Vishadmay*
Glorification	*Keertigan*
Glorified	*Surkhroo*
Glorious	*Gauravshalee, Pratapee, Tajomay, Tajasswee*
Glory	*Keerti, Pratap*
Glottis	*Kakal*

Glow-worm	*Khadyot*
Glucose	*Draksh-sharkara*
Gluey	*Laslasa*
Gluttonous	*Patoo, Khau*
Gluttony	*Patoopan*
Glycerin	*Glisareen*
Gnat	*Dans*
Gnaw	*Kutarna*
Go	*Jana*
(to) go back by one's world	*Natna, Mukarna*
(to) go crazy	*Sanakna*
(to) go on lamenting like a sickly child	*Pinpinana*
(to) gobble gulp down	*Gapakna*
Goal keeper	*Golkee*
Goblet of wine	*Surapattr*
God	*Eeshshwar, Prabhu, Dev, Parmatma, Bhagwan*
God Ganesh	*Ganapati*
God Vishnu	*Jaggnath*
God father	*Dharmpita*
God hood	*Ishshvarattv*
God mother	*Dharmmata*
God of Death	*Yam*
God of wealth	*Dhanpati*
God son	*Dharmputr*
God's play	*Maya*
Goddess	*Devee*
Goddess Durga	*Sinhvahinee, Candika, Bhavanee, Jagdamba*
Goddess Kali	*Kalee, Kapalika*

Goddess Lakshmi	*Padma, Sarvmangla*
Goddess Parvati	*Mahadevee*
Goddess of Learning	*Sharda, Sarasswatee*
Goddess of a forest	*Vandevee*
Goddess of victory	*Vijay-lakshmee, Jayshree*
Goddess of war	*Rancandee*
Godliness	*Khudaee*
Godly	*Daivee*
Godown	*Bhandar, Malgodam*
Gods and demons	*Surasur*
Going	*Gavan, Chalta*
Going ahead	*Purogamee*
Going along	*Sahcar*
Going along with	*Sahgaman*
Going backwards	*Pashcgamee*
Going fast	*Drutgamee*
Going round	*Vivartan*
Going together	*Hamrah*
Goitre	*Galgand, Ghagha*
Gold	*Sona, Svarn*
Gold coin	*Asharfee, Swarn mudra*
Gold or silver thread	*Salma, Tilla*
Gold smith	*Sunar, Swarnkar*
Golden	*Sunehla, Kancan*
Golden Jubilee	*Svarn-jayantee*
Golden age	*Svarn yug*
Golden colour	*Svarn-varn*
Golden letter	*Swarnakshar*
Goldness	*Sonal*
Gomootr	*Urine of a cow*
Gone aside	*Parshvgat*
Gong	*Ghant, Dhootoo*
Good	*Nek, Bhala, Accha*

Good Government	*Surajjy*
Good Name	*Sunam, Satkeerti*
Good and evil	*Hit ahit, Nakee vadee, Bhala bura*
Good character	*Carittree*
Good company	*Susangati*
Good conduct	*Sadacaran, Nakcalan*
Good counsel	*Sadupdash*
Good deed	*Sukarm*
Good fortune	*Saubhaggy*
Good luck	*Khushnaseebee*
Good morning	*Suprabhat*
Good news	*Khushkhambree*
Good opportunity	*Suavsar*
Good sense	*Subuddhi*
Good shot	*Nishanabaz, Nishancee*
Good taste	*Suruci*
Good trait	*Sadgun*
Good use	*Sadupyog*
Good wife	*Supatnee*
Good-looking	*Khushnuma*
Good-situation	*Susthiti*
Goodness	*Nakee, Acchaee, Bhalaee*
Goods	*Saman*
Goods clerk	*Malbaboo*
Goods train	*Malgaree*
Gorilla	*Gorilla*
Gossip	*Gap*
Gossipper	*Gapora, Gappee*
Got	*Apt*
Gourd	*Tumba*
Gout	*Amvat*
Governance	*Abhishasan*
Governed	*Abhishasit*

Governing body	*Shasan-nikay*
Government	*Sarkar, Hukoomat, Shasan*
Government house	*Rajbhawan*
Government post	*Rajpad*
Governmental	*Shasanik*
Governor	*Rajypal*
Governor General	*Gavarnar janral*
Governor of a province	*Soobadar*
Gown	*Gaun*
Grab	*Hathiyana, Khasotna*
Grabbing	*Khasot*
Grace	*Shaleenta, Mahar, Barkat, Niyaz, Phagunahat*
Grace of body	*Angsaushthav*
Graceful	*Shobhan, Sajeela, Shaleen*
Gracing with one's presence	*Virajit*
Gracious arrival	*Shubhagaman*
Gracious benediction	*Shubhasheesh*
Graded	*kotibaddh*
Gradual	*Kramik*
Gradually	*Shanaih shanaih, Kramshah, Rafta-rafta*
Graduate	*Snatak*
Grain	*Ann*
Grain of corn	*Kanika*
Gram	*Cana*
Gram glour	*Besan*
Grammarian	*Vaiyakaran*
Grammatical	*Vyakarnik*
Grammatical discipline	*Shabdanushasan*
Gramophone	*Gramofon*

Granary	*Dhannyagar*
Grand	*Vishal, Aleeshan*
Grand daughter	*Pautree*
Grand eloquence	*Vagjal*
Grand father	*Dada, Baba*
Grand mother	*Dadee*
Grand son	*Pautr*
Grandeur	*Vibhooti, Vishalta*
Grandiloquent	*Vagvilasee*
Grant	*Anudan*
Granulated wheat	*Soojee*
Grape	*Angoor*
Grass	*Ghas, Kush*
Grasshopper	*Tidda*
Grassy	*Trinmay*
Grateful	*Shukkrguzar, Ehsanmand, Namak-halal*
Gratefulness	*Abhar, Namakhalalee*
Grater	*Ghiyakash*
Gratification	*Toshan*
Gratified	*Aptkam*
Gratified and happy	*Kritkritty*
Gratis	*Santmant man*
Gratuity	*Anutoshik*
Grave	*Mazar, Kabr*
Gravel	*Bajree, Kankree*
Graveyard	*Kabristan*
Gravitation	*Guruttvakarshan*
Gravity	*Guruta*
Graze	*Carna*
Grazier	*Carvaha*
Great	*Mahan, Brihat*
Great ascetic	*Taponidhi*

Great grand father	*Pardada*
Great grand son	*Parpota*
Great hermit	*Muneendr, Muneeshwar*
Great man	*Mahapurush*
Great ocean	*Maharnav*
Great perseverance	*Sadhna*
Great power	*Mahashakti*
Great sage	*Mahamuni*
Great scholar	*Mahopaddhyay*
Great sin	*Mahapapee*
Great sinner	*Mahapatakee*
Great war	*Mahayuddh*
Great warrior	*Maharathee*
Great zeal	*Josh-kharosh*
Greater	*Mahattar, Brihattar*
Greatest	*Sarvadhik, Mahattam*
Greatness	*Mahima, Mahatta, Baraee*
Greed	*Lobh, Lalac, Trishna, Lipsa*
Greediness	*Lobheepan*
Greedy	*Lalcee, Lobhee*
Green	*Hara, Harit*
Green coconut	*Dabh*
Green gram	*Hola, Horaha*
Green grocer	*Kunjra*
Green leaves vegetable	*Sag*
Green lentil	*Moong*
Green manure	*Haree khad*
Green twig	*Tallo*
Green vegetable	*Taroee, Parval*
Green vitriol	*Kasees*
Greenery	*Hariyalee*
Greenness	*Harapan*

Greet	*Juharana*
Greeting	*Salam*
Grey	*Dhoosar*
Greyish brown	*Phakhtaee*
Griddle	*Tava*
Grief	*Dukh, Gam*
Grief stricken	*Shokvihhval, Shokmagn*
Grieved	*Art*
Grin (as a sign of helplesssness)	*Khees*
Grind	*Peesna*
(to) grind coarsely	*Dalna, Darna*
(to) grind the teeth in anger	*Kachkachana*
Grinding	*Pisaee, Pashan*
Grindling mill	*Cakkee*
Grit	*Balookan*
Groan	*Kankhna*
Grocer	*Pansaree, Parcooniya*
Grocery	*Parcoon*
Grocery market	*Pansarhatta*
Groom	*Saees*
Groove	*Khancha*
Grotesque	*Dhondha*
Ground	*Maidan, Pisht*
Ground meal of vetch	*Dhuvans*
Ground pulse	*Peethee*
Ground sacrified by austerities	*Tapobhoomi*
Ground-nut	*Moong-phalee*
Group	*Samooh, Gan, Yooth*
Group of four	*Caunkree*
Group of seven	*Saptak*

Grouping	*Samoohan*
Groupism	*Gutbandee*
Grouse	*Shikva*
Grove	*Kunj, Upvan*
Grove lane	*Kunjgalee*
Grow	*Ugna*
(to) grow	*Upajana, Barhna*
(to) grow fat	*Motana*
Growing	*Vardhman, Prarohan*
Growl	*Gurrahat*
(to) growl	*Gurrana*
Grown up	*Sayana*
Growth	*Barh, Vriddhi*
Growth of the family	*Vanshvriddhi*
Grudge	*Kuneh*
Grumble	*Jheekhna*
(to) grumble unavailingly	*Pitpitana*
Guarantee	*Prattyabhooti*
Guard	*Pehra, Rakhvala, Praharee*
(to) guard	*Rakhana*
Guardian	*Abhibhavak, Sarparast, Sanrakshak*
Guardian of a minor	*Mutvallee*
Guardianship	*Sarparasttee, Abhibhavakta*
Guarding	*Pasbanee*
Guerilla	*Gurilla*
Guerilla warfare	*Chapamar laraee*
Guess	*Andaz*
(to) guess	*Bhanpna*
Guest	*Atithi, Mehman*
Guffaw	*Attahas*
Guidance	*Margdarshan, Disha-nirdash*

Guide	*Margdarshak, Pathpradarshak*
Guide-book	*Sandarshika*
Guiltless	*Doshmukt, Nirapradh, Bekasoor, Nishpap*
Guilty	*Doshee*
Guinea	*Ginee*
Guinea worm	*Nehrua*
Guise to another	*Swang*
Guitar	*Gitar*
Gulf	*Akhat*
Gullet	*Halak, Bhojanalika*
Gulp down	*Gatakna*
Gurgle	*Gargarana*
Gum	*Niryas, Gond*
Gum-pot	*Gonddanee*
Gums	*Masoora*
Gun	*Bandook*
Gun-carriage	*Topgaree*
Gunman	*Bandookcee, Bandookdharee*
Gunner	*Topchee, Golandaz*
Gunnery	*Top viddya, Golandazee*
Gunny	*Gannee*
Gunpowder	*Barood*
Gurgling sound	*Gatgat*
Gush through	*Jhakorna*
Gush of wind	*Jhakora*
Gust	*Jhonka*
Gusto	*Zor-shor*
Gut	*Tant*
Guttapercha	*Gataparcha*
Gutter	*Panala, Nabdan*
Guttural	*Kanthy*
Gutturo-labial	*Kanthyaushthy*

Gutturopalatal	*Kanth talavvy*
Gymkhana	*Jimkhana*
Gymnasium	*Vyayamshala*
Gynarchy	*Stree-rajy*
Gypsum	*Ciroree*

H

Habit	*Adat*
Habit of drinking	*Sharabkhoree*
Habit of lecturing	*Lakcarbazee*
Habit of picking pockets	*Jebkatree*
Habit of roving	*Sailaneepan*
Habit of stealing	*Caurry vritti*
Habit of wenching with prostitutes	*Randeebazee*
Habitation	*Bastee*
Habitually	*Adatan*
Habituated to kicks	*Letkhor*
Hackneyed	*Ghisapita*
Haemorrhage	*Raktstraw*
Haft	*Mooth*
Haggling	*Molbhav*
Hagiology	*Sant-carit*
Hail	*Ola*
Hair	*Kesh*
Hair dressing	*Keshvinnyas*
Hair-do	*Kanghee cotee*
Hair-dye	*Khizab*
Hairy	*Roandar*
Hairy-dye	*Keshkalp*
Hakeem	*Hakeem*
Hale and hearty	*Bhala canga*
Half	*Addha*
Half a century	*Pacasa*
Half cooked	*Kachcha pakka*
Half moon	*Ardhchandr*
Half moon shaped	*Ardhchandrakar*
Half-bloomed	*Adhkhila*
Half-burnt	*Adhjala*

Half-dead	*Adhmara*
Half-grounded	*Dardara*
Half-naked	*Adhnanga*
Half-open	*Adhkhula*
Half-pants	*Nikar*
Half-ripe	*Adhahkachra*
Half-rupee coin	*Athannee*
Half-said	*Adhkaha*
Half-yearly	*Chamahee*
Hall	*Haul*
Hall of private audience	*Deevan-a-khas*
Hallucination	*Matibhram*
Halo	*Abhamandal*
Halt	*Thamak*
(to) halt suddenly due to fear etc.	*Thamkana*
Halting place	*Adda, Tikan*
Hammer	*Hathora*
Hand	*Hath, Hast*
Hand impression	*Hatha*
Hand saw	*Aree*
Hand span	*Bitta*
Hand to hand fight	*Bahuyuddh*
Hand-bag	*Haindbaig*
Hand-cart	*Saggar*
Hand-clapping	*Kartal dhwani*
Hand-fan	*Hathpankhee*
Hand-glove	*Dastana*
Hand-grenade	*Hathgola*
Hand-made	*Hathbana*
Hand-practice	*Hast-kriya*
Hand-pump	*Nalka*

Hand-span	*Balisht*
Hand-spun	*Hathbuna*
Hand-stitching	*Turpna*
Hand-writing	*Likhavat*
Handbook	*Gutka*
Handicraft	*Dastkaree, Hastkala, Hastshilp*
Handing over	*Hastantaran*
Handkerchief	*Rumal*
Handle	*Dandee, Hattha, Haindil*
Handle of knife, etc.	*Bant*
Handloom	*Hathkargha*
Handsome	*Roopvan, Haseen*
Handwriting	*Hastlipi, Hastlekh*
Handwritten	*Hastlikhit*
Handy	*Jabee*
Handy gadget	*Soop*
Hang	*Latkana, Tangna*
Hanging light-lamp	*Kandeel*
Hank	*Laccha*
Hanuman	*Pavan putr, Bajrang*
Haphazard	*Alal-tappoo, Ootak-natak*
Haphazard livelihood	*Akashvritti*
Happened	*Ghatit*
Happening	*Ghatan*
Happily	*Sukhpoorvak*
Happiness	*Khushee, Prasannta*
Happiness and prosperity	*Sukh-sampatti*
Happiness and welfare	*Anand mangal*
Happy	*Prasann, Khush, Sukhee*
Happy coincidence	*Suyog*
Happy times	*Sudin*
Harass	*Padana*

Harassed	*Parashan, Halakan*
Harassment	*Halakanee, Pareshanee*
Harbour	*Bandargha, Godee*
Hard	*Kathor, Sakht*
Hard struggle	*Jaddojahad*
Hard to please	*Nakcarha*
Hard to understand	*Klisht*
Hard-hearted	*Bedardee, Nithur*
Hard-working	*Shramsheel*
Hardness	*Kathorta*
Hardworking	*Jangartor, Mashakkatee*
Harem	*Ranivas*
Harlot	*Rambha, Varangna*
Harm	*Ahit, Harj*
Harmful	*Hanikar*
Harmless	*Ahinsar*
Harmonious pair	*Jugal-joree*
Harmonium	*Harmoniyam*
Harmony	*Samrasta*
Harsh	*Karkash, Karnkatu*
Harshness	*Karkashta*
Harvest a crop	*Lavna*
Hastiness	*Jaldbazee*
Hasty	*Jaldbaz, Harbariya*
Hat	*Topa, Hait*
Hatchet	*Kuthar, Kulharee*
Hate	*Nafrat*
Hated	*Ghrinit*
Hateful	*Ghrinaspad*
Hatred	*Ghrina*
Haunted	*Bhutaha*
Have a burning sensation	*Charcharana*

(to) have a hearty laugh	*Khikhilana*
(to) have a lingering pain	*Kasakna*
(to) have a pungent irritation	*Carparana*
(to) have a sight	*Deedar*
(to) have returned	*Firvana*
(to) have set or joined	*Jurvana*
(to) have something ground coarsely	*Dalvana*
(to) have the head shaved	*Mundna*
(to) hav th jitters	*Pinakna*
Having Apertures	*Jhireedar*
Having a family	*Parivarwala*
Having a good voice	*Sukanth*
Having a heart	*Hridayvan*
Having a keen intellect	*Kushaggrbuddhi*
Having a knot	*Ganthdar*
Having a tragic finale	*Viyogant*
Having an axis	*Saksh*
Having an ear cut off	*Kankata*
Having an honest purpose	*Nakneeyat*
Having been	*Shuda*
Having brown hair	*Kapil*
Having excellent disposition	*Carusheel*
Having exclusive right	*Akadhikaree*
Having experience of sufferings	*Bhuktbhogee*

Having face like that of a cow	*Gomukh*
Having faith	*Shraddhavan*
Having fish like eyes	*Meenakshi*
Having four teeth	*Caudanta*
Having fulfilled mission	*Siddhkam*
Having gone astray	*Gumrah*
Having good eye sight	*Sujhakha*
Having good-features	*Sumukhee*
Having head bowed down (in respect)	*Natmastak*
Having joint(s)	*Jordar*
Having just bathed	*Saddyahsnat*
Having large nails	*Nakhee*
Having leaves	*Saparn*
Having life vitality	*Pranvan*
Having lust for war	*Jigeeshu*
Having much to do	*Kam kajee*
Having no posterity	*Nirbansee*
Having no regard and consideration	*Balihaz*
Having one meaning	*Akarthak*
Having only one eye	*Kana*
Having overcome attachment	*Veetrag*
Having plenty of knots	*Gatheela*
Having seven chains	*Satlara*
Having seven sons	*Satpootee*
Having shapely arms	*Subahu*
Having similar function	*Sadharmee*
Having six fingers	*Changa*
Having the name	*Namak*

Having the same religion	*Sadharmik*
Having two folds	*Dohara*
Having two kinds of flavour or taste	*Dorasa*
Having two layers	*Dupalla*
Having two minds	*Dodila*
Having two mouths	*Dumunha*
Having uncombed hair	*Muktkash*
Having unproportionately small eyes	*Cundha*
Having windows	*Khirkeedar*
Having wings	*Sapaksh*
Hawk	*Baz*
Hawker	*Phareevala*
Hay	*Phoos*
Haytrusser	*Ghasiyara*
Haziness	*Dhundhlapan*
Hazzy	*Dhundhla*
Heat	*Garmana*
(to) heat	*Tapana*
He-calf	*Bachra*
He-cat	*Biral*
He-goat	*Bakra*
He-quail	*Bater*
Head	*Pradhan, Shir, Mund*
Head clerk	*Meermunshee*
Head of a monastery	*Mandalashshwar, Mathadheesh*
Head of an animal slaughtered for meat	*Siree*
Head office	*Mukhyalay*
Headache	*Sirdard*

Heading	*Sheershak*
Heading towards end	*Maranonmukh*
Headless	*Sirkata*
Headless trunk	*Kabandh*
Headline of the letters	*Shirorakha*
Headman	*Caudhree, Mukhiya, Nambardar*
Headman of a village	*Patel*
Headmanship	*Caudhreepan*
Headmaster	*Pradhanadhyapak*
Health	*Svasthy*
Health Minister	*Svasthymantree*
Health-Ministry	*Svasthymantralay*
Health-certificate	*Aroggy pramanak*
Healthy	*Tandurust, Svasth, Neerog*
Healthy and powerful	*Pusht*
Heap	*Dher*
Heaping	*Ganjaee*
Heard	*Shrut*
Hearing	*Sunvaee*
Heart	*Kaleja, Citt, jee, Dil, Man, Hariday*
Heart and soul	*Jee-jan*
Heart burning	*Antardah*
Heart-disease	*Hridrog*
Heart-piercing	*Hriday-vadhee*
Heart-rending	*Marmbhadee*
Heart-rending	*Hriday-vidarak*
Heartiness	*Hardikta*
Heartless	*Bedard, Bedil*
Heartless miser	*Arthpishac*
Heartlessness	*Nirmamta*
Hearty	*Hardik*
Heat	*Tap, Taw*
Heat treatment	*Tapopcar*

Heated	*Tapt*
Heated discussion	*Garmagarmee*
Heater	*Ooshmak*
Heathenism	*Kuffr*
Heaven	*Devlok*
Heavenly	*Divvy*
Heavily rubbed	*Gharshit*
Heaviness	*Bhareepan*
Heavy	*Bharee, Vajnee*
Heavy hearted	*Khinn*
Heavy water	*Gurujal*
Hectic and restless (person)	*Cilbila*
Hedge	*Bar*
Hedonism	*Indriyvad*
Heel	*Aree*
Hefty fellow	*Mustanda*
Height	*Unchai, Kad*
Heinous	*Jaghanny*
Heir	*Varis, Namlava*
Heir apparent	*Yuvraj*
Heirless (person)	*Lavaris*
Held up	*Atakna*
Hell	*Narak*
Hell-pond	*Narak-kund*
Hellish	*Narkeey*
Helmet	*Shirastran*
Helmsman	*Karndhar*
Help	*Sahayata, Madad*
(to) help in delivery	*Janmana*
Help to wear	*Pehanvana*
Helper	*Madadgar*
Helpless	*Asahhay, Bebas, Majboor, Lacar*

Helplessness	*Bebasee, Majbooree, Lacaree*
Helter-shelter	*Titar-bitar*
Hem	*Magzee*
Hemisphere	*Golardh*
Hemp	*San*
Hemp or jute string	*Sutlee*
Hemp plant	*Ganja*
Hemp-smoker	*Ganjakhor*
Hen	*Murgee*
Hence	*Atah, Av*
Henchman	*Pichlaggoo, Gurga*
Herald	*Aggrdoot*
Herald of a revolution	*Krantidoot*
Herb	*Jareebootee*
Herbaceous	*Shakeey*
Herbs and vegetables	*Sag-pat*
Herculean effort	*Bhageerath prayatn*
Herd	*Lehanra*
Here	*Yahan, Idhar*
Here and there	*Idhar udhar*
Hereditary	*Anuvanshik, Pushtainee*
Heretic	*Vidharmee*
Heritage	*Virasat, Bapautee*
Hermit	*Tapasswee*
Hermitage	*Ashshram*
Hero	*Nayak*
Hero of India	*Rustam-e-hind*
Hero-worship	*Veer-pooja*
Heroic	*Veertapoorn*
Heroic end	*Veergati*
Heroic posture	*Veerasan*
Heroine	*Nayika*
Heroism	*Shaurry*

Heron	*Bagla, Bak*
Herpetology	*Sareesripviggyan*
Hesitancy	*Achkachahat*
Hesitant	*Sankocee, Achkachana*
Hesitation	*Jhijhak*
Hexagon	*Shatkon*
Hexagonal	*Shatkoneey*
Hibernation	*Parishayan*
Hiccup	*Hickee*
Hide	*Chipana, Lukna*
Hidden	*Chipna, Ojhal*
Hidden compartment	*Corkhana*
Hidden meaning	*Lag-lapat*
Hidden or secret lock	*Cor tala*
Hidden part (of something)	*Corpat*
Hidden pit	*Cor garha*
Hide and seek	*Luka-chipee, Ankhmichauni*
Hide of a hairy beast	*Posteen*
Hiding	*Chipaw*
Hierarchy	*Purohit-tantr, Dharm-tantr*
High	*Uchch*
High commission	*Uchchayog*
High commissioner	*Uchchayukt*
High court	*Uchchnyayalay*
High education	*Uchchshiksha*
High ideal	*Uchchadarsh*
High officer	*Uchchadhikaree*
High personage	*Mahajan*
High priest	*Dharmacary, Mahant*
High school	*Haee skool*
High words	*Jharpa-jharpee*
High-handed	*Seenazor*

High-handedness	*Seena-zoree*
Highest	*Sarvocc*
Highest form of philosophy as per Vedas	*Vedant*
Highest septet in Music	*Tarsaptak*
Highly educated	*Sushikshit*
Highly manipulative	*Tikrambaz*
Highway	*Rajmarg*
Highway robbery	*Rahzanee*
Highwayman	*Batmar*
Hile	*Bil*
Hill in Gujrat	*Girnar*
Hillock	*Teela, Dongar*
Hilly	*Paharee*
Him	*Use, Ise*
Himalaya	*Giriraj*
Hindi	*Hindee*
Hindi spoken in Mithila	*Maithilee*
Hindrance	*Rukavat, Atkav*
Hindu Priest	*Pujaree, Purohit*
Hindu Tantrik cult	*Vammarg*
Hindu calender	*Pancang, Patra*
Hindu convent	*Math*
Hindu festival of lights	*Deepavali*
Hindu mythology	*Puran*
Hindu ritualist	*Karmkandee*
Hinduism	*Hinduttw*
Hint	*Ishara, Ingit*
Hinted	*Lakshit*
Hip	*Kulha, Nitamb*
His excellency	*Mahamahim*

His Majesty	*Tatbhavan*
Hiss (of a snake)	*Phuphkar*
(to) hiss	*Phuphkarna*
Hissing sound	*San-san, Siskaree*
Histology	*Ootakvigyan*
Historian	*Itihaskar*
Historical	*Aitihasik*
Historical city of Afghanistan	*Kandhar*
Historicity	*Aitihasikta*
History	*Itihas*
Hit in the vitals	*Marmahat*
Hitter	*Upghatak*
Hitting range	*Capat*
Hitting the target	*Lakshyavadh*
Hive	*Chatta*
Hoarder	*Jama-khor*
Hoarding	*Jama-khoree*
Hob-nob	*Hilna-milna*
Hob-nobbing	*Hal-mal*
Hobby	*Shauk*
Hockey	*Hakee*
Hoe	*Kudal*
Hoeing charges	*Guraee*
Hogdeer	*Parha*
Hoist	*Phephrana*
Hold	*Pakarna, Thamna*
(to) hold oon	*Datna*
Holdall	*Bistarband*
Holder	*Dharak*
Hole	*Soorakh, Chidr*
Hole made in a house for burglary	*Sendh*

Holi festival	*Phag*
Holiday	*Chuttee*
Holiness	*Pavanta*
Hollow	*Khokh, Pola, Thotha*
Hollow of a receptacle	*Samputt*
Hollow of a tree	*Kottar*
Hollow of the palm	*Anjali, Culloo*
Hollow piece of land	*Cor jameen*
Hollow threat	*Geedar-bhabhkee*
Hollowness	*Pol*
Holy	*Pavitr*
Holy place	*Teerth*
Holy scriptures	*Nigamagam*
Homage	*Shraddhanjali*
Home	*Ghar*
Home Minister	*Grih-mantri*
Home Ministry	*Grihmantralay*
Home Secretary	*Grih Sachiv*
Home-guard	*Grihrakshan*
Homeless	*Beghar*
Homeopathy	*Homiyopaithee*
Homestick	*Grihasakt*
Hominy	*Daliya*
Homogeneity	*Sazateeyta*
Homogeneous	*Samang*
Homogeniety	*Samangta*
Homonym	*Samdhwanik*
Honest	*Eemandar*
Honesty	*Eemandaree, Eeman*
Honesty of purpose	*Nakneeyatee*
Honey	*Madhu*
Honey-bee	*Madhumakkhee*
Honey-comb	*Madhukosh*

Honeymoon night	*Madhuyaminee*
Honorarium	*Manday*
Honorary	*Avaitanik*
Honoraium paid to a priest	*Dakshina*
Honorific	*Sammansoocak*
Honorofic used for women	*Sushshree*
Honour	*Samman*
Honourable	*Sammanneey, Manneey*
Honoured	*Gauravanvit*
Honouring	*Abhinandan*
Hood of a carriage	*Tap*
Hood of a snake	*Phan*
Hoodwink	*Jhansa*
Hoof	*Sum*
Hoof-beat	*Tap*
Hook	*Kulaba, Huk*
Hookah	*Gargarana*
Hookworm	*Cuncuna*
Hooligan	*Gunda, Joojoo*
Hooliganism	*Gundagardi*
Hoot like an owl	*Ghughuana*
Hope	*Ummeed, Asha*
Hope and despair	*Asha nirasha*
Hope of acquisition	*Praptyasha*
Hopeful	*Ashavan*
Horizon	*Kshitij*
Horizontal	*Ara*
Horn	*Bhonpoo, Vishan*
Horned	*Shringee*
Horoscope	*Janm-pattree*
Horrible	*Vikat*

Horrid	*Beebhats*
Horridness	*Beebhatsta*
Horrified	*Bhayakul*
Horripilated	*Romancit*
Horripilating	*Romharshak*
Horripilation	*Romanc*
Horripilatory	*Lomharshak*
Horse	*Ghora*
Horse carriage	*Tanga, Ghora-garee*
Horse-faced	*Ghurmunha*
Horse-race	*Ghurdaur*
Horse-rider	*Ghursavar*
Horse-riding	*Ghursavaree*
Horse-trainer	*Cabuk-savar*
Horsemanship	*Shagsavaree*
Horsewhip	*Cabuk*
Hospitable	*Mehmandar*
Hospital	*Aspatal*
Hospitality	*Atithisatkar, Mehmandaree, Avbhagat, Khatir*
Host	*Mezban*
Hostage	*Ol*
Hostel	*Chatravas*
Hostility	*Riputa*
Hot	*Garam, Ushm*
Hot ash	*Bhoobhal*
Hot from the oven	*Garmagaram*
Hot haste	*Mara-maree*
Hot news	*Garam khabar*
Hot wind	*Loo*
Hot-tempered	*Krodhee, Gussail*
Hotel	*Hotal*
Hour	*Ghanta*

House	*Makan, Sadan, Kothee*
House all entire	*Khirkee-band*
House of Music	*Sangeetalay*
House of learning	*Viddyapeeth*
House of mirrors	*Sheeshmahal*
House of prostitution	*Kasbee khana*
House of the people	*Loksabha*
House owner	*Makanmalik*
House search	*Khana talashee*
House servant	*Mehra*
House-breaking	*Nakab*
House-building mortar	*Gach*
House-holder	*Kautumbik, Ghardwar, Grihasthee*
Housewife	*Grihanee, Grihlakshmi*
How	*Kaisa*
How many	*Kai*
How much	*Kitna*
However	*Prattyut*
Hubbub	*Ror*
Huge	*Bara*
Huge bundle	*Gatthar*
Huge drum	*Nagara, Nakkara*
Huge frying pan	*Karaha*
Huge whale	*Timingil*
Hulla-Balloo	*Haytoba, Utkrosh*
Human	*Manushee, Manav, Manushik*
Human being	*Banda, Insan*
Human excreta	*Goo-moot*
Human sacrifice	*Narbali*
Human size	*Adamkad*
Humane	*Insanee, Manaveey, Manushshyocit*
Humanisation	*Manaveekaran*
Humanism	*Manavtavad*

Humanistic	*Manavtavadee*
Humanities	*Manavshastr*
Humanity	*Admeeyat, Insaniyat, Manavta*
Humble	*Vinammrtapoorn*
Humble abode	*Gareebkhana*
Humble submission	*Savinay nivedan*
Humbly	*Savinay, Sanunay*
Humid	*Nameedar*
Humidity	*Adrata*
Humiliated	*Zaleel*
Humiliation	*Zillat, Manmardan*
Humility	*Vinaysheelta*
Humming sound	*Ninad, Gunjar*
Humorous	*Mazakiya, Vinodee, Hasykar*
Humorous temperament	*Vinodvritti*
Humorousness	*Vinodsheelta*
Humour and satire	*Hassy vyangy*
Hump	*Koobar*
Hump of a camel	*Kohan*
Humpbacked	*Kubj, Kubra*
Hundred	*Shat, Sainkra*
Hundred billion	*Kharab*
Hundred thousand	*Lakh*
Hundredth	*Sauvan*
Hunger	*Bhookh, Bubhuksha*
Hunger-strike	*Anshan, Bhookhartal*
Hungry	*Nirann, Bhookha*
Hunt-out	*Toh*
Hunter	*Vyadh, Akhatak*
Hunting expedition	*Akhatyatra*
Huntsman	*Shikaree*
Hurdle race	*Rukavatee*

Hurled	*Prakshipt*
Hurling	*Prakshapan*
Hurricane	*Mahavat, Jhakkar*
Hurry	*Utavalee, Jaldee, Sheeghrata*
Hurry and scurry	*Daura dauree, Tarataree*
Hurt	*Ahat, Tilla, Chot*
(to) hurt	*Dukhna, Khalna*
Hurtful	*Akharna*
Husband	*Piya, Pati, Gharwala, Khasam, Shohar*
Husband and wife	*Dampati*
Husband of husband's sister	*Nandoee*
Husband of mother's sister	*Mausa*
Husband's sister	*Nanad*
Husband's younger brother	*Devar*
Husbandry	*Kisanee*
Hush money	*Munh-bharaee*
Husk	*Toos, Bhoosa*
Husk of pulses	*Karaee*
Hustle and bustle	*Bhag-daur*
Hut	*Jhugee, Kutee, Jhonpra*
Hutment	*Kutiya, Marhee, Maraiya*
Hybrid	*Sankar*
Hybridity	*Sankarta*
Hydrocele	*Andavriddhi*
Hydroelectricity	*Jalviddyut, Panbijlee*
Hydrogen	*Udjan*
Hydrometer	*Jalmapak*
Hydrophobia	*Jaltras, Jalbheeti*
Hydrous	*Sajal*

Hyena	*Lakarbaggha*
Hygrometer	*Adratamapee*
Hymn	*Stottr*
Hymn book	*Bhajnavalee*
Hyphen	*Yojika, Haifan, Viyojika*
Hypnotised	*Sammohit*
Hypnotises weapon	*Sammohanastr*
Hypnotising agent	*Sammohnee*
Hypnotism	*Sammohan-vidya*
Hypochondria	*Pittonmad*
Hypocrisy	*Pakhand, Vak-vritti*
Hypocrite	*Bagla bhagat, Dharm dhwajee*
Hypocritical	*Dhongee, Pakhandee*
Hypocritical act	*Dhakosala*
Hyprocisy	*Dhong*

I

I	*Main*
Ice-age	*Himyug*
Ice-berg	*Himshail*
Ice-cream frozen in a conical container	*Kulfee*
Ichthyology	*Matsyviggyan*
Iconoclast	*Butshikan*
Icy	*Barfeela*
Ideal	*Adarsh*
Idealism	*Adarshvad*
Identical	*Akatm, Avikal*
Identification	*Shanakht*
Identity	*Pehcan*
Identity Card	*Paricay-patr*
Ideogram	*Bhavcittr*
Ideography	*Bhavankan*
Ideological	*Vaicarik*
Ideology	*Vicardhara*
Idiom	*Muhavra*
Idiomatic	*Muhavredar*
Idiot	*Gobar ganesh, Jarmati*
Idiotic	*Bhucc*
Idler	*Nigora*
Idol	*Pratima*
Idol-breaking	*Pratima-bhanjan*
Idol-worship	*Pratima-pooja*
Idol-worshipper	*Pratima-poojak*
Idolator	*Butparast*
If	*Yadi*
If you please	*Caha*
Ignite	*Sulgana*
Ignobility	*Adhamta*
Ignobility of descent	*Akuleenta*

Ignoble	*Kameena, Adham*
Ignorance	*Aggyta, Aviddya*
Ignorant	*Aggyanee*
Iguana species of lizard	*Goh*
Ill	*Manda*
Ill luck	*Badkismatee*
Ill temper	*Badmizajee*
Ill-advised	*Kumantrit*
Ill-fame	*Kuyash*
Ill-fated	*Naseebonjala*
Ill-intent	*Badneeyati*
Ill-motived	*Badneeyat*
Ill-natured	*Dush-prakriti*
Ill-omen	*Kusagun*
Ill-repute	*Akeerti*
Ill-speaking	*Astuti*
Ill-will	*Dvesh, Asadbhav*
Illegal	*Avaidh, Gairkanooni*
Illegal practice	*Avaidhacaran*
Illegality	*Avaidhta*
Illegible	*Aspasht*
Illegible scrawling or scribbling	*Ghaseet*
Illegitimacy	*Zarajta*
Illegitimate	*Haramee, Jaraj*
Illiteracy	*Jahalat*
Illiterate	*Anparh*
Illiterate person	*Dehkan*
Illness	*Rugnta*
Illogical	*Tarkheen, Besir*
Illomen	*Apshakun*
Illuminated	*Deepit, Udbhasit*
Illumination	*Udbhas*

Illusion Supreme	*Mahamaya*
Illusioned	*Bhramit*
Illusionism	*Mayavad*
Illusionist	*Mayavadee*
Illusive	*Mayabee, Bhramjanak*
Illusoriness	*Bhramatmakta*
Illusory	*Bhramatmak*
Illustrated	*Nidarshit*
Illustration	*Drishtant*
Illustration	*Nidarshan*
Imagery	*Bimb-yojna*
Imaginable	*Kalpaneey*
Imaginary	*Kalpanik*
Imagination	*Kalpana*
Imaginative	*Kalpanamay*
Imagined	*Kalpit*
Imbalance	*Asantulan*
Imcomparable	*Atul*
Imersed in joy	*Anand magn*
Imitation	*Anukaran*
Imitator	*Nakkal*
Immaculate	*Nishkalank*
Immanence	*Antaryamita*
Immanent	*Antaryamee*
Immeasurable	*Amapaneey*
Immediate	*Tatkal, Jhat, Fauran*
Immense	*Amit, Atatoot*
Immense riches	*Karoron ka khazana*
Immersion	*Avgahan*
Immigration	*Appravas*
Immoderate	*Amaryadit*
Immodesty	*Avinay*
Immoral	*Papee*

Immortal	*Amar, Mrittyunjay*
Immovable	*Sthavar, Achal*
Immune	*Nirapad*
Impact	*Sanghat*
Impartial	*Nishpaksh*
Impartiality	*Nishpakshta*
Imparting of knowledge	*Viddyadan*
Impassable	*Agammy, Alanghy, Durlanghy*
Impatience	*Basabree, Utavalapan*
Impatiently eager	*Atur*
Impenetrable	*Abhaddy*
Imperative	*Aggyarthak*
Imperative need	*Garaz, Gaun*
Imperceptible	*Agochar*
Imperialism	*Samrajjyavad*
Imperialistic	*Samrajjyavadee*
Imperishable	*Avinashshwar*
Impersonal	*Avvyaktik*
Impersonal use	*Bhava prayog*
Impertinence	*Baadbee, Shokhee*
Impertinent	*Munh-laga, Shokh*
Imperturbable	*Avichalit*
Implementation	*Abhipoorti, Palan, Kriyanviti*
Implemented	*Kriyanvit*
Implication	*Nihitarth, Vivaksha*
Implied	*Dhwanit*
Impolite	*Avinayee*
Import	*Ayat*
Import and export	*Ayat Niryat*
Import duty	*Ayat shulk*
Importance	*Mahatw*
Important	*Aham*
Imported	*Ayatit*

Importunity	*Duraggrah*
Impossible	*Namumkin, Asambhav*
Impostor	*Bahuroopiya*
Impotence	*Namardee*
Impotent	*Hijra, Namard*
Impracticability	*Avyavharikta*
Impracticable	*Avvyavharry*
Imprecatory	*Shapatmak*
Impregnable	*Durdamneey*
Impregnation	*Garbhadhan*
Impressed	*Prabhavit*
Impression	*Chap*
Impression of the full hand	*Thapa, Panjak*
Imprest	*Aggrday*
Imprint	*Chapna*
Imprinted	*Naksh*
Imprisonment	*Kaid, Karavas*
Improbability	*Asambhavna*
Improbable	*Asambhavvy*
Improper	*Ayukt, Ulta seedha, Namunasib*
Improper utterence	*Kehnee-ankehnee*
Impropreity	*Bekayadgee*
Impropriety	*Ayuktta*
Impudence	*Gustakhee, Kumatti*
Impudent	*Munhzor*
Impulse	*Bhavavash, Jhonk*
Impulsive	*Tawdar, Tarangee*
Impure	*Ashuddh*
Impurity	*Ashuddhta*
Imtimacy	*Ghantishthta*
In case	*Agar*
In cash	*Nagdee*

In charge	*Karry bharee*
In comparison with	*Banisbat*
In detail	*Savistar, Byoravar*
In distress	*Sankatapann*
In due course	*Yathasamay*
In due order	*Kramanusar*
In fact	*Hakeekat, Tatthytah*
In front of	*Sammukh*
In ful bloom	*Sarsabz*
In heaps	*Dheron*
In honour of	*Sammanarth*
In open court	*Saradarbar*
In opposition	*Barkhilaf*
In place of	*Bajay*
In possession	*Kabiz*
In proper order	*Tarteebvar*
In quick succession	*Danadan, Taratar*
In short	*Kissa kotah*
In spite of	*Bavajood*
In the Morning	*Sabera, Subah*
In the form of a verse	*Paddyatmak*
In the grip of frustration	*Kunthagrast*
In the opposite direction	*Ulta*
In the presence of	*Sanmukh*
In vain	*Nahak*
In what direction	*Kidhar*
In-charge	*Incarj*
Inability	*Asamarthta, Ayoggyta*
Inaccessible	*Durgam, Gehvar*
Inactive	*Acasht, Akriy*
Inactivity	*Jaddy, Akriyta*

Inactivity due to lassitude	*Mutmardee*
Inadvertently	*Akamte*
Inanimate	*Jar*
Inanimate matter	*Jar-padarth*
Inarticulate	*Asphut*
Inaugurated	*Udghatit*
Inauguration	*Udghatan*
Inauguration ceremony	*Udghatanotsav*
Inauspicious	*Ashubh*
Inauspicious interrogation	*Tok*
Inauspicious or bad characteristic	*Kulakshan*
Inborn	*Janmsiddh*
Incalculable	*Behisab*
Incantations accompanied by rituals	*Mantr-tantr*
Incarnate	*Shareerdharee*
Incarnation	*Avtar*
Incense	*Dhoonee*
Incensory	*Dhoopdan*
Incessant downpour	*Tarara*
Incest	*Agammyagaman*
Inch	*Inc*
Incharge	*Incarj*
Incident	*Ghatna*
Incidental	*Anushangik*
Incis	*Pachna*
Incision	*Katan, Ceera*
Inciting and abetting quarrels	*Lagaee-bujhaee*

Incivility	*Ashishtta, Asabbhyta*
Inclination	*Pravritti, Abhinati*
Inclined	*Pravritt, Abhinat*
Inclined to doubt	*Shakalu*
Included	*Shamil, Antrabhoot*
Inclusion	*Sannivash, Antarbhav*
Incoherent talk	*Pralap*
Incombustible	*Adahhy*
Income	*Amdanee, Ay*
Income and expenditure	*Ay-vyay*
Income tax	*Ay kar*
Incomimg	*Avak*
Incomparable	*Nirupam*
Incompatibility	*Asamanjassy*
Incomplete	*Adhoora, Apoorn*
Incomprehensible	*Aboddhy*
Inconceivable	*Achinty*
Incongruous and irrelevant	*Ool-jalool*
Inconsiderate	*Bemuravvat*
Inconvenience	*Asuvidha*
Incorporating	*Samavashan*
Incorporation	*Samavesh*
Increase	*Vriddhi, Tarakee, Barhotaree*
Increase in a tax	*Kar vriddhi*
Increased	*Vardhit*
Increasing	*Vardhansheel*
Increment	*Vetan-vriddhi*
Incurable	*Asaddhy, La ilaj*
Indebted	*Ringrast*
Indecency	*Abhaddrta*
Indecent	*Abhaddr*

Indecisive reflection	*Oohapoh*
Indeclinable	*Avikaree, Avvyay*
Indelible	*Amit*
Independence	*Swatantrata, Azadi*
Independent	*Swatantr, Azad, Nirdal*
Index	*Anukkramanika*
Index number	*Soocakank*
Indian	*Hindostanee, Bharatvasee*
Indian guitar	*Tamboora*
Indian Penal Code	*Tazeerata hind*
Indian abuse	*Munh-jhaunsa*
Indian bean	*Bora*
Indian clarionet	*Shehnaee*
Indian cuckoo	*Koel, Papeeha*
Indian intoxicant	*Turanta*
Indian musical instrument	*Sarod*
Indian tree	*Peepal*
Indian shirt	*Kurta*
Indian stringed musical instrument	*Sarangee*
Indian sweet	*Jalebee*
Indian sweet	*Panjeeree*
Indian sweet made from cheese	*Rasgulla*
Indian tree	*Tamal*
Indian trousers	*Payjama*
Indian type of pudding	*Pakvan*
Indian vareity of Saltish pastry	*Samosa*
Indian weight	*Ratee*
Indianisation	*Bharteeykaran*
Indianised	*Bharteeykrit*

Indianness	*Bharteeyta*
Indicated	*Dyotit*
Indication	*Dyotan*
Indicative	*Dyotak*
Indicator	*Bodhak*
Indictment	*Abbhyaropan*
Indifference	*Udaseenta*
Indifferent	*Udaseen*
Indigence	*Deenta*
Indigenous	*Swadashee*
Indigent	*Dariddr, Muhtaj, Bhukkha*
Indigestion	*Apach, Ajeern, Badhazmee*
Indirect	*Paroksh*
Indiscipline	*Anushasanheenta*
Indiscreet	*Kuvicharee*
Indiscretion	*Avivak*
Indiscriminately	*Andhadhundh*
Indisposal	*Aswasth*
Indisposed	*Aleel, Rugn*
Indisposition	*Aswasthata*
Indisputable	*Nirvivad, Avivaddy*
Individual	*Vyashti*
Individualisation	*Vyakteekaran*
Individualism	*Vyaktivad*
Individualistic	*Vyakti-pradha*
Individuality	*Vyaktittw, Vaiyaktikta*
Indivisible	*Abhajjy*
Indo-European	*Bharopeey*
Indolent	*Akarmanny, Dhillar*
Indologist	*Bharatvid*
Indology	*Bharatviddya*
Indomitable	*Durgharsh*
Indra's thunderbolt	*Vajjr*

Indrapuri	*Surpur*
Inductive	*Agamanatmak*
Indulge in drinking	*Peena-pilana*
Indulgence	*Lar-pyar*
Indulgence in gay life	*Vilasita*
Indulgence in luxury	*Bhogvilas*
Indus Valley	*Sindhu ghatee*
Industrial	*Auddhyogik*
Industrialisation	*Auddyogee karan*
Industrialism	*Audhyogikta*
Industrious	*Uddyogee*
Ineffective	*Nishprabhav*
Ineffectual	*Akarath*
Inefficiency	*Adakshta*
Inefficient	*Adaksh*
Inequality	*Asamanta*
Inestimable	*Akoot*
Inevitability	*Avashshyambhavita*
Inevitable	*Avashshyambhavee, Honhar*
Inexcusable	*Akshammy*
Inexperienced	*Nausikhua*
Inexpressible	*Avarnaneey*
Infallible	*Amogh*
Infancy	*Shishuta*
Infant	*Shishu*
Infanticide	*Balvadh*
Infantryman	*Padik*
Infatuated	*Vyamohit, Vimugdh*
Infatuated with sexual love	*Kamasakt*
Infatuating	*Vimugdhkaree*
Infatuation	*Vyamoh*
Infeasible	*Ashakky*

Infectious	*Sankramak*
Infer correctly	*Boojhna*
Inferior	*Ghatiya, Avar*
Inferiority	*Laghuta*
Inferiority complex	*Heenattw*
Infernal world	*Yamlok*
Infiltration	*Ghuspaith*
Infiltrator	*Ghuspaithiya*
Inflammation of udder	*Thanalee*
Inflammatory	*Dahak*
Inflate	*Phulana*
Inflation	*Phulaw*
Inflation of currency	*Muddra-spheeti*
Inflexion	*Karak chihn*
Inflict pain	*Shoolna*
Inflicted	*Zada*
Influence	*Prabhav*
Influence of evil spirit	*Bhootbadha*
Influential	*Prabhavshalee, Prabhavpoorn*
Influenza	*Influenza*
Inform	*Kehlana, Janvana*
Informal	*Areetik*
Informality	*Batakallufee*
Information	*Ittala*
Information	*Soocna*
Information centre	*Soocnalay*
Informative	*Gyapak*
Informed	*Gyapit*
Informer	*Mukhbir*
Infrangible	*Abhangur*
Ingenuous	*Bhola-bhala, Nishkapat*
Ingratitude	*Namakharamee*
Ingredient	*Upadan*

Inhabitant	*Vasee*
Inhabitant of Maharashtra	*Maratha*
Inhabitants of a town	*Purjan*
Inhaling and exhaling	*Shwas-prashshwas*
Inherent	*Antarnihit*
Inherent duty of a woman	*Streedharm*
Inheritance	*Dayadhikar*
Inheritor	*Daybhagee*
Inhuman	*Amanveey*
Inimical	*Shatrootapoorn*
Initials	*Addyakshar*
Initiated	*Deekshit*
Initiation	*Deekshan*
Initiative	*Abhikkram*
Injection	*Injekshan*
Injunction	*Nishedhaggya*
Injured	*Ghayal*
Injustice	*Gair-insafee*
Ink	*Roshnaee*
Inkling	*Abhas*
Inkpot	*Davat*
Inkstand	*Kalamdan*
Inland	*Antardasheey*
Inlay	*Jarat*
(to) inlay	*Jarna*
Inlaying work	*Panceekaree*
Inn	*Saray*
Inn-keeper	*Bhatiyara*
Innate	*Janmjat*
Innate modesty	*Haya*
Innate quality	*Swadharm*

Innate sense	*Sahaj buddhi*
Innate tendency	*Sahajbhav*
Innately modest	*Hayadar*
Inner	*Antrang, Antar, Abbhyantar*
Inner circle	*Antarcakkr*
Inner conflict	*Antardvandv*
Inner feeling	*Antarbhavana*
Inner light	*Antarjyoti*
Inner sole	*Paytaba*
Inner urge	*Antahprarna*
Inner world	*Antarjagat*
Innocence	*Nirdoshta*
Innocent	*Abodh, Nasamajh, Nirdosh, Masoom, Begunah*
Innocent heroine	*Mugdha*
Innovation	*Abhinavan*
Innter being	*Antahsatta*
Innumerable	*Bashumar*
Inopportune	*Bemauka, Asamayocit*
Inorganic	*Ajaiw*
Inpudent	*Gustakh*
Inquire and find out	*Dariyaft*
Inquisitive	*Kutoohalee*
Inquisitiveness	*Kutoohal*
Insanity	*Unmad*
Insatiable	*Asantoshee*
Insatiable lust	*Havas*
Insect	*Patanga, Keet*
Insect which eats grains	*Sursuree*
Insect which infests vegetables	*Sunda*
Insecticide	*Keetnashak, kriminashak*
Insectivorous	*Keetbhakshee*

Insects and moths	*Keet patang*
Insecure	*Arakshit, Asurakshit*
Insecurity	*Asuraksha*
Insemination	*Sansecan*
Insense-stick	*Dhoop battee*
Inseparable	*Abhinn*
Insetting	*Jaraee*
Inside	*Andar*
Insight	*Antardrishti, Soojh, Paith*
Insignia of royalty	*Rajcinh*
Insignificance	*Asarta, Tucchta*
Insignificant	*Aisa vaisa, Chuchoo, Naceez*
Insipid	*Viras*
Insipidity	*Virasta*
Insistence	*Zid, Israr*
Insistence on truth	*Sattyagrah*
Insolence	*Dhrishta*
Insolent	*Dhrisht*
Insolvency	*Divala*
Insolvent	*Divaliya*
Inspection	*Muayna*
Inspector	*Daroga, Nireekshak*
Inspiration	*Prerna*
Inspired	*Prerit*
Inspirer	*Prerak*
Instability	*Cancalta, Asthirta*
Installation	*Prasthapan*
Installed	*Prasthapit*
Installer	*Prasthapak*
Instalment	*Kist*
Instance	*Nazeer*
Instantaneous	*Tatkshanik*
Instantaneously	*Jhatpat, Ananfanan*

Instantly	*Akdam, Tatkshan*
Instigate	*Uksana*
(to) instigate	*Harkana*
Instigation	*Uksav*
Instinct	*Sehaj-vritti*
Instinctive	*Sahaj gyan*
Institute	*Sansthan*
Institution	*Sanstha*
Institutional	*Sansthagat, Sansthanik*
Instruct	*Sikhana*
Instruction	*Anudesh, Hidayat, Nirdesh*
Instrument	*Yantr*
Instrumental case	*Karankarak*
Instrumental music	*Vaddysangeet*
Instrumentalist	*Vadạk*
Insult	*Apman*
Insurance	*Beema*
Insured	*Beemakrit*
Insurer	*Beemakarta*
Insurgent	*Vidrohee*
Inteference	*Dastandazee*
Integration	*Samakta, Samakalan*
Intellect	*Medha, Pragya*
Intellectual	*Buddhijeevee, Sudhee, Buddhivadee*
Intellectual class	*Buddhivarg*
Intellectual power	*Buddhibal*
Intellectualism	*Buddhivad, Pravvyavad, Bauddhikta*
Intellectualist	*Buddhivadee*
Intelligence	*Buddhi, Samajh*
Intelligent	*Zaheen, Medhavee*
Intelligentsia	*Viddwajjan*
Intelligible	*Bodhgammyta, Subodhta, Buddhigammay*

Intemperance	*Badparhezee*
Intemperate	*Badparhez*
Intense	*Teevvr*
Intensity	*Shiddat, Teevvrta*
Intent	*Amada, Mansha, Mantavvy*
Intention	*Irada*
Intentional disregard	*Avhelna*
Inter provincial	*Antarprantiy*
Inter-Regional	*Antarpradashik*
Intercalary month	*Malmas, Purushottam mas*
Intercaste	*Antarjateey*
Intercepted	*Antaravarodhit*
Interception	*Antaravarodhan*
Interchange	*Adalbadal*
Interest	*Sood, Abhiruci*
Interesting	*Rocak, Dilcasp, Rucikar*
Interference	*Hastakshep*
Interferes	*Dakhalandaz*
Interim	*Antarim*
Interior	*Bhoogarbh*
Intermediary	*Antasth*
Intermediate	*Antarvartee*
Intermittent fever	*Tijra*
Intermittent pain	*Thanak*
Internal	*Bheetree*
Internal Secretion	*Antahstrav*
Internal angle	*Antahkon*
International	*Antarrashtreey*
Internecine quarrel	*Kaleh*
Interpolation	*Kshepak*
Interpretation	*Vivriti, Nirvecan*
Interrogate inauspiciously	*Tokna*

Interrogative	*Prashnvacak, Savaliya, Prashnatmak*
Interruption of relish	*Rangbhang*
Intersection	*Praticchad*
Interval	*Kalantar, Maddhyantar*
Interval time	*Antaral, Samayantar*
Interview	*Bhentvarta, Shakshatkar*
Intestine	*Aant*
Intimacy	*Lagaw, Meljol*
Intimate	*Dilee*
Intimidate	*Dhamkana*
Intimidation	*Dhamkee*
Intolerable	*Nagavar*
Intolerance	*Asahishunta, Asehansheelta*
Intolerant	*Asahishnu, Asehansheel*
Intonation	*Lehja*
Intoxicated	*Tann, Matt, Pramadee, Madmatt*
Intoxicating	*Nasheela, Madak, Madir*
Intoxicating leafy drug	*Bhang*
Intoxication	*Nasha, Saroor, Madakta*
Intoxication of wealth	*Dhanmad*
Intransitive	*Akarmak*
Intricate Problem	*Marhala*
Intricate affair	*Gorakhdhandha*
Intrigue	*Kuchakkr, Kootyojna*
Intriguing	*Kucakkree*
Introduction	*Bhoomika, Paricay*
Introduction of a vowel	*Swaragam*
Introspection	*Antardarshan, Atmsameeksha*
Introvertive	*Antarmukhee*
Intuitive	*Pratibh*
Inundation	*Applavan*
Invalidation	*Amanyakaran*

Invectives	*Galee-galauj*
Inveigle	*Behkana*
Inveiglement	*Behkava*
Invented	*Avishkrit*
Inventing	*Avishkaree*
Invention	*Eejad, Avishkar*
Inventor	*Avishkarta*
Inventory list	*Suchee, Soocee*
Inverse	*Prateep, Pratilom*
Inverted	*Aundha*
Investigation	*Tehkeekat, Janc-partal*
Investigator	*Gavashak*
Investiture	*Manabhishek*
Investment	*Nivesh, Viniyog, Laggat*
Invigilator	*Abhijagar*
Invigorating	*Balkarak*
Invincible	*Durdant, Durjay*
Invisibility	*Adarshan, Adrishshyta*
Invisible	*Alakshy, Addrishshy*
Invitation	*Nyota, Nimantran*
Invitation card	*Nimantran-patr*
Invite	*Nyotna*
Invited	*Nimantrit*
Invocation	*Duhaee*
Invocatory prologue	*Mangalacaran*
Invoice	*Beejak*
Invok a curse	*Kosna*
Involuntarily	*Basakhta*
Involved	*Antagrast*
Involved in an accident	*Durghatnagrast*
Iota	*Lavlash*
Ire	*Krodhagni*
Iron	*Loha, Istree*

Iron bar	*Seekhca, Sariya*
Iron fillings	*Lauh-coorn*
Iron-man	*Lauhpurush*
Ironical censure	*Vyajninda*
Ironical commendation	*Vyajastuti*
Ironical statement	*Vyajokti*
Irony	*Vyangy*
Irrefutable	*Akatty*
Irregular	*Aniyat*
Irregularly	*Bekayda*
Irrelavance	*Asangati*
Irrelevant	*Ant shant, Asangat, Batuka, Visangat*
Irrelevant talking	*Behak*
Irreligious	*Vaidharmik, Adharmee*
Irrepressible	*Adammy*
Irresponsibility	*Gair-zimmedaree*
Irresponsible	*Gair-zimmedar*
Irrigated	*Sincit, Sacit, Sikt*
Irrigation	*Sincan*
Irrigate	*Seencna*
Irritability	*Circirapan*
Irritating sensation	*Rarak, Cuncunahat*
Irritation	*Jhunjhlahat, Kheej*
Is	*Hai*
Islamic	*Islam*
Island	*Dveep, Jazeera*
Isolated	*Vivikt*
Isolation	*Vivikti*
Issue	*Ijra, Santan, Vad-vishay*
Issued	*Nirgat*
Issueless	*Nirvansh, Nissantan, Beaulad*
Issues	*Santan, Aulad*

Isthmus	*Jaldamrumaddhy, Sthal-damroo-madhy*
Itch	*Kharish, Khujlee*
(to) itch slightly	*Sursurana*
Itches	*Kandu*
Itching sensation	*Salsalahat, Khujlahat*
Ivory	*Hathee-dant*

J

Jabber	*Tany-Tany*
(to) jabber	*Budbudana*
Jack tree fruit	*Kathal*
Jackal	*Siyar, Geedar*
Jacket	*Jakit, Bandee, Mirjaee*
Jacket worn by women	*Salooka*
Jaggery	*Gur*
Jail	*Jal*
Jailor	*Karapal*
Jambolan	*Jamun*
January	*Janvaree*
Jar	*Marataban*
Jasmine	*Joohee, Camelee*
Jaundice	*Peeliya, Kamalbaee*
Jaw	*Jabra*
Jealous	*Eershya, Irshyalu*
Jelly	*Avlah*
Jerk	*Dhacka*
(to) jerk (as a vehicle in motion	*Dacakna*
Jerky	*Dhackedar*
Jester	*Bhanr*
Jesting	*Thitholee, Maskharee*
Jesting and laughing	*Hansee-thattha*
Jesus Christ	*Eesa, khreesht*
Jet black	*Koylee, Kajrara*
Jevenile literature	*Bal-sahitty*
Jew	*Yahoodee*
Jewel	*Ratn, Mani, Nag*
Jeweller	*Ratnkar, Jauharee*
Jewess	*Yahoodin*
Jewish	*Yehodee*
Jingle	*Cham, Jhunjhun*

(to) jingle	*Khanakna, Chamkna*
Jingled	*Jhankrit*
Jingling	*Jhankar, Khanak*
Jingling bell	*Ghunghroo*
Jingling sound	*Thanthan, Thanka*
Jittery	*Pinkee*
Jocular	*Hansor, Vinodpriy*
Jocularity	*Dillageebazee*
Joinery	*Joraee*
Joining	*Yojan*
Joint	*Sanyukt*
Joint-account	*Sanyukt khata*
Joke	*Dillagee, Mazak, Parihas*
Joker	*Makhauliya, Dillageebaz, Thathol*
Jollity	*Cuhal*
Jolt	*Hickola*
Jostling	*Thalamthal*
Journalism	*Patrkarita*
Journalist	*Patrakar*
Journey	*Safar, Yatra*
Joy	*Harsh*
Joyful temperament	*Khushdil*
Joyous hilarity	*Haha-hoohoo*
Joyous screech	*Kilkaree*
Jubilant	*Ullas, Gehgeha*
Jubilation	*Hulas*
Jubilee	*Jayantee*
Judge	*Nyaykarta, Nyayadheesh*
Judgement	*Nirnay*
Judicially	*Nyaytah*
Judiciary	*Nyayang, Nyaytantr, Nyaypalika*
Judicious	*Nyayparayan*
Juggler	*Madaree, Bajeegar*

Juice	*Ras, Joos*
Juice of date-tree	*Neera*
Juiciness	*Rasatmakta*
Juicy	*Rasdar, Rasmay*
Jujube	*Ber*
Jujube tree	*Beree*
July	*Julaee*
Jump	*Phandna, Tapna, Chalang, Kudana, Uchalna*
(to) jump	*Koodnal, Phandna, Phudakna*
(to) jump off	*Chatakana*
(to) jump over	*Tapna*
Junction of three roads	*Tiraha*
Jungle	*Sehra, Dav, Aranny, Jangalik*
Junior	*Jooniyar, Kanishth*
Junk	*Kabar, Angar-Khangar*
Junk dealer	*Kabaree*
Jupiter	*Brihaspati*
Jurisdiction	*Kshetradhikar*
Jurisprudence	*Nyayshastr*
Jurist	*Nyayaggy, Vidhishastree*
Jury	*Jooree*
Just	*Mauzoon*
Just in time	*Ain*
Just like	*Bataur*
Just now	*Abhee*
Just performed	*Saddyahkrit*
Justice	*Insaf, Nyay*
Justice-loving	*Nyaypriy*
Jute	*Patsan, Joot*
Juvenile	*Kamummr*

K

Kabaddi	*Kabadee*
Kangaroo	*Kangaroo*
Keep	*Rakhnee*
(to) keep away	*Durana*
(to) keep things ship-shape	*Sanjona*
Keep man	*Dharala*
Keep watch	*Agorna*
Keeping aloof	*Kinara kashee*
Kept	*Gharbasee, Rakhalee*
Kept for a long time	*Dharaoo*
Kerosene oil	*Mittee ka tal*
Kettle	*Dagca*
Kettledrum	*Danka, Dagar*
Kettledrum house	*Nakkarkhana*
Key	*Cabee*
Key-note	*Moolmantr*
Khaki	*Khakee*
Khalif	*Khaleefa*
Kharif	*Khareef*
Kharoshthi	*Kharoshthee*
Kick	*Dulattee, Padprahar, Thokar*
Kidnapping	*Apharan*
Kidney	*Gurda, Vrikk*
Kill	*Marna*
Killed	*Halak*
Killed and wounded	*Hatahat*
Killer	*Hanta, Ghatee*
Killing	*Vadh, Maran, Pranghat, Hattya*
Kilogram	*Kilo*
Kilometer	*Kilomeetar*
Kilowatt	*Kilowat*
Kind	*Kripalu, Tarah, Kism, Maharban*

Kind of flute	*Algoza*
Kind-hearted	*Dayalu, Dayasagar*
Kindly Attitude	*Kripadrishti*
Kindly feeling	*Sadbhav, Sadbhavna*
Kindness	*Raham, Maharbanee*
Kinetic	*Gatij*
King	*Prajapati, Naresh, Badshah, Raja*
King cobra	*Nagraj*
King of Kings	*Maharaja, Shenshah*
King's court	*Darbar*
King's physician	*Rajvaidya*
King-fisher	*Kirkila*
Kingdom	*Saltnat*
Kingly	*Shahee*
Kingship	*Rajasv*
Kinsfolk	*Kutumb*
Kinship	*Bandhu bhaw, Swajanta*
Kinsman	*Kutumbee*
Kissing	*Cumban*
Kitchen	*Pakshala, Rasoee-ghar*
Kitchen room	*Cauka*
Kite	*Patang, Guddee*
Kite bird	*Ceel*
Kite-flier	*Patangbaz*
Kite-flying	*Patangbazee*
Kite-swoop	*Ceel-jhapatta*
Kitten	*Bilota*
Knapsack	*Jhola*
Knead	*Goondhna, Beendna*
(to) knead (flour)	*Manrna*
Knee	*Tihunee*
Knife	*Churee, Cakoo*
Knifer	*Churebaz*

Knock	*Dastak*
(to) knock	*Khat khatana*
Knock out	*Dharana*
Knocking	*Khat khat*
Knot	*Gireh, Antee, Ganth*
Knotty	*Girehdar, Ganthil, Ghundeedar*
Know	*Janna*
Knowability	*Gayta*
Knowable	*Gyay*
Knowledge	*Viddya, Maloomat, Jankaree, Gyan*
Knowledge divine	*Brahmvidya*
Knowledge little	*Alpaggy*
Knowledge of the future	*Bhavishygyan*
Knowlege of the Supreme	*Brahmgyan*
Known	*Vidit, Gyat, Maloom*
Known since long	*Cir-paricit*
Kohlrabi	*Ganthgobhee*
Koil	*Kokil*
Kuber	*Dhanesh*
Kurukshetra	*Dharm-kshetr*

L

Label	*Lebil*
Labial	*Oshthy*
Laboratory	*Prayogshala*
Laborious	*Mehnatee, Shramee*
Labour	*Parishram, Mehnat, Shram*
(to) labour hard	*Palna*
Labour Department	*Shramvibhag*
Labour dispute	*Shramvivad*
Labour laws	*Shramvidhi*
Labour of delivery	*Prasooti*
Labour welfare	*Shramkalyan*
Labourer	*Mazdoor, Shramik*
Lac	*Laksha*
Lace of clarity	*Aspashtta*
Lacerated	*Videern*
Lack	*Abhav*
Lack lustre	*Berang, Beraunak*
Lack of confidence	*Avishshwas*
Lack of faith	*Ashraddha*
Lack of understanding	*Nasakjhee*
Lackey	*Khidmatgar*
Lackeying	*Piththoopan*
Lacking in colour	*Shreeheen*
Lacky	*Tehlua*
Laconic	*Alpaksharik*
Lactometer	*Dugdhmapak*
Ladder	*Seerhee, Nasainee*
Ladle	*Karcchee*
Lady	*Mahila, Memsahab*
Lady finger	*Bhindee*
Lady owner	*Malkin*
Lady teacher	*Addhyapika*
Lady-fly	*Beerbahootee*

Lag behind	*Picharna*
Lake	*Jheel, Sarovar*
Lakshmi	*Lakshmee*
Lamb	*Memna*
Lame	*Langra*
Lament grumblingly	*Kalapna*
Lame and maimed	*Langra-loola*
Lamella	*Patalika*
Lameness	*Langrapan*
Lament	*Bilakhna*
Lamentation	*Krandan*
Lamp	*Deepak, Cirag, Deeya, Lamp*
Lamp black	*Kajal*
Lamp stand	*Deeyat, Deevat, Deepadhar*
Lamp-house	*Deep-ghar*
Lance	*Naza, Ballam*
Lancer	*Nazabardar*
Lancet	*Nashtar*
Land	*Bhoomi, Zameen, Thal*
Land and sea	*Jal-thal*
Land animal	*Thalcar*
Land revenue	*Bhoorajjassw, Malguzaree*
Land route	*Sthalmarg*
Land warfare	*Sthal-yuddh*
Landing	*Avtaran*
Landlord	*Bhooswami, Zameendar*
Landslide	*Bhooskhalan*
Language	*Bhasha*
Lantern	*Laltan*
Lap	*God*
Large	*Kunda*
Large Kettle	*Pateela*
Large ant	*Makora*

Large drum	*Toor, Dhaka*
Large kettledrum	*Dhaunsa*
Large ladle	*Kalcha*
Large metal dish	*Parat*
Large pack	*Gadda*
Large pliers	*Janboora*
Large sickle	*Hansua*
Large wooden tub	*Kathra*
Large-hearted	*Dilvala, Dariyadil*
Lassitude	*Tandralas*
Lasso	*Phansa, Kamand*
Last	*Antim, Akhiree*
Last moment	*Antkal*
Last month of the Hindu Calendar	*Phagun*
Latch	*Sitkine*
Late	*Swargeey, Vilambit, Marhoom, Parlokvasee*
Late fee	*Vilamb-shulk*
Latency	*Pracchannta*
Latest	*Adhuniktam*
Lathe	*Kharad*
Lathi	*Lathee*
Latin	*Lateenee*
Latitude	*Akshansh*
Latrine	*Shaucgrih, Pakhana*
Latrine pot	*Sandas*
Latter	*Maska*
Latter half of winter	*Shishir*
Latter half part	*Uttarardh*
Latticed	*Jhanjhareedar*
Latticed window	*Jhanjhree*
Laudatory	*Prashansatmak*

Laughter	*Hansee*
Launching	*Jalavatran*
Lava (volcano)	*Lava*
Lavatory	*Shaucalay, Peshabkhana*
Lavender	*Cameliya*
Law	*Vidan, Kanoon*
Law of adoption	*Dattak-vidhan*
Law-suit	*Nalish*
Lawfully	*Kanoonan*
Lawn	*Lan*
Lax	*Shithil*
Laxity	*Dheel, Shithilta*
Lay down	*Letna*
Laying bricks in a wall etc.	*Cunaee*
Laymen	*Jansadharan*
Laziness	*Nithallapan, Alas*
Lazy	*Sust, Alsee*
Lead	*Seesa*
Leader	*Nata, Sargana, Jannayak*
Leadership	*Sardaree, Netrittw, Netageeree*
Leading article	*Aggrlekh*
Leaf	*Varek, Patee, Parn, Patta*
Leaf of a toddy tree	*Tarpatr*
Leaf-bowl	*Dona*
Leafless tree	*Thoontha*
Leaflet	*Patrak*
Leak heavily	*Taptapana*
Lean	*Dubla*
Lean and feeble	*Krish*
Lean and lanky	*Lamtarang*
Lean and thin	*Tanu, Ksheen*
Lean and thin person	*Laklak, Seenk salaee*

Leanness	*Dublapan*
Leap	*Ucchal, Uchakana*
Leap month	*Adhimas*
Learn	*Seekhna*
(to) learn by rote	*Ghokhna*
Learned	*Gyanee*
Learning	*Ilm, Vaidushshy*
Lease	*Patta*
Lease holder	*Pattedar, Ijaradar*
Leather	*Camra*
Leather bag	*Mot*
Leather belt	*Pashband*
Leather bucket	*Purvat*
Leather water bag	*Mashak*
Leave	*Rukhsat*
Leave of absence from work	*Muhalat*
Leaven	*Khameer*
Leaves	*Pati*
Leavings of food	*Joothan*
Lecherous	*Lampat*
Lecture	*Vyakhyan*
Leech	*Jonk, Jalauka*
Leechee	*Leecee*
Left	*Bayan*
Left over	*Baca-khuca*
Left side	*Vampaksh*
Leg	*Tang, Lat*
Leg of a chair	*Pava, Paya*
Legacy	*Rikth, Uttardan*
Legal	*Vaidh, Vidhik*
Legal agent	*Mukhtar*
Legal document	*Vilakh*

Legal expert	*Vidhiggy*
Legality	*Vidhikta*
Legend	*Dantkatha*
Legendary person	*Kathapurush*
Legislation	*Vidhan*
Legislator	*Vidhayak*
Legislature	*Vyavasthapika, Vidhayika*
Leisure	*Mohlat, Avkash*
Lementation	*Vilap*
Lemon	*Neeboo*
Lemon-juice	*Lemancoos*
Lemon-pickle	*Nibo ka achar*
Length	*Lamban, Lambaee*
Lens	*Lens*
Lentil	*Masoor*
Leopard	*Tendua*
Leper	*Korhee, Kushtee*
Leper asylum	*Kushtalay*
Leprosy	*Korh, Kusht*
Lesee	*Pattadharee*
Less	*Kam, Nyoon*
Lesson	*Sabak*
Let alone	*Darkinar*
Lethargic	*Laddhar*
Lethargy	*Laddharpan*
Lethargy due to intoxication	*Pinak*
Letter	*Haraf, Patr, Khat, Chitthee*
Letter-bearer	*Patrvahak*
Letter-box	*Patrpetee*
Leucoderma	*Shvatkushth*
Leucorrhoea	*Pradar*
Level	*Hamvar, Star, Cauras, Sateh*

Level-headed	*Samras*
Levelling	*Samtalan*
Lever	*Leevar*
Lewdness	*Lampatta*
Lexicographer	*Koshkar*
Lexicology	*Koshkala*
Lexicon	*Nighantu*
Liability	*Daittw, Dendaree*
Liable to kick	*Latiyal*
Liar	*Mitthyavadee*
Liberal	*Mukthast*
Liberalism	*Udartavad*
Liberality	*Udarta*
Liberated	*Unmochit*
Liberation	*Unmochan*
Liberator	*Muktidata*
Libertine	*Swacchandcaree*
Librarian	*Pustakalayadhyaksh*
Library	*Pustakalay*
Licence	*Anuggyapti*
Lick	*Catna*
Lid	*Dhakkan*
Lie and relax	*Paurhna*
Lieutenant	*Leftinent*
Life	*Pran, Jeevan, Jan, Zindgee*
Life Insurance	*Jevan-beema*
Life and death	*Jeevan maran*
Life long	*Ajeevan*
Life of a householder	*Grihasth ashshram*
Life of the common man	*Janjeevan*
Life sentence	*Damal*
Life-boat	*Jeevan-nauka*

Life-companion	*Jeevan-sangee*
Life-cycle	*Jeevan-cakr*
Life-history	*Jeevan-katha, Jeevan vrit*
Life-line	*Ghurnas*
Life-long celibate	*Bal-brahmacaree*
Life-time	*Jeevan-kal*
Lifeless	*Murdane, Nishprán*
Lift	*Uthana, Lift, Uttolak*
Lifting up	*Unnayan*
Light	*Halka fulka, Candna, Lait, Roshnee, Prakash*
Light and delightful	*Bheena*
Light blow of fist	*Mukkee*
Light cold	*Khunkee*
Light drizzle	*Rimjhim*
Light fomentation	*Takor*
Light green	*Dhanee*
Light maroon	*Unnabee*
Light music	*Saral sangeet*
Light red	*Sataluee*
Light refreshment	*Cay panee, Jalpan*
Light rosy	*Sharbatee*
Light thud	*Dhap*
Light-house	*Prakash stambh*
Lighted	*Alokit, Ujala*
Lighting	*Tarit*
Lightness	*Halkapan*
Lightning	*Saudaminee, Capla, Daminee, Bijalee*
Like	*Jaisa, Manind*
Like a father	*Pitrituly*
Like that	*Tyon*
Like this	*Aisa*

Like-killing	*Janleva*
Likely	*Sambhavaneey*
Likeness	*Samy*
Lily	*Nalin*
Lily flower	*Kumud*
Limb	*Avyav*
Limb of minor limb	*Upang*
Limbed	*Angee*
Lime	*Coona*
Lime-stone	*Coona-patthar*
Limelight	*Prakashshy*
Limit	*Intha, Parimiti, Seema, Maryada*
Limitation of time	*Tamadee*
Limited	*Sant, Saseem, Maryadit, Parimit, Pariseemit*
Limitedness	*Seemitta*
Limitless	*Niravadhi, Niseem*
Limitlessness	*Nissemta*
Limp	*Lang, Bhacak*
(to) limp	*Langrana*
Limpid	*Vimal*
Limpidity	*Vimalta*
Line	*Rekha, Pankti*
Line of fate	*Brahmlekh, Karmrekha, Brahmrekha*
Line of stiches	*Seeyan*
Line on the palm	*Hastrekha*
Lineage	*Nasal, Gottr*
Lineament	*Cehra mohra*
Linear	*Rakhakar*
Lined	*Rakhit*
Linen wrapper	*Dupatta*
Lines	*Padee*

Lingual	*Bhasheey*
Linguist	*Bhashavid*
Linguistic	*Bhashaik*
Linguistic expertise	*Zabandanee*
Lining	*Astar*
Lining of a cloth	*Bhitalla*
Link	*Karee*
Linseed	*Alsee, Teesee*
Lintel	*Lintar*
Lion	*Vanraj, Sinh, Sherbabar*
Lion-hearted	*Sherdil*
Lion-like	*Sinhvat*
Lionet	*Sinhshasak*
Lip	*Dashanacchad*
Liquefiable	*Dravneey*
Liquid	*Taral, Drav*
Liquidation	*Parisamapti*
Liquidity	*Dravta, Taralta*
Liquor	*Sharab, Hala, Tharra*
Liquor and meat	*Sharab-kabab*
Lisp	*Tutlana*
Lisping	*Totla, Tutlahat*
List	*Talika, List, Fehrist*
List of words	*Shabdavalee, Shabdsoocee*
Listen	*Sunna*
(to) listen and assimilate	*Sunna-gunna*
Listener	*Shrota, Sunvaiya*
Listlessness	*Chatpatahat*
Literacy	*Saksharta*
Literal	*Shabdik, Aksharik*
Literal meaning	*Vaccyarth*
Literal translation	*Shabdanuvad*

Literary	*Sahityik*
Literate	*Sakshar*
Literateur	*Sahittyakar*
Literature	*Sahity*
Litho	*Leetho*
Litigant	*Adalatbaz, Mukadmebaz*
Litigation	*Adalatbazee, Mukaddamebazee*
Litre	*Litar*
Little	*Thora, Zara, Tanik*
Little finger	*Changulee, Kanishthika*
Littoral	*Samudrvartee*
Liturgy	*Poojanvidhi*
Live	*Sajeev*
(to) live	*Jeena*
Live coal	*Angara*
Livelihood	*Abodana, Jeevika*
Liveliness	*Sajeevta, Sphoorti*
Lively	*Jeevant*
Liver	*Kaleja, Jigar, Yakkrit*
Livestock	*Pashudhan*
Living	*Jeevit*
Living being	*Jeev, Pranee*
Living dead	*Jeevan-mrit*
Living in an islands	*Dweepee*
Living in hell	*Narakvas*
Living in solitude	*Akantvas*
Living on land	*Sthalcar*
Living together	*Akjaee, Sehvas*
Lizard	*Chipkalee*
Load	*Ladan, Bhar, Bojh*
(to) load	*Ladna*
Load-stone	*Cumbak-patthar*
Loaf of bread	*Pawrotee, Dabal rotee*

Loafer	*Lofar, Avara, Lafanga*
Loam	*Domat*
Lobby	*Upantika*
Local	*Sthaneey*
Local people	*Yahanvala*
Locality	*Tola, Muhalla*
Lock	*Tala*
Lock and key	*Tala-kunjee*
Lock of braid	*Joora*
Lock of hair	*Zulf, Lat*
Lock of hair along the temple	*Kakpaksh*
Lock-out	*Talabandee*
Lock-up	*Jail, Havalat*
Locket	*Lakat*
Locomotion	*Sancalan*
Locomotive	*Calittr*
Locust	*Tiddee*
Lodging place of a marriage party	*Janvasa*
Loftiness	*Uccta, Bulandee*
Lofty	*Tung, Udatt*
Log of wood	*Lakkar*
Logic	*Tarkshastr*
Logical	*Tarkik, Tarksangat*
Logician	*Siddhantee, Naiyayik*
Loin cloth	*Tehmat, Dhotee, Lungee*
Loneliness	*Soonapan, Akelapan, Tanhaee*
Lonely	*Nirjan, Sunsan*
Long	*Lamba*
Long and thin needle	*Sooja*
Long coat	*Sharvanee, Achkan*
Long drawn eulogy	*Virudavalee*

Long for	*Lalakna*
Long horn	*Pon*
Long jump	*Kulanch*
Long life	*Zindabad*
Long lived	*Ciranjeev*
Long necked jar	*Surahee*
Long period	*Yug*
Long robe	*Cola*
Long separation	*Cir-viyog*
Long tail	*Puchalla*
Long term	*Deerghkaleen*
Long wooden staff	*Ballee*
Long-awaited	*Cir-prateekshit*
Long-cherished	*Cirkankshit*
Long-cherished desire	*Sadh*
Long-drawn ailment	*Rajrog*
Long-drawn breath	*Ucchwas*
Long-lived	*Deerghayu, Cir, Deerghjeevee*
Long-sighted	*Giddh-drishti*
Long-term	*Doorgamee*
Longed for	*Mancaha*
Longing	*Lalak, Arzoo, Manokamna*
Longish	*Lambotara*
Longish pair of scissors	*Kaincha*
Look	*Citvan*
(to) look	*Dekhna*
(to) look askance	*Tararna*
(to) look fine	*Bilasna*
(to) look for	*Johna*
(to) look intently	*Bhalna*
Look intently	*Niharna*
Look-out	*Tak*
Looking after	*Sanbhal*

Looking all round	*Sinhavalokan*
Looking at others for help	*Mukhapekshee*
Looking glass	*Makur*
Looking towards	*Unmukh*
Looks	*Rangroop*
Loom	*Kargha*
Loose	*Dheela, Dhildhila*
Loose-motion	*Dast*
Loosen	*Dheelna*
(to) loosen (outer skin)	*Thalakna*
Looseness	*Dhilaee*
Loot	*Loot*
Loquat	*Lukat*
Lord	*Malik*
Lord Brahma	*Brahma*
Lord Buddha	*Buddh, Arhant, Tathagat*
Lord Ganesh	*Ganesh*
Lord Indra	*Surendra*
Lord Indra's Elephant	*Airavat*
Lord Krishna	*Murleedhar, Natvar, Giridhar, Kanhaiya*
Lord Krishna's Mother	*Nandranee*
Lord Shiv	*Bholanath, Shankar, Mahadev, Neelkanth*
Lord Vishnu	*Vankatesh, Vishnu, Narayan*
Lord of all	*Sarveshwar*
Lord the Great	*Mahalshwar*
Lordly	*Sahebee*
Lorry	*Laree*
Lose	*Khona*

(to) lose one's self control in anger	*Baukhlahat*
(to) lose the jointgrip	*Hackana*
(to) lose through fraud	*Dehkana*
Loss	*Hani, Tota, Ghata*
Loss of direction	*Disha-bhram*
Loss of the joint-grip	*Hacak*
Lost	*Gum*
Lost for war	*Jigeesha*
Lost in ecstasy	*Anand vibhoor*
Lost in meditation	*Dhyanavasthit*
Lottery	*Latree*
Lotus	*Pankaj, Padm, Neeraj, Kamal*
Lotus flower	*Kamal*
Lotus lake	*Padmakar*
Lotus like face	*Mukhkamal*
Lotus-like feet	*Carankamal*
Loud	*Buland*
Loud and piercing	*Gagan bhedee*
Loud bang	*Dhdmaka*
Loud call	*Tar*
Loud crash	*Karaka*
Loud cry	*Dhad*
Loud laughter	*Kehkaha, Thahaka*
Loud merriment	*Ceh-ceh*
Loud report	*Dan*
Loud scream	*Ciciyahat*
Loud sound of drum etc.	*Ghamar*
Loud tinkling sound	*Thanaka*
Loudspeaker	*Laudspeekar*
Lounge	*Vishramkaksh*

Lounging of a horse	*Kava*
Louse	*Naroo, Joon, Ceelar*
Lovability	*Priyta*
Love	*Muhabbat, Prem*
Love stalk	*Premalap*
Love-affair	*Premvyapar*
Love-lorn person	*Majnoon*
Love-sick	*Kamart, Prematur*
Loveliness	*Lavanny, Manoramta*
Lovely	*Manoram*
Lovely eyes	*Sunayan*
Lovely young woman	*Ramnee*
Lover	*Premee, Sajan, Ashik*
Lover of art	*Kalapremee*
Lover of solitude	*Aikant priy*
Low	*Heen, Neecha*
Low caste	*Kujati*
Low ground marsh	*Dabar*
Low level	*Neecaee*
Low mentality	*Heen-bhavna*
Low or faint ring	*Bhanak*
Low stool	*Peerha*
Low tide	*Bhata*
Low wicker stool	*Maciya*
Low wooden seat	*Patra*
Low-minded	*Kshudr-hriday*
Low-priced	*Sastee*
Lower	*Nicla*
Lower end of a cot	*Paitana*
Lower end of a reed	*Santa*
Lower lip	*Adhar*
Lower stone of a grinder	*Tarauta*

Lower-undergarment	*Janghiya*
Lowliness	*Tuccapan, Heenta, Neecta*
Lowminded	*Tucca*
Loyal	*Vafadar, Nishth*
Loyal to Truth	*Sattyanishth*
Loyalist	*Rajbhakt*
Loyalty	*Vafadaree*
Lubricant	*Snehak*
Lubrication	*Snehan*
Lubricate the wheels of a vehicle	*Toolna*
Luckless	*Karmheen, Bhaggyheen*
Lucky	*Bhaggyvan, Kismatvar, Takdeervar*
Lucky person	*Mahabhag*
Lucky thread	*Mangalsootr*
Ludeness	*Bhoglipsa*
Ludicrous	*Hassyaspad*
Luggage	*Saj-saman, Mal-asbab*
Luke-warm	*Gunguna*
Lullaby	*Loree*
Lumber	*Kath kabar*
Lumber market	*Gudree bazar*
Luminious	*Prakashman*
Lump	*Bhala, Dhala, Thakka*
Lump of dung	*Coth*
Lump of flesh	*Lothra*
Lunar eclipse	*Candrgrahan*
Lunch	*Lanc*
Lung	*Phephra*
Lurching	*Dagmag*
Lush with greenery	*Hara-bhara*
Lusterless	*Beab*
Lustful	*Kamee, Lipsu*

Lustre	*Raunak, Abha, Kanti*
Lustreless	*Nistej, Kantiheen*
Lustrous	*Jyotirmay, Kantiman*
Lusture	*Vibha*
Lusty	*Hatta-katta*
Luxurious	*Vilasmay, Aishparast*
Luxurious bed	*Saj*
Luxury	*Aish, Vilas*
Lying down	*Shayee*
Lying-in chamber	*Sauree, Sootikagar*
Lying-in home	*Sootika-grih*
Lying-in room	*Sootika prakoshth*
Lying-in ward	*Sootika-kaksh*
Lying-in woman	*Sootika*
Lynx	*Banbilaw*
Lyrical poem	*Geeti kavvy*

M

Mace	*Gada*
Mace spice	*Javittree*
Machine	*Masheen*
Machine part	*Kalpurza*
Machine-age	*Yantr-yug*
Machine-gun	*Masheengan*
Machine-maker	*Yantrkar*
Machine-man	*Masheenman*
Machine-operated	*Yantrcalit*
Machine-room	*Yantralay*
Machinery	*Masheenaree*
Mad	*Bavra, Pagal*
Mad cap	*Buram*
Maddening desire	*Harak*
Made from raisins	*Kishmishee*
Made to order	*Farmaishee*
Made to wear	*Sila-silaya*
Made-up and adorned	*Saja-dhaja*
Madness	*Junoon, Pagalpan*
Magazine	*Patrika*
Magic	*Jadoo, Indrjal*
Magical	*Jaduee*
Magical spell	*Tilism*
Magician	*Jadoogar, Indrjalak*
Magistracy	*Magistratee*
Magistrate	*Majistrat, Dandadhikaree*
Magnet	*Cumbak*
Magnification	*Sanvardhan, Avardhan, Pravardhan*
Magnificence	*Shanban*
Magnificent	*Shandar*
Magnifying	*Sanvardhak*
Maid servant	*Mehree, Dasee*
Maiden	*Kumaree, Kannyka*

Mail	*Dak*
Mail train	*Dak-garee*
Maimed	*Booca*
Maimed hand	*Loola*
Main	*Sadar*
Mainstay	*Adharstambh*
Maintain	*Palna*
Maintainable	*Pratipalaneey*
Maintained	*Palit, Pratipalit*
Maintainer	*Palankarata, Pratipal*
Maintainer female	*Palika*
Maintaining	*Palan, Pratipalak*
Maintenance	*Rakh rakhav, Pratipalan, Bharan-poshan*
Maintenance allowance	*Kharchee*
Maize	*Makka, Makaee*
Majestic	*Diggaj, Shahana*
Major	*Vayask*
Major (army)	*Majar*
Majority	*Bahumat*
Make a crackling sound while burning	*Catcatana*
(to) make a hissing sound	*Chanchanana, Siskarna*
(to) make a humming sound	*Gunjarna*
(to) make a rattling noise	*Kharbarana*
(to) make a sound like that of a big drum	*Dhamakna*
(to) make a splashing sound	*Chapchapana*

(to) make a tapping sound	*Tahakna*
(to) make a thorough search	*Dhandhora*
(to) make a tinkling sound	*Tankarna*
(to) make conquettish gestures	*Matkana*
(to) make dirty by rough and wrong use	*Latharna*
(to) make laugh	*Hansana*
(to) make one dance	*Nacana*
(to) make one hold	*Thamana*
(to) make turbid by stirring	*Ghangholna*
(to) make understand	*Samjhana*
(to) make undue haste	*Harbarana*
(to) make up	*Sajna-sanvarna*
(to) make wet	*Bhigona*
(to) make-up	*Singarna*
Make up	*Roopsajja, Mekap, Banavat*
Make up aids	*Prasadhan*
Makeup-box	*Singardan*
Making a tinkling sound	*Ghanaghan*
Making an effort	*Yatnsheel*
Making pretences	*Tallanaveesee*
Making tree	*Bhilavan*
Maladministration	*Kushasan, Kuprashasan*
Malaria	*Maleria*
Male	*Nar*
Male accompanyist of a dancer	*Meerasee*

Male organ	*Lingandriy*
Male sparrow	*Ciraunta*
Male-Buffalo	*Bhainsa*
Malc-sheep	*Bhera*
Male-spider	*Makra*
Malformed	*Viroop*
Malice	*Ranjish*
Malicious	*Viddwashee, Dweshpoorn, Kucal, Dushtatma*
Malicious fault-finding	*Chalchiddr*
Maliciously secretive	*Ghunna*
Malnutrition	*Kuposhan*
Malta	*Malta*
Maltreatment	*Kuvyavhar, Badsulookee*
Malva	*Malva*
Mamager	*Prabandhak*
Mammal	*Stanee, Standharee*
Mammon	*Kubar*
Man	*Manushshy, Purush, Nar*
Man of action	*Karmyogee*
Man of the age	*Yugpurush*
Man-eater	*Adamkhor*
Man-in-charge	*Karyadhikaree*
Man-power	*Janshakti*
Man-slaughter	*Narvadh*
Manacle	*Hathkaree*
Management	*Prabandh, Bandobast*
Mandate	*Aadesh*
Mandatory	*Adeshatmak*
Mane	*Ayal*
Mane of a lion	*Sinhkesar*
Manganese	*Maingneez*
Manger	*Carnee*

Mango	*Aam*
Mango juice	*Aamras*
Mango powder	*Amcoor*
Manifest	*Ujagar*
Manifestation	*Prakateekaran, Unmesh, Prakatan*
Manipulation to fulfil one's ends	*Tippas*
Mankind	*Manushshyjati*
Manliness	*Punsattw*
Manner	*Dhab*
Manner of going	*Cal*
Mannerless	*Besaleeka, Kudhanga*
Mannerly	*Saleekedar*
Manners	*Tameez, Shaoor*
Manoeuvres	*Danw-pac*
Manoeuvres of war	*Yuddhabbhyas*
Manoeuvring	*Paintrabazee*
Manrac	*Saudaee*
Mansion	*Saudh*
Manual labour	*Mehnatmazdooree*
Manual labourer	*Beldar*
Manual skill	*Hastkaushal*
Manufacturing cost	*Parta*
Manure	*Khad*
Manuscript	*Pandulipi*
Many	*Bahu, Akadhik*
Map	*Naksha, Mancitr*
Mapping	*Mancittran*
Marble	*Sangmarmar, Marbal*
March	*Yatra, March, Prayan*
March for victory	*Vijay-yatra*
Mare	*Ghoree, Ghoriya*
Margin	*Hashiya*

Marginal heading	*Parshw-sheershak*
Marginal note	*Parshwtippnee*
Marigold	*Gainda*
Marine	*Samudr, Samudrik*
Marine fire	*Barvanal*
Marital	*Dampatik*
Mark	*Marka, Ank, Cinh*
Mark of bruise made by pinching	*Bakota*
Mark of the hoof	*Khuree*
Mark put on the forehead	*Teeka*
Marked	*Cihnit*
Market	*Mandee, Hatt, Bajar*
Market-rate	*Bajar-bhaw*
Marketability	*Vipannyta*
Marketing	*Vipanan*
Marksmanship	*Nishanabazee*
Marl viscous soil	*Ciknee mittee*
Marriage	*Shadee, Vivah, Byah, Nikah, Parinay*
Marriage celebration	*Vivahotsav*
Marriage procession	*Barat*
Married	*Parineet, Vivahit*
Marrow	*Majja*
Mars	*Mangalgrih*
Martial	*Marshal, Lashkaree*
Martial music	*Maroo*
Martyr	*Shaheed, Hutatma*
Martyrdom	*Pranotsarg*
Marxism	*Marks vad*
Masculine gender	*Punling*
Masculine man	*Sharmard*

Masculinity	*Mardangee*
Mash	*Bharta*
Mask	*Nakab, Mukhauta*
Masked	*Avgunthit*
Masked person	*Nakabposh*
Masochist	*Atmpeerak*
Mason	*Rajgeer*
Masonry	*Rajgeeree*
Mass	*Dravvyman*
Mass murder	*Katlaam*
Mass of clouds	*Dalbadal*
Mass prayer	*Missa-pooja*
Massage	*Malish, Campee*
Massaging	*Mardan*
Massive	*Bhareebharkam*
Mast	*Mastool*
Maste of Music	*Sangeetacarya*
Master	*Master, Nath*
Master commentary	*Mahabhashy*
Master-stroke	*Ustadee hath*
Masticate	*Cabana*
Mat	*Cataee, Boriya*
Match	*Maic*
Match stick	*Teelee, Deeyasalaee*
Matches	*Macis*
Matching	*Sanee*
Matchless	*Anupam, Bejor*
Mate	*Mat*
Material cause	*Upadan karan*
Materialism	*Jarvad, Dehatmvad*
Materialist	*Dehatmvadee*
Materialistic	*Jarvadee, Bhautikvadee*
Materialistic tendency	*Bhautikvadita*

Maternal	*Matrik*
Maternal aunt	*Mamee*
Maternal great grandfather	*Nana*
Maternal uncle	*Mama*
Maternity home	*Zaccakhana*
Mathematician	*Ganitagy*
Mathematics	*Ganit*
Mating	*Mithun*
Mating season	*Ritukal*
Matriarchy	*Mattritantr*
Matricide	*Mattrihatya*
Matrimonial	*Vaivahik*
Matron	*Matran, Matrika*
Matted hair	*Jatazoot*
Matter	*Majra, Dravvy, Padarth*
Mattock	*Gaitee*
Mattress	*Tosh*
Mature	*Praurh, Paripakkw*
Maturity	*Praurhta*
Mausoleum	*Makbara, Roza*
Maxim	*Misal*
Maximum	*Adhiktam*
May	*Maee*
Mayor	*Mayar, Nagar-pramukh*
Maze	*Bhool-bhulaiya*
Me	*Mujhe*
(to) me	*Mujhe*
Meagre offering	*Panpatta*
Mean	*Kamina*
Meandering	*Visarpan*
Meaning	*Arth*
Meaningful	*Sarth, Sarthak*

Meaningfulness	*Sarthakta*
Meaningless	*Arthheen, Anarthak*
Meaningless complication	*Tanta*
Meaningless talk	*Jalp*
Means	*Sadhan, Upay, Zariya*
Means of livelihood	*Rozeerotee*
Meant for show	*Dikhaua*
Measles	*Khasra*
Measure	*Map, Nap*
(to) measure	*Napna, Mapna*
Measure of distance	*Leeg*
Measure of five cubits	*Pursa*
Measurement	*Paimaish, Napjokh*
Measurer	*Mapak*
Measuring	*Mapan*
Meat	*Gosht, Mans*
Meat-curry	*Kaliya*
Mechanic	*Yantraggy*
Mechanical	*Yantrik*
Mechanics	*Yantrikee*
Mechanised	*Yantrit*
Mechanism	*Yantrikta, Yantrracna*
Mechanization	*Yantreekaran*
Mechanized	*Yantrsajjit*
Medal	*Padak, Tagma, Tamga*
Mediation	*Maddhyasthta, Beec-bacaw*
Mediator	*Maddhyasth*
Medical	*Medikal*
Medical leave	*Cikitsavkash*
Medical liquid	*Ghuttee*
Medical science	*Cikitsa vigyan*
Medical store	*Aushadhalaya*

Medical treatment	*Cikitsa*
Medicated stream	*Baphara*
Medicinal	*Aushadheey*
Medicinal decoction	*Karha*
Medicinal plant	*Kachoor*
Medicinal root (of plant)	*Jaree*
Medicine	*Dava*
Medieval	*Maddykaleen*
Medieval era	*Maddhyyug*
Meditation	*Manan, Pranidhan*
Mediterranean Sea	*Bhoomaddhysagar*
Medium	*Miyana, Majhola, Maddhyam*
Medley	*Gaparchauth*
Meek and borbearing	*Sahishnu*
Meekness	*Vinamrta*
Meet	*Milna*
Meeting	*Mulakat, Milan, Meeting*
Melancholic	*Vishadpoorn*
Melathesis	*Varn-viparyay*
Melee	*Rel-pel*
Melodious	*Karnpriy, Sumadhur*
Melodious sound	*Kalnad*
Melon	*Kharbooza*
Melt	*Galna*
(to) melt	*Pighalna*
Melted	*Dravit, Draveebhoot*
Melting	*Dravan, Vigalan*
Member	*Membar, Sadasy*
Member of an assembly	*Sabhasad*
Member of the bride's party	*Larkeevala*

Member of the bridegroom's party	*Larkavala*
Membership	*Sadasyata*
Membership-fee	*Sadasyata-shulk*
Membrane	*Jhillee*
Memento	*Smriti cihn*
Memoirs	*Sansmaran*
Memorable	*Smaraneey*
Memorandum	*Smriti pattr, Smarika, Smaranpattr*
Memorandum of demands	*Mangpattr*
Memorial	*Mamoriyal*
Memory	*Smaran shakti, Smrit, Yad, Yaddasht*
Men and property	*Jandhan*
Mendicancy	*Fakeeree, Bhimshavritti*
Mendicant	*Fakeer*
Menial service	*Tehal*
Meningitis	*Gardantor bukhar*
Menopause	*Rajonivritti*
Menses	*Rajodharm*
Mensuration	*Kshattrmiti*
Mental	*Mansik, Dimagee, Manogat*
Mental aberration	*Manovikkriti*
Mental agony	*Manovyatha*
Mental complex	*Manogranthi*
Mental faculty	*Maneesha*
Mental hospital	*Pagalkhana*
Mental picture	*Smriticittr*
Mental satisfaction	*Manastosh*
Mentally	*Manobhav, Mansa*
Mentally wearied	*Uchat*
Mention	*Ullekh*

Mentioned twice	*Dvirukt*
Mercantile association	*Vyapar-sangh*
Merchant	*Vanij*
Merciful	*Deendayalu, Dayamay, Rehamdil*
Merciless	*Beraham*
Mercury	*Para*
Mercy	*Daya*
Mere show	*Dikhavat*
Merged	*Leen*
Meridian	*Yammyottar*
Meritorious	*Gunvan*
Meritorious of classical work	*Gauravgranth*
Merriment	*Tafreeh*
Merry making	*Hansna khelna*
Merry making children	*Chagan magan*
Meshed	*Jaleedar*
Mess	*Mes, Kabara, Ghal-mel*
Mess of things	*Khatrag*
Mess-mate	*Sehbhojee*
Message	*Sanvad, Paigam, Sandesh*
Message of condolence	*Shoksandesh*
Messenger	*Harkara, Sandeshvahak, Sandeshkar*
Messenger of death	*Yamdoot*
Messenger of gods	*Devdoot*
Messiah	*Maseeha*
Messrs	*Sarvshree*
Metal	*Dhatu*
Metal bowl	*Katora*
Metal bowl with a lid	*Katordan*
Metallic	*Dhatavik*

Metallic age	*Dhatu yug*
Metallic bar	*Salakh*
Metallurgy	*Dhatu-vigyan*
Metaphor	*Roopak*
Metaphysician	*Tattwvata*
Metaphysics	*Tattwvata, Tattw-meemansa*
Meteor	*Ulka*
Meteoric fall	*Ulka pat*
Meteorite	*Ulkashm*
Meteorology	*Antariksh vigyan*
Meter	*Meetar*
Method	*Vidhi, Dhang, Paddhati*
Method of teaching	*Shikshavidhi*
Method of use	*Sevan vidhi*
Methodically	*Vidhivat, Vidhipoorvak*
Methylated	*Uphat*
Metonymy	*Lakshana*
Metre	*Chand*
Metrical	*Chandobaddh*
Metropolis	*Mahanagar*
Metropolitan	*Rajdhaneey*
Mezzanine	*Miyanee*
Michelia champaca	*Campak*
Microscope	*Sookshmdarshee*
Mid-day	*Maddhyanh*
Middle	*Midil, Maddhy, Majhla, Darmiyan, Bicla*
Middle aged	*Adhar*
Middle class	*Maddhyvarg*
Middle finger	*Maddhyma*
Middle path	*Maddhy marg*
Middle-east	*Maddhypoorv*
Middleman	*Bichauliya*

Midnight	*Maddhyrattri*
Midstream	*Manjhdhar*
Midwife	*Daee*
Might and grandeur	*Bal-vaibhav*
Mighty	*Mahabalee, Shaktiman*
Migration	*Pravasan, Pravrajan*
Migratory	*Pravasee*
Milch cow	*Lavaree*
Mild jolt	*Hacka*
Mile	*Meel*
Militarisation	*Astreekaran, Sainikeekaran*
Militarism	*Sainyvad, Samarikta, Samrikvad*
Military exercise	*Shatrabhyas*
Military officer	*Sanadhikaree*
Military science	*Shastrvidya*
Military strength	*Sanybal*
Milk	*Dugdh, Doodh*
(to) milk (a cow etc.)	*Doohna*
Milkman	*Doodhvala*
Milky	*Dudhiya, Doodhiya*
Milky way	*Vyom ganga, Surtaranginee*
Mill	*Mil*
Millenium	*Sehassrabd*
Millet	*Bajra, Jondhree*
Millionaire	*Lakhpati*
Millions	*Lakhokha*
Minaret	*Meenar*
Minced meat	*Keema*
Mind	*Manas*
Minded	*Manask*
Mine	*Khan, Surang*
Mine and thine	*Mera-tera*
Miner	*Khan mazdoor*

Mineral	*Khanij*
Mineralogy	*Khanij vigyan*
Mingled	*Vimishshrit*
Minimum	*Alpatam, Nyoontam*
Minister	*Vazeer, Mantree, Ministar*
Minister of Communication	*Sancar Mantree*
Minister of a state	*Deevan*
Minister of defence	*Yuddhmantree*
Ministry	*Ministree, Mantralay*
Ministry of Education	*Shiksha-mantralay*
Ministry of Labour	*Shram-mantralay*
Minor	*Nabalig, Avyask*
Minority	*Alpamat, Alpsankhyak*
Minority of age	*Alpavayaskta*
Mint-house	*Taksal*
Minted rupee	*Kaldar*
Minute	*Minat, Sookshm*
Minuteness	*Sookshmta*
Miracle	*Karishma, Camatkar*
Miraculous	*Karamatee, Camatkaree*
Mirage	*Mareecika, Mrigjal, Mrigtrishna*
Mirror	*Arsee, Darpan*
Misapplication	*Dushprayog*
Misapprehension	*Andesha*
Misbehaviour	*Durvyavhar*
Miscarriage	*Garbhpat*
Miscellaneous	*Vividh*
Miscellany	*Agrambagram*
Mischief	*Utpat*
Mischiefmaker	*Khurchali*
Mischievous	*Utpatee, Shaitan, Shararatee*
Misconduct	*Duracaran, Dushcarittr*

Misdeed	*Dushkarm, Karastanee,*
Miserable	*Damneey*
Miserable plight	*Cheechaledar*
Miserliness	*Kripanta, Khaseesee*
Miserly	*Kanjus, Kripan*
Misfortune	*Badnaseebee*
Mishap	*Hadsa*
Misled	*Bhrant*
Mismanagement	*Kuprabandh*
Mismatched	*Bamal*
Missile	*Kshappyastr*
Missing	*Lapata*
Mission	*Mishan*
Missionary	*Mishnaree*
Mist	*Neehar*
Mistake	*Galtee, Ashuddhi*
Mistress	*Swaminee*
Mistress of a house	*Gharnee*
Mistrusted	*Beitbar*
Misunderstanding	*Galatfehmi*
Misuse	*Durupyog*
Mite	*Damree*
Mix	*Milana*
(to) mix by pouring	*Gadd-madd*
(to) mix together inextricably	*Samona*
Mixed	*Mishshr*
Mixed flour	*Missa*
Mixture	*Mishshran*
Mixture of seven grains	*Satnaja*
Mixture of wheat and barley	*Gojaee*

Moan	*Karah*
(to) moan	*Karahna*
Moat	*Khaee, Parikha*
Mobile	*Chal, Gatisheel*
Mobile theatre	*Mandua*
Mobilisation of the people	*Loksangreh*
Mobility	*Gatisheelta*
Mobilization	*Lambandee*
Mobmentality	*Bhariya-dhasan*
Mockery	*Vidambna*
Mode	*Tareeka*
Model	*Pratiman*
Moderate	*Maddhim*
Modern	*Arvaceen, Navvy, Adhunik*
Modern Hindi	*Kharee bolee*
Modernity	*Adhunikta*
Modernization	*Adhunikeekaran*
Modest	*Vinammr, Vinaysheel, Vineet, Namrtapoorn*
Modest and humble	*Lajjasheel*
Modesty	*Vineetta, Namrta, Lajja*
Modulation	*Moorchna*
Modulation of voice in reciting	*Tarannum*
Moghal	*Mugal*
Mohammadan	*Yavan*
Mohammedan form of address	*Miyan*
Molar tooth	*Darh*
Molasses	*Sheera, Joosee, Rab*
Mole	*Chachundar*
Molecular	*Anvik*

Moment	*Sait, Lamha, Kshan, Chan*
Momentary	*Kshanik*
Momento	*Yadgar*
Momentum	*Avag, Samvag*
Monarchical	*Aktantreey, Rajtantreey*
Monarchy	*Aktantr, Rajtantr*
Moneky	*Bander, Vanar*
Monetary punishment	*Arthdand*
Money	*Rupaya, Mudra, Paisa, Dhan*
Money and possessions	*Dhan-daulat, Dhan-sampatti*
Money giving by way of thanks	*Shukrana*
Money order	*Dhanadesh, Maneearder*
Money-bag	*Batua*
Money-bill	*Dhanvidhayak*
Moneyless	*Dhanheen*
Mongoose	*Navla*
Monism	*Adwaitvad*
Monistic	*Adwait*
Monkey	*Bandar, Vanar*
Monkey-God	*Hanuman*
Monogamy	*Aikvivah, Aikpatneettv*
Monolingual	*Aikbhashee*
Monologue	*Aikalap*
Monopolised	*Aikadhikrit*
Monopoly	*Aikadhikar*
Monotheism	*Aikashshvarvad*
Monotonous	*Aikras, Aksura*
Monotony	*Aikrasta, Aksurapan*
Monsoon	*Pavas, Mansoon*
Monster	*Nar-pashu*
Monstrosity	*Vikralta*
Month	*Mahena, Mas, Mah*

Month regarded by Hindus as inauspicious	*Kharmas*
Monthly	*Masik, Mahwar, Mahvaree*
Monument	*Smarak, Keertistambh*
Mood	*Mizaj, Tabeeyat*
Moon	*Som, Cand, Candr, Candrma*
Moon light	*Candnee*
Moon-stuck	*Candra*
Moonshine	*Candrika*
Moral	*Naitik*
Moral code	*Acharsanhita*
Moral consideration	*Dharmadharm*
Morale	*Manobal*
Morality	*Naitikta*
Mordant	*Rangsthapak*
More	*Adhik, Jyada*
More or less	*Nyoonadhik*
Morning	*Subah, Pratah, Bhor, Sabera*
Morning and evening	*Subah-sham*
Morning bath	*Pratahsnan*
Morning circumambulation	*Prabhat-pheree*
Morning duties	*Pratahkarm*
Morning song	*Prabhatee*
Morning walk	*Tehlan*
Morphia	*Marfiya*
Morphology	*Roopvigyan*
Morsel	*Nivala, Kaur*
Mortal	*Okhlee, Kharal*
Mortal world	*Martylok*
Mortality	*Nashwarta*
Mortar	*Gara*
Mortar and pestle	*Imam dasta*

Mortgage	*Rehan, Bandhak*
Mortgage deed	*Rehannama*
Mortgage with possession	*Bhogbandhak*
Mortgaged	*Girvee*
Mortgagedeed	*Girveenama*
Mortgagee	*Girveedar, Rehandar*
Mortise	*Cool*
Mortuary	*Murdaghar, Shavshala*
Moslem judge	*Kazee*
Mosque	*Masjid*
Mosquito	*Macchar*
Mosquito net	*Macchardanee*
Moss	*Kaee, Shaival*
Most excellent	*Attyuttam*
Most prominent	*Shreshthtam*
Mote	*Arhat*
Moth	*Shalabh*
Mother	*Mata, Mamee, Maiya, Jananee, Mehtaree*
Mother India	*Bhart mata*
Mother and new born baby	*Zacca bacca*
Mother hood	*Mattrittw*
Mother land	*Vatan, Mattribhoomi, Janmbhoomi*
Mother of Christ	*Mariyam*
Mother of Duryodhan in Mahabharata	*Gandharee*
Mother of an unworthy son	*Kupooti*
Mother of the brave	*Veerprasoo*
Mother's brother	*Mama*
Mother's father	*Nana*

Mother's home	*Nanhal, Mayka*
Mother's mother	*Nanee*
Mother's sister	*Mausee*
Mother-in-law of daughter/son	*Samdhin*
Mother-tongue	*Matri-bhasha*
Motion	*Gati, Jumbish*
Motion picture	*Calcitr*
Motionless	*Gatiheen, Nishcal*
Motivation	*Abhipraran*
Motive	*Uddashshy*
Motor	*Motar*
Motor car	*Motar car, Kar*
Motor-bicycle	*Phatphatiya*
Motor-cycle	*Motar-saikil*
Motor-driver	*Motardriver*
Mould	*Bhukree*
(to) mould	*Dhalna*
Moulded	*Dhalvan*
Mound	*Stoop, Dhuss, Bheeta*
Mountain	*Giri, Parvat, Pahar*
Mountain Pass	*Darra*
Mountaneer	*Parvatarohee*
Mounted	*Savar*
Mourning	*Gamee, Matam*
Mouse	*Cooha, Moosa*
Moustaches	*Moonch*
Mouth	*Munh, Mukh*
Mouth of a river	*Nadeemukh*
Mouth of a water-bag	*Dahana*
Mouthful	*Gassa, Gras*
Movable	*Jangam*

Movable and immovable	*Caracar, Calacal*
Move	*Hilna, Khisakna*
(to) move away	*Hatna*
(to) move to and fro	*Dulana*
(to) move to and fro, to wave	*Jhoomna*
Move this way or that	*Hatana-barhana*
Moved	*Karunardr*
Movement	*Gatividhi, Sancaran, Harkat*
Moving	*Chalayman, Gamee*
Moving quality	*Marmikta*
Moving upwards	*Oordhvgami*
Mucus	*Shleshma, Anv, Gid*
Mud	*Kando, keechar*
Mud-Plastering	*Gacckaree*
Muddy	*Gandla*
Mug	*Garua*
Mulberry fruit	*Shahtoot*
Mule	*Khachchar*
Multi coloured	*Bahuranga, Rang-biranga*
Multi form	*Bahuroop*
Multi linguist	*Bahubhashee*
Multi-millionaire	*Dhan kuber, Karorpati*
Multi-purpose	*Nanarth*
Multiple	*Gunaj*
Multiplicand	*Gunny*
Multiplication	*Guna, Gunan*
Multiplier	*Gunak*
Multipronged attack	*Caturdik*
Mumble	*Cuphlana*
Mummy	*Momiya*
Mumps	*Kanpera, Galsua*

Municipal corporation	*Nagar-palika*
Municipality	*Myunisipaltee*
Munificence	*Dansheelta*
Munsif	*Munsif*
Murder	*Katl, Hattya*
(to) murder	*Hanna*
Murderer	*Katil, Halakoo*
Murderous	*Katilana*
Muscle	*Manspeshee*
Museum	*Ajayabghar*
Mushroom	*Chatrak*
Music	*Sangeet*
Musical	*Sangeetatmak*
Musical instrument	*Been, Vady, Baja*
Musical pipe	*Tootee*
Musical-merrymaking	*Gana-bajana*
Musicologist	*Sangeetshastree*
Musing	*Manovilas*
Musk	*Kastooree*
Musk deer	*Kastooree mrig*
Musky	*Mushti*
Muslim	*Musalman*
Muslim Crusader	*Gazee*
Muslim era	*Hijree*
Muslim festival	*Id, Bakreed*
Muslim form of salutation	*Salam*
Muslim mendicant	*Kalandar*
Muslim prayermat	*Musalla*
Muslim priest	*Mulla*
Muslim religious ruling	*Fatva*
Muslim weaver class	*Momin*
Muslin	*Malmal*

Mustard oil	*Sarso ka tel, Karva tel*
Mustard seeds	*Sarson*
Mutation	*Dakhil-kharij*
Mute	*Bezaban*
Mute and motionless	*Gumsum*
Mutiny	*Gadar*
Mutter	*Barbar*
(to) mutter	*Barbarana*
Mutual	*Apsee, Parasparik*
Mutual affection	*Malmuhabbat*
Mutual oaths and promises	*Kasma-kasmee*
Mutual relationship	*Apas daree*
Mutuality	*Parasparta, Parakparikta*
Mutually	*Itratar, Paraspar*
My	*Mara*
My dear sir	*Janabaman*
Myrobalan	*Harr*
Myrtle	*Manhdee, Hina*
Mysterious	*Rahasypoorn, Rahasybhara*
Mystic	*Rahasyvadee*
Mystical	*Rahesyatmak*
Myth	*Devkatha, Purankatha*
Mythological	*Pauranik*
Mythological demigod	*Yaksh*
Mythological demon	*Katu*

N

Nadir	*Adhahswastik*
Nail	*Keel, Nakhoon*
Nail-cutter	*Nehnee*
Naked	*Digambar, Nagn, Vivastr*
Name	*Nam*
Name-plate	*Nam-patt*
Name-sake	*Namnam, Namrasee*
Narcissus	*Nargis*
Nard	*Jatit*
Narrative	*Kathatmak*
Narrative of glorious deeds	*Yashogatha*
Narrator	*Vacak*
Narrow	*Sankeern, Tang, Sankara*
Narrow lane	*Corgalee*
Narrow street	*Koocha*
Narrowness	*Sankeernta*
Nasal	*Nassy*
Nasal accent	*Nakkee*
Nasal vowel	*Candrbindu*
Nation	*Rashtr*
National	*Kaumee*
National anthem	*Rashtrgeet*
National emblem	*Rashtrcinh*
National flag	*Rashtrdhwaj*
National language	*Rashtrbhasha*
National poet	*Rashtrkavi*
Nationalisation	*Rashtreekaran*
Nationalism	*Rashtrvad*
Nationalist	*Rashtrvadee*
Nationality	*Rashtreeyta*
Native	*Deshee, Deshaj*
Native land	*Swadesh*

Natural	*Swabhavik, Prakrit*
Natural beauty	*Sushama*
Naturally	*Swabhavtah, Nisargtah*
Naturalness	*Swabhvikta*
Nature	*Swabhav, Kudrat, Prakriti*
Naughtiness	*Shararat*
Naughty	*Shareer*
Nausea	*Matlee, Vaman-pravritti*
Nauseate	*Miclana*
Nautical science	*Nau-viggyan*
Naval	*Jahazee*
Naval fleet	*Naubara*
Naval service	*Nauseva*
Naval war	*Jalyuddh*
Navel	*Naf, Tundee*
Navel-string	*Anvalnal*
Navigation	*Naucalan, Jahazranee*
Navy	*Nausena, Jalsena*
Nazi	*Natsee*
Nazism	*Natseevad*
Ncbula	*Neeharika*
Near	*Sameep, Pas, Nikat, Nazdeekee*
Near and dear relatives	*Swajan*
Near by	*Kareeb, Sameepasth*
Near relations	*Bhaeebandh*
Nearest	*Nikattam, Sameeptam*
Nearness	*Sameeppy, Sameepta, Nikatta*
Necessary	*Zarooree, Avashshyak*
Neck	*Gardan*
Neck-ring	*Tauk*
Neck-tie	*Taee*
Necklace	*Kanthee, Kanthhar*
Necromancy	*Pratsiddhi*

Nectar	*Sudha, Amrit*
Nectareous	*Amritmay*
Need	*Darkar, Zaroorat*
Needing Shelter	*Sharany*
Needing repairs	*Marammatee*
Needle	*Soocika, Suee*
Needle work	*Sooeekaree*
Needless wrangle	*Hujjat*
Needs	*Zarooriyat*
Needy	*Zarooratmand, Garazmand*
Neem tree	*Neem*
Neeromancy	*Pishac-vidya*
Negative	*Nakaratmaakta, Rinatmak*
Negative reply	*Na-nukar*
Neglect	*Berukhee, Upeksha*
Neglected	*Upekshit*
Negligence	*Gaflat*
Negligent	*Gafil*
Negligent of duty	*Kartavya-vimukh*
Negligibility	*Upekshaneeyta*
Negligible	*Tucch, Naganny*
Neigh	*Hinhinana*
Neighbour	*Parosee, Hamsaya, Muhalledar*
Neighbour hood	*Muhalledaree, Arosparos*
Neighin	*Hinhinahat*
Neo-literate	*Navsakshar*
Nepal	*Nepal*
Nepotism	*Kunbaparastee, Bhaeebhateejavad*
Nerve	*Snayu, Tantrika*
Nervous system	*Snayusansthan*
Nest	*Ashiyana, Neer, Ghonsla*
Net	*Jal, Sikka*
Nether world	*Patal lok*

Netted	*Jaldar*
Neuter	*Alingee*
Never	*Kadapi*
Nevertheless	*Albatta*
New	*Naveen, Acir, Naya*
New Testament	*Injeel*
New born	*Navjat*
New comer	*Agantuk*
New era	*Yugantar*
Newly married man	*Navaorh*
Newly married woman	*Navvadhoo*
Newness	*Nootanta, Nayapan, Navalta*
News	*Khabar, Samacar*
News reel	*Samacar-film*
News reporter	*Samacardata*
News-agent	*Samacar-agent*
Newspaper	*Akhbar, Samacarpattr*
Newspaper man	*Akhbarvala*
Next birth	*Parjanm*
Nib	*Nib*
Nib of a pen	*Jeebhee*
Nice	*Sijal*
Nice-hearted	*Suman*
Niche	*Takha*
Nick name	*Upnam*
Nickel	*Gilat, Nikal*
Niggardliness	*Soompana*
Night	*Ratri, Rat*
Night of Annihilation	*Kalratri*
Night of ceremonious consummation	*Suhag-rat*
Night-blind	*Ratondh*

Night-blindedness	*Rataundhee*
Night-shelter	*Rain-basara*
Night-wayman	*Rahjan*
Nihilism	*Nashvad, Shoonnyvad*
Nihilist	*Nashvadee*
Nihilistic	*Shoonyvadee*
Nine	*Nau*
Nine kinds of precious stones	*Navratn*
Nine of cards	*Nehla*
Nine planets	*Navgrah*
Nine-storeyed	*Nau-khanda*
Nineteen	*Unnees*
Ninety	*Nabbe*
Ninety-five	*Pancanbe*
Ninety-four	*Cauranbe*
Ninety-nine	*Ninnyanbe*
Ninety-six	*Chiyanbe*
Ninety-three	*Tiranbe*
Ninth	*Navam*
Ninth month of Hindu calendar	*Margsheersh*
Ninth month of the Muslim Calendar	*Ramzan*
Ninth sign of the zodiac	*Dhanu*
Nipple	*Cucuk, Coocee, Cusnee*
Nobility	*Kuleenta, Sharafat*
Noble	*Shareef, Abhijat, Mahamana*
Noble lady	*Bhadra*
Noble person	*Bhadrjan*
Noble soul	*Mahapran*
Nocturnal being	*Rajneecar, Ratricar*

Nodding acquaintance	*Dekhadekhee*
Noise	*Halla, Shor*
Noisy	*Kolahalpoorn*
Noisy exchange of words	*Cakhcakh*
Nomad	*Banjara, Khanabadosh*
Nomadic life	*Khanabadoshi*
Nomenclature	*Namavalee*
Nominal	*Farzee*
Nominally	*Jhunthon*
Nominated	*Namzad, Namankit*
Nomination	*Namzadgee, Namankan*
Nominative case	*Prathma*
Non Indian	*Abharteey*
Non classical	*Ashastreey*
Non official	*Gairsarkaree*
Non persuance	*Adampairvee*
Non vegetarian	*Amishbhoji*
Non-Brahmin	*Abbrahman*
Non-Ferrous	*Alauh*
Non-Hindi	*Ahindi*
Non-Hindu	*Ahindoo*
Non-Materiality	*Abhautikta*
Non-acceptability	*Amanyata*
Non-agricultural	*Akrishik*
Non-alignment	*Tatasthta*
Non-appreciation	*Bekaddree*
Non-attachment	*Aliptta*
Non-communal	*Asampradayik*
Non-conformist	*Rind*
Non-cooperation	*Asahyog*
Non-cumbustible	*Adahy*
Non-doer	*Akarta*

Non-existent	*Nast, Abhoot*
Non-gazetted	*Arajpatrit*
Non-interference	*Ahastakshep*
Non-metal	*Adhatu*
Non-physical	*Abhautik*
Non-placental	*Ayonij*
Non-poisonous	*Vishheen*
Non-political	*Arajneetik*
Non-proficient	*Gunheen*
Non-rectification	*Amarjan*
Non-stop	*Aviram*
Non-transferable	*Aday*
Non-vegetarian	*Mansaharee, Samish*
Non-vegetarian food	*Mansahar*
Non-violence	*Ahinsavad*
Non-violent	*Ahinsak*
Non-white	*Ashshwet*
Noon	*Dupahar*
Noose	*Galphansee*
Normal	*Prasam*
North	*Uttar*
North-east	*Eeshan, Poorvottar*
North-western	*Uttar-Pashcim*
Northern	*Uttaree*
Nose	*Nak*
Nose-bag	*Tobra*
Nose-bleeding	*Nakseer*
Nose-pendant	*Bulak*
Nose-pipe	*Chucchee*
Nose-ring	*Nathnee, Nath, Nakel*
Nostril	*Nathna*
Not	*Naheen*
Not accepting	*Asweekaran*

Not edited	*Asampadit*
Not expressed	*Avvyakt*
Not favoured by luck	*Mandbhaggy*
Not present	*Avidyman*
Not prosperous	*Asampann*
Not transferable	*Ahastantareey*
Not ungrateful	*Akrittaghn*
Not-transferred	*Ahastantarit*
Note book	*Notbook*
Nothingness	*Shoonyta*
Notice	*Notis*
Notice board	*Soocna-patt*
Notification	*Adhisoochan*
Notion	*Dharna*
Nought	*Phis*
Noun	*Ism*
Novel	*Upannyas*
Novelist	*Upannyaskar*
Novelty	*Naveenta*
November	*Navambar*
Novena	*Navahn*
Novercal	*Vimattreey*
Novice	*Rangroot*
Now	*Ab*
Now-a-days	*Ajkal*
Nozzle	*Tauntee*
Nucleus	*Kandrak*
Nude	*Nirvasan*
Nude-dance	*Nagn-nritty*
Nudism	*Nagnvad*
Nudist	*Nagnvadee*
Number	*Sankhya, Tadad*
Numbered	*Sankhyankit*

Numberless	*Asankhy*
Numbness	*Jhunjhunee*
Numeral	*Sankhyank*
Numerical	*Sankhy, Sankhyatmak, Sankhyavacak*
Numerous	*Bahusankhyak*
Numismatics	*Mudrashastr*
Nurse	*Paricarika, Aya*
Nursery	*Shishubala*
Nursing	*Upcarya, Teemardaree*
Nursing home	*Aroggy shala*
Nurture	*Parvarish*
Nurturing the subjects	*Prajapalan*
Nut socket	*Dhibree*
Nut-cracker	*Sarauta*
Nutmeg	*Jayphal*
Nutritious	*Paushtik*
Nutritive	*Poshak*
Nutritive diet	*Giza*
Nutritiveness	*Paushtikta*
Nux vomica	*Kuchla*
Nymph	*Paree, Devkanya*
Nymphal	*Apsarik*

O

Oak	*Baloot*
Oaken	*Balootee*
Oar	*Cappoo*
Oarsman	*Khavanhar*
Oarsmanship	*Kavtaee*
Oasis	*Marudyan, Nakhlistan, Marudweep*
Oat	*Jaee*
Oath	*Halaf, Kasam, Shapath*
Oathtaking	*Shapathgrehan*
Obdurate	*Duraggrahee*
Obeahism	*Jadoo-tona*
Obedience	*Agyakarita, Agyapalan*
Obedient	*Agyakaree, Agyapalak*
Obedient servant	*Hukmbardar*
Obediently	*Yathagya*
Obeissance	*Sijda*
Object	*Vastu*
(to) object to something said	*Dulakhna*
Object of pity	*Daya patr*
Objection	*Apati, Aitraz*
Objectionable	*Apattijanak*
Objective	*Vastugat, Vastunishth*
Objectivity	*Vastunishtha*
Objurate	*Dapatna*
Objuration	*Dapat*
Oblation	*Havi*
Obligation	*Ehsan*
Obliged	*Anugrihzet, Upkrit, Abharee*
Oblique	*Tiryak, Bhagrekha*
Obliquity	*Tirchapan*
Oblivion	*Faramoshee*
Oblivious	*Faramosh, Vismaransheel*

Obscene	*Ashleel*
Obsequies	*Antyashti, Mritak-karm*
Observance	*Paripalan*
Observance of formalities	*Khanapuree*
Observation	*Nireekshan*
Observatory	*Manmandir, Vaidhshala*
Observed	*Nireekshit, Prakshit*
Observer	*Prakshak*
Observing	*Darshee*
Obsession	*Dhun*
Obstacle	*Alsat, Arcan*
Obstetrics	*Dhatree-vidya*
Obstinacy	*Ar, Hath*
Obstinacy and illtemper	*Tarrapan*
Obstinate	*Takee, Hatheela*
Obstinately shameless	*Bahaya*
Obstructed	*Bandhit, Pratiruddh, Avruddh, Niruddh*
Obstructing	*Vighnkaree*
Obstruction	*Pratirodh, Avrodh*
Obstructionist	*Arangebaz*
Obstructive	*Badhak*
Obtainable	*Prapy*
Obtained	*Prapann*
Obtuse	*Bhothra*
Obtuseness	*Bhothrapan*
Obvious	*Pratyaksh*
Occasional	*Naimittik*
Occult science	*Tantr shastr, Jantar-mantar*
Occupant	*Dakhalkar*
Occupation	*Rozgar, Kamkaz*

Occupied	*Adhikkrit*
Occupying a seat	*Padaseen, Virajman*
Occuring after every five years	*Pansala*
Ocean	*Sagar, Samudr*
Ocean of Milk	*Doodhsagar*
Oceanography	*Samuddrviggyan*
Oceanus	*Samuddra-davata*
Ochlocracy	*Bheershahee*
Ochrous	*Garua*
Octagon	*Ashtbhuj*
Octavo	*Athpejee*
October	*Aktoobar*
Octopod	*Ashtpad*
Octopus	*Ashtbahu*
Octroi	*Cungee*
Octroi post	*Cungee-ghar*
Ocular	*Naittrik*
Odalisque	*Bandee*
Odd	*Atpata, Vilakshan*
Odd sort	*Bedhab*
Oddity	*Vicitrata*
Odious	*Ghinauna*
Odontology	*Dant-vigyan*
Odourless	*Nirgandh*
Of that kind	*Vaisa*
Of the other side	*Parla*
Of the same age	*Hamummr*
Ofcourse	*Beshak*
Off-season	*Bemausim*
Offence	*Apradh, Jurm*
Offered	*Arpit*
Offering	*Pinddan*

Offering as a sacrifice	*Balidan*
Offering made to a deity	*Prasadee*
Offering of condolence	*Matam-pursee*
Offering of flowers	*Pushpanjali*
Office	*Karyalaya, Daftar*
Office-bearer	*Paddharee*
Officer	*Afsar*
Official	*Shaskeey, Padadhikarik, Sarkaree*
Officiating	*Kartvahak, Sthanapann*
Offspring	*Balbacca, Santati*
Oil	*Tail*
Oil colour	*Tailrang*
Oil painting	*Tailcitr*
Oil-cake	*Khalee*
Oil-cloth	*Momjama*
Oil-seed	*Tilhan*
Oil-tanker	*Tailpot*
Oilman	*Tailee*
Oily	*Cikna, Taliya*
Ointment	*Lep, Ubtan, Malham*
Old	*Vrid, Jaree, Purana,*
Old age	*Burhapa, Vriddhavastha, Jara*
Old man	*Burha*
Old woman	*Vriddha, Boorhee, Burhiya*
Oligarchy	*Kultantr*
Olive	*Jaitoon*
Olympic	*Olampik*
Ominous	*Manhoos*
Ominous conjunction of planets	*Markash*
Ominousness	*Manhoosee*
Occupied	*Akaran*

Omnipresence	*Vibhuta*
Omnipresent	*Vibhu*
Omniscience	*Sarvagyta*
Omniscient	*Sarvagy*
On behalf of	*Maddha*
On left hand side	*Bain*
On the horns of a dilemma	*Kartavya vimoorh*
On the other hand	*Varan*
On the point of death	*Maranasann*
Once	*Aikbar*
One	*Aik*
One above the other	*Tarpar*
One act play	*Akankee*
One after another	*Ghamagham*
One and a half	*Dyorha, Darh*
One and a quarter	*Sava, Savaya*
One colour	*Akranga*
One given to affection	*Coclabaz*
One given to creating problems	*Jhamaliya*
One having greyish blue eyes	*Kanja*
One hundred	*Shatak*
One month old	*Masy*
One who adopts	*Dattak grahee*
One who appreciates	*Kaddrdan*
One who donates his land	*Bhoodanee*
One who holds	*Dharta*
One who is eager to know	*Jigyasu*
One's all	*Sarvasw*

One's deeds	*Swakarm*
One's own	*Apas vala, Swakeey*
One's liking	*Manpasand*
One's utmost	*Bharsak*
One's own right	*Swedhikar*
One's own self story	*Apbeeti*
One's own volition	*Sweccha*
One-eighth part of a day	*Pehar*
One-eyed person	*Kana*
One-fourth part	*Cauth, Caturthansh*
One-limbed	*Aikang*
One-sided	*Aikpaksheey, Aiktarfa*
One-storeyed	*Aikmanzila*
One-stringed musical instrument	*Iktara*
One-tenth part	*Dashamansh*
One-third	*Tihaee*
Oneness with divinity	*Kaivalya*
Onerous	*Durveh, Kashtsadhy*
Onion	*Kanda, Pyaj*
Only	*Matr, Keval*
Only if	*Basharta*
Only you	*Tumhee*
Onstentatious	*Numaishee*
Oozing	*Ksharan, Sravan*
Open	*Khula*
(to) open	*Kholna*
Open door	*Khuladwar*
Opened	*Unmeelit*
Opening balance	*Rokar jama*
Openly	*Khullam khulla*
Operated	*Paricalit*

Operation	*Pracalan, Aprashan, Daran*
Operation process	*Sankriya*
Operational	*Sankriyatmak*
Operator	*Pracalak*
Ophthalmology	*Nettrvigyan*
Opinion	*Ray*
Opium	*Afeem, Ciniya bagam*
Opponent	*Vipakshee, Pratipakshee*
Opportune	*Samayocit, Avsaranukool*
Opportunism	*Avsarvad*
Opportunist	*Avsarvadee*
Opportunity	*Avsar, Mauka*
Opposed	*Paranmukh*
Opposite	*Pratikool*
Opposite party	*Vipaksh, Pratipaksh*
Opposition	*Pratipakshta, Pratikoolta*
Oppress	*Satana*
Oppressed	*Utpeerit, Durgat*
Oppressed with burden	*Bharakrant*
Oppressed with hunger	*Kshudhapeerit*
Oppressing	*Peeran*
Oppression	*Daman, Utpeeran*
Oppressive	*Utpeerak, Damankaree*
Optical	*Prakashikeey*
Optical illusion	*Drishtibhram*
Optics	*Prakashikee*
Optimism	*Ashavad*
Optimistic	*Ashavadee*
Option	*Vikalp*
Optional	*Aicchik*
Opulent	*Sampattishalee*
Or	*Athva*
Oral	*Zabanee, Maukhik*

Orally	*Munh-zabanee*
Oramental ear-ring	*karanphool*
Orange	*Narangee, Santara*
Orator	*Vagmee*
Oratory	*Vagmita*
Orchestra	*Vadyvrind*
Orchestration	*Vrindvahan*
Ordained	*Vihit*
Ordeal	*Divvy-pareeksha*
Order	*Agya, Kram*
Ordered	*Adisht*
Orderliness	*Krambaddhta*
Orderly	*Krambaddh*
Ordinarily	*Sadharantah*
Ordinary	*Mamoolee*
Ordnance	*Sanny-sajja*
Organ	*Indriy, Mukhpattr*
Organ of action	*Karmandriy*
Organ of hearing	*Shravanandriy*
Organic	*Sandriy*
Organisation	*Sangathan, Vyavasthapan*
Organised	*Sangathit, Ayojit, Vyavasthit*
Organiser	*Ayojak, Vyavasthapak*
Orient	*Pracee*
Oriental	*Praccy*
Orientation	*Saj*
Origin	*Udbhav, Pradurbhav*
Original	*Maulik*
Original home	*Moolsthan*
Originality	*Maulikta*
Ornament	*Jevar, Gehna, Abhooshan*
Ornament worn on the head	*Curamani*

Ornament worn on the toe	*Bichooa*
Ornament worn on the wrist	*Pahuncee*
Ornamentation	*Alankriti*
Ornamented	*Vibhooshit, Bhooshit*
Ornithology	*Pakshee-vigyan*
Orography	*Parvat-viggyan*
Orphan	*Anath, Yateem*
Orphange	*Yateem khana*
Orthodox	*Kattar*
Orthodoxy	*Kattarta*
Oscillate	*Dolna*
Oscillated	*Lolit*
Oscillating	*Dolayman*
Ostentation	*Bharakeelapan, Dolan, Teemtam*
Ostentatious	*Adambaree, Bharkeela*
Ostrich	*Shuturmurg*
Other	*Paraya, Doosra*
Other wordly	*Parlaukik*
Otherwise	*Varna*
Otter	*Ood vilav*
Ounce	*Auns*
Our	*Hamara*
Out of curiosity	*Kutuhalvash*
Out of date	*Dinateet*
Out of sense	*Moorchit*
Out of tune	*Besura, Betal, Tal-betal*
Outer covering	*Uparna, Chadan*
Outer space	*Antariksh*
Outflow	*Nissaran*
Outline	*Bahirrakha, Parirakha*
Outrage of modesty	*Sheelbhang*

Outside world	*Bahirjagat*
Outsider	*Begana, Gair, Baharwala*
Outskirts	*Bahhyancal*
Outstanding	*Shirasth*
Outward	*Vahy, Javak, Bahirgat*
Outward appearance	*Dhaj*
Outward show	*Teeptap*
Ovary	*Andashay, Shukkrashay*
Oven	*Damkala, Coolha, Tandoor*
Over-awe	*Dehlana*
Over bearing	*Uddhat*
Over burdened	*Lada-phanda*
Over clouding	*Ghata*
Over coat	*Ovarkot*
Over crowded	*Khachakhach, Thasathas*
Over drawing	*Atiranjan*
Over drawn	*Atiranjit*
Over due	*Attyavadhik*
Over haul	*Kayapalat*
Over head	*Oopree*
Over lapped	*Parivyapt*
Over powering	*Galib*
Over production	*Atyutpadan*
Over stimulating	*Vicarottajak*
Over time	*Samayopari*
Overturn	*Aundhana*
Over whelmed with emotion	*Bhavvibhor*
Over whelmed with grief	*Shɔkakul*
Over whelming influence	*Dabdaba*
Over-cooling	*Atisheetan*

Over-fond of spicy dishes	*Catorapan, Catora*
Over-garment	*Labada*
Over-greedy	*Dhanpishac*
Owl	*Ulloo*
Own	*Atm, Nij*
Owner	*Malik*
Owner of a factory	*Karkhanedar*
Owner of a house	*Grihsvamee*
Owner of an estate	*Jageerdar*
Ownership	*Swamittw*
Oxygen	*Akseejan*
Oyster	*Shukti*

P

Pacified	*Upshamit*
Pacifying	*Upshamak, Shantidayak*
Packer	*Samvashtak*
Packet	*Paket*
Packing	*Paiking, Samvashtan*
Pad	*Paid*
Paddy	*Dhan*
Page	*Prishth*
Pagoda tree	*Gulcheen*
Paid up	*Cukta*
Pain	*Dard, Peera*
Pain relieving	*Peeranashak, Peerashamak*
Painc	*Bheeshika*
Painful	*kashtprad, Dukhad*
Painful separation	*Bichoh*
Painfully restless	*Tilmilana*
Paint	*Rogan*
(to) paint	*Citarna*
Paint and varnish	*Rang-rogan*
Painted	*Citrit*
Painter	*Citrakar, Rangsaz*
Painter's brush	*Toolika*
Painting	*Rangsazee, Citrakaree, Citrakala*
Pair	*Jut, Joree, Yugm*
Pair of scissors	*Kartnee, Kainchi*
Pair of spectacles	*Cashma*
Palace	*Rajgrih, Prasad, Bhavan, Mahal*
Palaeographist	*Puralipigy*
Palaeography	*Puralipi*
Palanquin	*Shivika*
Palatable	*Asswady*
Palatal	*Talavy*
Palatial building	*Havelee*

Palestine	*Filisteen*
Palm of a hand	*Kartal*
Palpitation	*Dharkan, Hritkamp*
Paltoon	*Paltan*
Pamphlet	*Caupanna*
Pancake	*Malpua*
Pancreas	*Agnyashay*
Pandal	*Pandal*
Panegyric	*Prashasti*
Panegyrist	*Stota*
Panel of door	*Dilla*
Panel of names	*Namika*
Panelled	*Dilladar*
Pannier	*Jhaba*
Panorama	*Paridrishshy*
Pantheon	*Devgan*
Pant	*Hanphna*
Pantomimic coquetry	*Camkaual*
Papaya fruit	*Papeeta*
Paper	*Kagaz, Paper*
Paper currency	*Not*
Paper pulp	*Lugdee*
Paper work	*Kagzee karyavaee*
Papyrus	*Patara*
Parachute	*Parashoot, Havaee-chatree*
Parade	*Parad*
Paradise	*Bihisht, Swarg, Baikunth*
Paradox	*Virodhabhas*
Paragraph	*Anucched*
Parallel	*Samanantar*
Parallelism	*Samanantarta*
Paralysis	*Lakva, Pakshaghat*
Paramour	*Dhagra*

Paramour woman	*Dhagree*
Parapet	*Mundara*
Paraphernalia	*Tamjham*
Paraphrasing	*Padanvay*
Parapsychology	*Paramanovigyan*
Parasite	*Parjeevee, Tukark-tor*
Parasite creeper	*Amarbel*
Parasitic way of living	*Muftkhoree*
Paratrooper	*Chatreebaz*
Paratroops	*Chatreesena*
Parcel	*Parsal*
Parch	*Bhoonjna*
Parched and puffed rice	*Murmura*
Parched barley	*Sattoo*
Parched corn	*Kheel*
Parched grain	*Bhoonja, Cabena*
Parched lotus seed	*Makhana*
Parched rice	*Ciura*
Parcher	*Bharbhoonja*
Parcher's oven	*Bharsaee*
Parching and loading	*Lad-phand*
Pardon	*Jan-bakshee*
Pare	*Tarashna*
Parental affection	*Mamta*
Parental residence	*Naihar, Peehar*
Parenthetical clause	*Nikshipt upvakky*
Parential affection	*Vatsally*
Parliament	*Sansad*
Parliamentary	*Sansadeey*
Parole	*Pairol*
Parrot	*Sugga, Tota, Mitthoo*
Parsing	*Pad-vyakhya, Shabdanvay*
Part	*Bhag*

Part of speech	*Shabdbhed*
Part-time	*Anshkalik*
Partial	*Pakshpatee, Anshik, Tarafdar*
Partial incarnation	*Anshavatar*
Partiality	*Tarafdaree, Pakshpat*
Participant	*Shirkat, Yogdan, Shareek*
Participle	*Kridant*
Particle	*Parakhaca, Kan, Zarra*
Partition	*Vibhajan, Bant, Batvara*
Partition of a country	*Deshvibhajan*
Partly	*Anshta*
Partly false	*Jhoth-sac*
Partner	*Hissedar*
Partnership	*Hissedaree, Sajha, Bhageedaree*
Partridge	*Teetar*
Parts of body	*Anjarpanjar*
Party	*Dal*
Party-politics	*Dalbandee*
Partywise	*Dalgat*
Pass	*Pravashpattr*
(to) pass	*Guzarna*
Pass-port	*Parpatr*
Pass stools	*Hagna*
Pass time	*Guzarna*
Pass wind	*Padna*
Passable	*Langhaneey*
Passed	*Parit, Uttern, Darguzar*
Passed away	*Ateet*
Passenger	*Pasinjar, Rasta-calta*
Passing	*Paran, Basar*
Passing of sarcastic remarks	*Cheentakashee*
Passing time	*Kalakshep*

Passive voice	*Karmvaccy*
Past	*Vigat, Bhoot*
Past ancestors	*Pitar*
Past participle	*Bhootkridant*
Past tense	*Bhootkal*
Paste	*Past*
(to) paste	*Cipkana*
Pasture	*Carbhoomi, Pashucar, Caragah*
Pat	*Thapkee*
(to) pat with the palm	*Thapthapana*
Patch	*Thiglee, Paiband, Caktte, Cippar*
Patched quilt	*Dudree*
Patent	*Patent*
Paternal ancestor	*Pitrit*
Paternal aunt	*Kakee*
Paternal grandfather	*Pitamah*
Paternal home	*Pitrigrih*
Paternal uncle	*Kaka*
Path	*Rah, Gail*
Path of a star	*Tarapath*
Path of devotion	*Bhaktimarg*
Path of salvation	*Muktipath*
Path of virtue	*Sanmarg*
Pathan	*Reading*
Pathetic	*Hridaysparshee, Karunajanak*
Pathway	*Dagar*
Patience	*Dheer, Sabbar, Dhairy*
Patient	*Rogee, Mareej*
Patient'ward	*Rogee-kaksh*
Patriarchical system	*Pitritantr*
Patricide	*Pitrihatya*
Patriot	*Swadashbhakt*
Patriotism	*Deshprem, Swadeshbhakti*

Patronage	*Prashray, Sanrakshakta*
Patronised	*Sanrakshit*
Patwari	*Patwaree*
Pause	*Viram*
Pavilion	*Mandap, Sabha-mandap*
Pay	*Tankhah, Vatan*
(to) pay up	*Bhugtana*
Pay-scale	*Vetanman*
Payee	*Panavala*
Paying fee	*Sashulk*
Paying off	*Rinshuddhi, Rinmochan*
Payment	*Bhugtan, Adayagee*
Pea	*Matar*
Peace	*Shanti*
Peace and happiness	*Sukh-shanti*
Peace force	*Shanti sena*
Peace loving	*Shantipriy*
Peace of mind	*Shanti*
Peace talks	*Shantivarta*
Peace treaty	*Shanti-sandhi*
Peaceful	*Shantimay, Shantipoorn*
Peach	*Aroo*
Peacock	*Mor, Mayoor*
Peacock feather	*Morpankh*
Peahen	*Mornee*
Peak	*Shikhar*
Peak of the Himalayas	*Kailas*
Pear	*Nashpati*
Pearl	*Gauhar, Motee, Mukta*
Peasant	*Kisan, Krishak*
Peasant caste	*Kunbee*
Pebbles and stones	*Kankar patthar*

Peck	*Thong*
(to) peck	*Condhna*
Peculiar	*Anokha, Vilakshan*
Peculiarity	*Vilakshanta*
Peculiarly attractive	*Albela*
Pedagogic	*Shikshashastreey*
Pedagogy	*Shikshashastr*
Pedantry	*Panditaoopan*
Pedestrian	*Padcaree*
Pedicel	*Nal*
Peel	*Chilka*
(to) peel	*Cheelna*
(to) peel of with the teeth	*Khutakana*
Peel of laughter	*Khilkhilahat*
Peep into	*Jhankna*
Peerless	*Lajawab*
Peevish	*Khunsee*
Peg	*Killee*
Pell-mell	*Dhakapal*
Pelting with stones	*Pathrav*
Pelvis	*Paroo*
Pen	*Kalam, Lekhnee*
Pen-friend	*Patr-mitr*
Pen-name	*Takhallus*
Penal-code	*Dand-sanhita*
Penalogy	*Dand-vigyan*
Penalty	*Dand*
Penalty parade	*Dalal*
Penance	*Tapasya*
Pencil	*Pensil*
Pendent	*Lolak, Latkan*
Pendulum	*Dolak*

Penetrate	*Ghonpna*
Penicillin	*Peneesilin*
Peninsula	*Praydweep*
Penis	*Land, Shishn*
Penniless	*Rank, Nanga-bucca, Kangal, Thanthan-gopal*
Penny	*Penee*
Pension	*Anuvritti, Penshan*
Pensive	*Cintamagn*
Pentagon	*Pancbhuj*
Penultimate	*Uppanty*
Penumbra	*Upacchaya*
Penury	*Kangalee*
Peon	*Ardalee, Caprasee*
People	*Log, Jan*
Peppermint	*Piparment*
Percent	*Pratishat*
Perceptible	*Nayangocar*
Perception	*Bodh, Indriygyan*
Percussion	*Samaghat*
Perennial	*Sarvakalik, Barahmasee, Varshanuvarshee*
Perenniality	*Sarvkalikta*
Perennially barren land	*Catiyal*
Perface	*Prastavana*
Perfect Incarnation	*Poornavtar*
Perfection	*Paripak, Poornta*
Perfectly clean	*Safacat*
Perfectly healthy	*Arogy, Tanmana*
Perfectly satisfied	*Nihal*
Perforated	*Viddh*
Perfume-manufacturer	*Gandhee*
Perfumed	*Vasit*

Perfumer	*Attar*
Perhaps	*Shayad, Kadacit*
Perify	*Pathrana*
Perihelion	*Ravi-neec*
Perimeter	*Parimap*
Period	*Time, Avdhi*
Period of famine	*Kehatsalee*
Period of forty days	*Caleesa*
Period of ill-luck	*Grehdasha*
Period of mourning	*Sogvaree*
Period of service	*Savakal*
Period of ten days	*Dashah*
Period of three hours	*Prahar*
Period of time	*Arsa*
Periodic	*Kalik*
Periodical	*Avadhik*
Perishable	*Vinashshwar, Kshar, Nashvan*
Permanent	*Cirasthaee, Davamee*
Permanent seat	*Thiya*
Permeability	*Pravashshyta*
Permeable	*Pravashy*
Permission	*Ijazat, Parvangee*
Permit	*Parmit*
Perpendicular	*Lamb*
Perpetual	*Ajasr, Cirantan*
Perpetrate	*Macana*
Perplexed	*Garbarana*
Perplexity	*Pasopash, Hairanee*
Perquisite	*Dastooree*
Perseverance	*Tandahee*
Persian	*Farsee*
Persian wheel	*Rehat*
Person	*Shakhs, Jana, Vyakti*

Person having very little capital	*Tutpunjiya*
Person of high and noble ideas	*Mahanubhav*
Person without any work	*Thala*
Personal	*Vyaktigat, Nijee, Apna*
Personal attendant	*Khavas*
Personal experience	*Swanobhooti*
Personal-bond	*Mucalka*
Personality	*Shakhsiyat*
Personified	*Moortiman*
Persons	*Sarvjan*
Perspective	*Sandarsh, Pariprakshy*
Perspiration	*Shramkan*
Perspired	*Swadit*
Pertaining to a bail	*Zamanatee*
Pertaining to a family	*Parivarik*
Pertaining to a kind	*Padshahee*
Pertaining to a month	*Masik*
Pertaining to a paternal uncle	*Cacera*
Pertaining to a question	*Prashnik*
Pertaining to a spirit	*Pretatmak*
Pertaining to a thousand	*Hazaree*
Pertaining to a tragedy	*Trasdeey*
Pertaining to adoption	*Dattakeey*
Pertaining to all	*Sarv, Sarvjaneen*
Pertaining to an agitation	*Andolankaree*
Pertaining to an application	*Darkhastee*

Pertaining to an assembly	*Majlisee*
Pertaining to an owner	*Malikana*
Pertaining to attendance	*Paricarak*
Pertaining to auction	*Neelamee*
Pertaining to events	*Ghatnatmak*
Pertaining to film	*Filmee*
Pertaining to forest	*Janglee*
Pertaining to jail	*Karagarik*
Pertaining to land	*Sthaleey*
Perturbance and agitation	*Kshobh*
Perturbation	*Vyakulta, Uddvag*
Perturbed	*Sankshubdh, Vyagr*
Perturbed and agitated	*Kshubdh*
Perturbed by doubt	*Shankakul*
Pervade	*Vyapna*
Pervaded	*Vyapt*
Pervading the world	*Vishwavyapee*
Pervasive	*Vyappy*
Pervasiveness	*Vyapti*
Pervert	*Ultee khopree*
Pestle	*Moosal*
(to) pestle	*Kutna*
(to) pestle (in a motar)	*Ghotna*
Pet	*Paltoo*
Petition	*Yacika*
Petition writer	*Arzeenavees*
Petrograph	*Shilalekh*
Petrol	*Petrol*
Petticoat	*Pettikot*
Petty	*Chichora, Chota-mota*

Petty person	*Chutbhaiya*
Petty thief	*Corkat*
Phaeton	*Fitan*
Phallicism	*Lingopasna*
Phallus	*Shivling*
Phantom	*Chayapurush, Manoleela*
Pharmacology	*Aushadh vigyan*
Pharmacy	*Bhaishjikee*
Phelgm	*Khakhar*
Phenyl	*Finail*
Phial	*Sheeshee*
Philander	*Ishkbazee*
Philanderer	*Ishkbaz*
Philanthropic	*Lokopakaree*
Philanthropy	*Lokopkar*
Philologist	*Bhasha-vigyanee*
Philology	*Bhasha-vigyan*
Philosopher	*Tattwgyani*
Philosopher's stone	*Paras*
Philosophical	*Darshanik*
Philosophy	*Tattwgyan*
Philosophy of action	*Karmyog*
Philosophy of religion	*Dharm-darshan*
Philosophy of ultimate good	*Parmarthvad*
Phlegm	*Balgam*
Phoneme	*Dhwanigram*
Phonetic	*Dhwannyatmak*
Phonetics	*Dhwani-vigyan*
Phosphate	*Fasfat*
Phosphorus	*Fasforas*
Photo	*Chaya, Foto*
Photographer	*Chayakar*

Photography	*Chayacitran*
Phrase	*Padbandh, Vakyansh*
Phrase used habitually	*Takiya kalam*
Phraseology	*Padavalee*
Phyrophobia	*Agnibheeti*
Physical	*Shareerik, Kayik, Daihik*
Physical bloom of youth	*Joban*
Physical exercise	*Vyayam, Kasrat*
Physical functions of the body	*Deh-dharm*
Physical power	*Bahubal*
Physical strength	*Pashubal*
Physically	*Sashareer*
Physician	*Kaychikitsak*
Physics	*Bhautikee*
Physiological	*Shareervaiggyanik*
Physiologist	*Shareerviggyanee*
Physiology	*Shareervigyan, Kayikee, Daihikee*
Physique	*Anglat*
Pick	*Khudnee*
(to) pick	*Cugna*
(to) pick out with the fingers	*Cutakna*
(to) pick up	*Beenna*
Pick-axe	*Gaintee, Pharsa*
Pick-pocket	*Jabkatra, Girehkat, Pakatmar*
Pick-pocketing	*Pakatmaree*
Picketing	*Dharna*
Pickles	*Acar*
Pictorial	*Citrmay, Sacitr*
Picture	*Citr, Tasveer*
Picturesque	*Citratkam*
Piece	*Tukra*

Piece of paper	*Parca*
Piece of poetry	*Muktak*
Piece of stone	*Shila, Rora, Batta*
Piece work	*Ujratee*
Pier	*Potghat*
Pierce	*Bhadna*
(to) pierce a hole into	*Badhna*
(to) pierce into	*Garana*
Pierceable	*Bhedy, Vadhneey*
Pierced	*Bhedit*
Piercing	*Vadhan, Ganseela, Bhedee*
Piercing a child's ear-lobe	*Karn vadh, Kancchedan*
Piercing thrust	*Hool*
Pig	*Shookar, Suar*
Pigeon	*Kabootar*
Pigeon fancier	*Kabootar baz*
Pigeon house	*Kabootar khana*
Pile	*Thak, Golee*
(to) pile up	*Ganjna*
Piles	*Bavaseer*
Pilferage	*Uthaigeeri*
Pilferer	*Lapka*
Pilgrim	*Teerthyatree*
Pilgrimage	*Teerthatan*
Pill-box	*Kavac kothree*
Pillage	*Loot-mar, Lootkhasot*
Pillar	*Khambha, Thamb*
Pillow	*Takiya, Sirhana*
Pillow case	*Gilaf*
Pilot	*Vimancalak*
Pimple	*Munhasa*
Pin	*Alpin, Pin*

Pincers	*Cimta*
Pinch	*Cikotee*
(to) pinch	*Bakotna*
(to) pinch with the nails	*Nicotna*
Pinching and snatching	*Noc-khasot*
Pine for	*Tarasna*
Pine tree	*Cheer*
Pineapple	*Anannas*
Pining for death	*Mumoorshu*
Pious	*Pootik*
Pious (person)	*Pavitratma*
Pipe	*Paip*
Piracy	*Jaldasyuta*
Pirate	*Jaldasyu*
Pirate ship	*Canciya jahaz*
Pisciculture	*Matsypalan*
Pish	*Chi, Chee*
Pistachio nut	*Pista*
Pistol	*Pistaul*
Pit	*Gart, Gaddha*
Pit for evacuation	*Khuddi*
Pitch	*Kaku*
Pitch dark	*Ghupp*
Pitcher	*Kumbh, Ghat*
Pith	*Gooda, Heer*
Pitiful	*Dardnak*
Pitiless	*Nirdayee*
Pity	*Taras*
Pivot	*Keelee*
Place	*Sthal, Thaur, Sthan, Jageh, Thanw*
(to) place	*Dharna*

Place for dumping refuse	*Kurakhana*
Place of accident	*Durghatnasthal*
Place of articulation	*Uchchasthan*
Place of murder	*Vadhasthal*
Place of sitting	*Asthan*
Place to stay	*Thikana*
Place which leads to salvation	*Muktidham*
Placenta	*Jarayu, Anval, Kharee*
Placid	*Saumy*
Placidity	*Saumyta*
Plagiarism	*Bhavharan*
Plague	*Taoon, Plag*
Plain and simple	*Seedha-sada*
Plaint	*Arzeedava*
Plaintiff	*Muddaee*
Plan	*Yojna, Ayojana*
Plance	*Randna*
Plane	*Sapat, Samtal*
Planet	*Greh*
Planetoid	*Kshudrgrah*
Plank	*Takht*
Planned	*Yojit, Yojnabaddh*
Planning commission	*Yojana ayog*
Plant	*Plant, Boota, Sanyantr, Takhta, Paudha*
(to) plant	*Ropna*
Plant ninsops dengi	*Maulsiree*
Plantation of tree	*Vrikshropan*
Planted	*Ropit*
Planter	*Ropak*
Planting	*Ropan*

Plaster	*Palastar*
(to) plaster (roughly) as mud on a wall	*Thopna*
Plastering	*Gilkaree, Gunthan*
White-washing	*Lipaee-putaee*
Plat form	*Alind, Platfarm*
Plate	*Palat, Tashtaree*
Plate made of copper	*Tamrpatr*
Plate worn on the belt	*Capras*
Plateau	*Pathar*
Plated	*Paletdar*
Plating	*Kalaee*
Platinum	*Platinam*
Platoon	*Risala*
Play	*Khelna*
Play back	*Pashcanayan*
Play-ground	*Kreerasthal*
Playback music	*Parshwsangeet*
Player	*Khilaree*
Playful	*Khilvaree*
Playful and restive	*Hurdangee*
Playful as a child	*Culbula*
Playing cards	*Tash*
Plea	*Yukti*
Pleader	*Abhivakta*
Pleading	*Abhivachan*
Pleasant	*Suhavna*
Pleasant love-play	*Surati*
Pleasant truth	*Soonrit*
Pleasantly saltish	*Mithlona*
Please come in	*Padharna*
Pleased	*Mudit*
Pleased to	*Kripya*

Pleasing	*Sukhad, Amodkaree, Ramneek*
Pleasing smell	*Sondhapan*
Pleasing to the populace	*Janranjan*
Pleasure	*Amod, Maza*
Pleasure and convenience	*Sukh-subheeta*
Pleasure garden	*Nazarbag*
Pleasure resort	*Vihar-sthalee*
Pleasure trip	*Amodyattra*
Pleasure-seeking	*Vilasee*
Pleasures and amenities	*Sukh-suvidha*
Pleasures and comforts	*Aish-o-aram*
Pledge	*Pratigya, Rehan, Dharohar*
Pledge of celibacy	*Kumarvrat*
Pledged	*Vagdatt*
Plenitude	*Bahuttw*
Plenteous	*Bharmar*
Plentiful	*Bahul, Pracur*
Plenty	*Adhikta, Bahut*
Pliable	*Anamy*
Pliers	*Jamboor, Sandsee*
Plight	*Durgati, Durdasha*
Plot of a drama	*Kathanak*
Plough	*Hal*
(to) plough	*Jotna*
Ploughing	*Jotaee*
Ploughman	*Halvaha, Haldhar*
Pluck	*Khoontna*
Pludering and destruction	*Loot-pat*
Plum	*Aloocha*
Plumb	*Sahul*
Plunder	*Lootna*

Plural	*Bahuvacan*
Plus half	*Sarha*
Plutocracy	*Dhaniktantr*
Pneumonia	*Nimoniya*
Poacher	*Corshikaree*
Pocket	*Jeb, Pakat*
Pocket-money	*Jeb-kharc*
Pocket-watch	*Jeb gharee*
Pod of pea	*Cheemee*
Poem	*Kavita*
Poet	*Kavi*
Poetess	*Kavayitree*
Poetic	*Kavvyatmak*
Poetic prose	*Gaddykavvya*
Poetic spirit	*Kavittw*
Poetic symposium	*Kavi Sammelan*
Poetics	*Kavvyshastr*
Poetry	*Kavita*
Poignant	*Marmantak*
Point	*Bindu, Nukta, Bindee*
Point aimed at	*Lakshyabindu*
Point of contact	*Sparsh bindu*
Pointed	*Nukeela*
Pointedness	*Nukeelapan*
Pointer	*Sanketak*
Poise	*Samasthiti*
Poison	*Vish, Garal, Zehar*
Poisonous	*Vishaila, Vishad, Zehreela*
Polar	*Dhurveey*
Polarisation	*Dhruveekaran*
Pole used for beating a trumpet	*Gaja*
Pole-star	*Dhruv-tara, Kutub*

Police	*Pulis*
Police rule	*Pulis-raj*
Police station	*Thana, Kotvalee*
Policy	*Palisee, Neeti*
Polish	*Palish*
Polite form of address	*Mahashay, Mahoday*
Politely	*Shishtapoorvak*
Politic	*Neetigy*
Political	*Siyasee*
Politics	*Rajneetee, Siyasat*
Polity	*Rajytantr, Rajyvyavastha*
Pollen	*Parag, Pushprag*
Pollination	*Paragan*
Polling booth	*Matdan koshth*
Polling station	*Matdan kendr*
Pollution	*Pradooshan*
Poltergeistic disturbance	*Pratleela*
Polutry-farming	*Murgee-palan*
Polyandry	*Bahupatittw*
Polygamist	*Bahupatneek*
Polygamy	*Bahuvivah*
Pomergranate	*Anar*
Pomp and show	*Dhoomdham , Chamak-dhamak*
Pond	*Pokhra, Talab, Kund*
Poniard	*Karaulee*
Pony	*Tangan*
Pooh	*Dur*
(to) pooh pooh	*Durdurana*
Poor	*Gareeb, Dariddree, Nirdhan*
Pope	*Pop*
Poppy seed	*Khaskhas*
Popular	*Janpriy, Lokpriy*
Popular custom	*Lokacar*

Popular saying	*Lokokti*
Popular song	*Calta gana*
Popularity	*Lokpriyta*
Populated	*Abad*
Population	*Abadee, Jansankhya*
Porcelam	*Ceenee mittee*
Porcupine	*Sahee*
Pore	*Randhr*
Porosity	*Chidralta*
Porous	*Chiddral, Sarandhr*
Porpoise	*Soons*
Port town	*Pattan*
Portable	*Uthaoo*
Porter	*Palledar*
Portfolio	*Samvibhag*
Portion between shoulder and elbow	*Khava*
Portionwise	*Khandshah*
Portrayal	*Citrankan*
Portugal	*Purtgal*
Portuguese	*Purtgalee*
Positiism	*Prattyakshvad*
Position	*Rutba*
Position of rest	*Viramavastha*
Positive	*Dhanatmak, Sakaratmak*
Positivist	*Pratyakshvadee*
Possessing a character	*Caritrvan*
Possessing a pleasing smile	*Caruhasee*
Possessing perennial youth	*Nirjar*
Possessing the three qualities	*Trigunatmak*

Possession	*Kabza*
Possibility	*Shakyta, Sambhavana*
Possible	*Sambhav, Mumkin, Shaky*
Possibly	*Sambhavtah*
Post	*Ohda, Post*
Post office	*Dak khana, Dakghar*
Post-Graduate	*Snatkottar*
Postal expenses	*Dak-Vyay*
Poster	*Postar*
Postgram	*Tarpatr*
Posthumous	*Maranotar*
Postman	*Pattrvah, Dakiya, Cittheerasan*
Postmortem	*Shavpareeksha*
Postpon	*Talna, Multave*
Postposition	*Parsarg, Vibhakti*
Postscript	*Pashclekh*
Postulation	*Abhidharan*
Posture	*Asan*
Pot	*Kamandal, Bhajan*
Pot belied	*Tundil, Tondal*
Potash	*Putash, Potas*
Potato	*Aloo, Batata*
Potter	*Kumhar*
Pottery	*Mrinpatr*
Pouch	*Thailee*
Poultice	*Pultis*
Pound	*Paund, Sarsee*
Pound sterling	*Paund*
Pounded	*Vimardit*
Pounding	*Vimardan*
Pounding and grinding	*Kutauni-pisauni*
Pounding of corn	*Kutaunee*
Pour	*Undalna*

Poverty	*Nirdhanta, Dainny, Gareebee, Dariddrta*
Powder	*Buknee, Coorn, Paudar*
(to) powder	*Bookna*
Powder of spices	*Garam masala*
Powdered	*Curkut, Coornit*
Power	*Zor, Pavar*
Power of attorney	*Mukhtarnama*
Power of digestion	*Hazma*
Power of endurance	*Bardasht*
Power of forbearance	*Sehan-shakti*
Power of imagination	*Kalpanashakti*
Power of reasoning	*Vicar-shakti*
Power of retention	*Dharan-shakti, Stambhan-shakti*
Power of speech	*Natka, Boltee*
Powerful	*Shaktisalee, Sabal, Balvan, Damdar, Tagra*
Powerfulness	*Shaktimatta*
Powerless	*Balheen, Shaktiheen*
Practicability	*Kriyatmakta, Vyavharryta*
Practicable	*Vyavharry*
Practical	*Vyavaharik*
Practical knowledge	*Praggyan*
Practical wisdom	*Vyavhar kushalta, Vyavhar buddhi*
Practicality	*Vyavharikta*
Practically	*Vyavhartah*
Practically unknown	*Jana-anjana*
Practice	*Maharat, Abbhyas*
Practice of yoga	*Yogabhyas*
Practised	*Abbhyasee*
Praise	*Gungan, Tareef*
(to) praise	*Sarahna*
Praiseworthy	*Abhinandaneey, Stutty, Sarahneey*

Prattle — *Bakbak, Bakvas, Capar-capar*
(to) prattle — *Tartarana*
(to) prattle for pain or sorrow — *Kurburana*
Prattler — *Bakvasee*
Prattling — *Pralapee*
Prawn — *Cingra*
Prayer — *Ardas, Prarthna*
Pre-cautionary measure — *Poorvopay*
Pre-conceived — *Poorvkalpit*
Pre-knowledge — *Poorvgyan*
Pre-planned — *Poorvayojit*
Preamble — *Amukh*
Precaution — *Ehtiyat*
Precautionary — *Nivarak, Ehtiyatee*
Precentage — *Pratishatta*
Preception — *Avbodhan*
Preceptor — *Guru, Deekshak*
Preceptor's secret message — *Gurumantr*
Precious — *Beshkeemat, Moolyvan, Anmol, Bahumooly*
Precipice — *Kagar*
Precise to the point — *Janca-tula*
Predicable — *Vaccy*
Predicament — *Auchat*
Prediction — *Bhavishyavani*
Preeminence — *Mukhyata*
Preferable — *Vareey*
Preference — *Tajeeh, Vareeyta*
Pregnancy — *Garbhavastha*
Pregnant — *Garbvati*
Prejudice — *Poorvagrah, Vidharana*

Prejudiced	*Vidharit*
Prelacy	*Dharmadhikar*
Prelate	*Dharmadhikaree*
Preliminary	*Prarambhik*
Premature delivery	*Akalprasav*
Prematurely aged	*Akalvriddh*
Premonition	*Poorvabhas*
Prenatal	*Janmpoorv*
Preparation	*Upakkraman, Taiyaree*
Prepared	*Uddyat*
Prepared and ready	*Tatpar*
Prerogative	*Parmadhikar, Vishashadhikar*
Prescribed by law	*Vidhivihit*
Prescription	*Nuskha*
Prescription of the scriptures	*Shastr-vidhan*
Presence	*Viddymanta, Upasthiti, Maujoodgee*
Present	*Vartman, Tohfa, Upasthit*
Presentation	*Prastuti, Avtarna, Peshee*
Preserved	*Parirakshit*
President	*Rashtrapati*
Presiding officer of a district	*Tehseeldar*
Press	*Dabna, Mudranalay*
(to) press down	*Dabana*
(to) press with a finger	*Teepna*
(to) press with feet for relieving pain	*Latarna*
Press reporter	*Khabarnees*
Pressure	*Dab, Dabaw*
Prestige	*Pratishtha, Gaurav*
Prestigious	*Manmaryadavala, Nakvala, Pratishthavan*

Presumed *Parikalpit*
Presumption *Parikalpna, Prakalpit*
Pretender *Heelabaz*
Pretext *Heela, Vyaj*
Prettiness *Manjulta*
Pretty *Manjul, Sucaru*
Pretty face *Mukharvind*
Pretty woman *Vanita*
Pretty young girl *Haseena*
Prevalence *Pracalan*
Prevalent *Pracalit*
Prevention *Nivaran, Rok-tham*
Preventive *Rognashak*
Previous one *Pehlevala*
Price *Dam, Keemat*
Price control *Mooly-niyantran*
Price index *Mooly-soocakank*
Price list *Moolysoocee*
Priceless *Amooly*
Prick *Cubhna*
Pricking sensation *Cuphan*
Prickly heat *Ghamauree*
Pride *Garv, Abhiman*
Prideless *Nirhankar*
Priest hood *Mahantee, Porohitty, Panditaee*
Primacy *Pramukhta*
Primarily *Pradhantaya*
Primarily emotional *Bhav-pradhan*
Primary *Praimaree*
Prime Minister *Pradhan mantree*
Primer *Praveshika*
Primeval *Adi*
Primeval man *Adipurush*

Primitive	*Adim*
Primitive man	*Baba adam*
Prince	*Rajkumar, Kunwar*
Prince among poets	*Kaviraj*
Princely	*Shahana*
Princess	*Rajkanya, Rajkumaree*
Principal	*Pracarry, Pradhanacarya*
Principal amount	*Mooldhan*
Principle	*Usool, Siddhant*
Print	*Chapna*
Printed	*Chapahova, Mudrit*
Printer	*Muddrak*
Printing press	*Chapakhana*
Printing type	*Mudra*
Prior to	*Peshtar*
Priority	*Agrta, Prathmikta*
Prison	*Bandeegrih, Jelkhana*
Prisoner	*Kaidee*
Prisoner of war	*Yud bandee*
Pristine	*Thath*
Private	*Asarvajanik*
Privy purse	*Rajvritti*
Prize	*Inam, Paritoshik*
Probability	*Prayikta*
Probable	*Sambhavit*
Probe	*Chan been*
Problem	*Samasya, Jhamela, Masla*
Procedure	*Prakriya, Karypranalee*
Proceedings	*Karyavivran*
Proceeds	*Arthagam*
Process	*Prakram*
Process of panelling	*Dillabandee*
Procession	*Jaloos*

Proclaimed	*Udghoshit*
Proclaimer	*Udghoshak*
Proclamation	*Munadee, Udghosh, Ghoshnapatr*
Procrastination	*Talmatol, Deerghsootrta*
Procreation	*Prajanan*
Procreative power	*Janankshamta*
Procurer	*Kutnee, Kutna*
Prodigal	*Khau-uraoo, Ghar-ganvaoo*
Produce	*Utpad, Upaj*
(to) produce	*Upjana*
(to) produce a jingling sound	*Jhamjhamana*
(to) produce a rattling sound	*Khurkhurana*
(to) produce a swishing sound	*Sansanana*
(to) produce irritating pain	*Rarakna*
Produced	*Utpadit*
Producer	*Utpadak*
Production	*Paidavar, Utpadan*
Productivity	*Utpadakta*
Profession	*Dhandha, Pesha*
Profession of a teacher	*Mastaree*
Profession of writing	*Naveesee*
Profession tax	*Vritti-kar*
Professional	*Peshevar*
Professional story-teller	*Kathakar*
Professional wrestler	*Danglee*
Professionally criminal	*Jarayampesha*
Professor	*Profesar, Acary, Pradhayapak*
Proficiency	*Sugharpan*
Proficient	*Nipun, Gunee*

Profit	*Labh, Munafa*
Profit and loss	*Labh Hanee*
Profitable	*Faydemand*
Profiteer	*Munafakhor*
Profiteering	*Munafakhoree*
Profound	*Prakand*
Profound colour	*Vacaspati*
Progency	*Aulad*
Progenitor	*Janmdata*
Programme	*Karykram*
Progress	*Unnati*
Progressive	*Unnatisheel, Pragatisheel*
Prohibition	*Varjet, Nishadh*
Project	*Prayojna*
Projected	*Kshipt*
Projected over-head rack/shelf	*Tand*
Projecting point	*Shosha*
Projector	*Prakshepak*
Prolegomenon	*Poorvpeethika*
Proletariate	*Sarvhara*
Prolific	*Dhakkar*
Prolonged discussion	*Behas-mubahisa*
Prolonging	*Lamban*
Prominence	*Pradhanta, Shreshthta*
Promiscuous spouse	*Harjaee*
Promise	*Vayda, Vada, Kaul*
Promising boy	*Naunihal*
Promissory	*Pratigyatmak*
Promoted	*Pravartit*
Promoter	*Pravartak*
Promulgation	*Prakhyapan*
Prone to bite	*Katha*

Prone to hit	*Markhana*
Prone to liquefy	*Dravansheel*
Prong	*Shool*
Pronominal	*Sarvnamik*
Pronote	*Pronot*
Pronoun	*Sarvnam*
Pronounced	*Uccarit*
Pronounced without a nasal touch	*Niranunasik*
Pronunceable	*Uchcharaneey*
Pronunciation	*Uccaran*
Proof	*Saboot, Proof*
Proof correction	*Proofshodhan*
Proof reader	*Proof reedar*
Prop	*Alamb*
(to) prop	*Takna*
Propaganda	*Prachar*
Propagator	*Pracarak*
Proper	*Theek, Ucit, Upyukt*
Proper Noun	*Vyaktivacak-sangya*
Property	*Jaydaa, Gundharm*
Property tax	*Sampatti-kar*
Property to a woman	*Streedhan*
Prophet	*Nabee, Mantr-drashta*
Propitiation	*Arcan*
Proportion	*Samanupat*
Proportional	*Anupatik, Samanupatik*
Proposal	*Prastav*
Proposer	*Prastavak*
Proprietor	*Adhipati*
Proprietory right	*Hak-malikana*
Propriety	*Upyuktta, Sameeceenta*
Proscribed	*Abhinishiddh*

Proscription	*Abhinishedh*
Prose	*Gaddyatmak*
Prosecutable	*Abhiyojjy*
Prosecution	*Abhiyojan*
Prosody	*Shastr, Pingal*
Prosper	*Sarasna*
Prosperity	*Sammriddhi*
Prosperity and success	*Riddhi Siddhi*
Prosperous	*Sammriddh, Sampann, Phala-phoola*
Prospertiy	*Sampannta*
Prostitute	*Tavayaf, Vaishya*
Prostration	*Dandvat*
Protected	*Rakshit*
Protection	*Suraksha, Sanrakshan*
Protective	*Rakshatmak*
Protector	*Raksthak*
Protectorate	*Sanrakshit rajjy*
Protest	*Abbhyapatti*
Prothesis	*Poorvagam*
Proto-historic	*Pragaitihasik*
Protractor	*Canda*
Proud	*Magroor, Abhiman*
Proved	*Siddh, Sabit, Pramanit*
Proverb	*Kahavat*
Provide a support	*Takana*
Providence	*Daivgati*
Provident fund	*Bhavishshyanidhi*
Providential	*Daivkrit*
Province	*Sooba*
Provincial	*Pranteey*
Provision	*Upbandh, Pravidhan*
Provisional	*Antahkaleen*
Provisions	*Rasad*

Provocative	*Bharkaoo, Uttejana, Uttejak*
Provoked	*Uttejit*
Proximity	*Sannidhdhy*
Prude	*Nakhreela*
Prudence	*Samajh daree, Samajh boojh*
Prune	*Khontna*
Pruning	*Kataee-chantaee*
Pseudonym	*Chadmnam*
Psychic element	*Manastattw*
Psychics	*Atmikee*
Psycho-analysis	*Manovishleshan*
Psychologist	*Manovaiggyanik*
Psychology	*Manoviggyan*
Psychopathy	*Manorog, Manovikar*
Psychosis	*Matibhransh*
Puberty	*Vayahsandhi*
Public	*Sarvajanik, Praja, Janta, Pancayatee*
Public censure	*Lokninda*
Public finance	*Rajvitt*
Public latrine	*Bampulis*
Public nuisance	*Lokkantak*
Public servant	*Jansevak*
Public service	*Lokseva, Janseva*
Publication	*Prakashan*
Publicly	*Sarebazar*
Published	*Prakashit*
Publisher	*Prakashak*
Puff	*Soota, Kash*
Pufification of mind	*Cit-shuddhi*
Pull	*Kheench*
(to) pull	*Kheenchna*
(to) pull through	*Saparna*

Pulley	*Charkhee, Gararee*
Pulling of hair	*Nucana*
Pulp	*Bhurkus*
Pulpy	*Goodedar*
Pulsated	*Spandit*
Pulsation	*Spandan*
Pulse	*Naree, Dal, Nabz*
Pulverized mica	*Bukka*
Pumping of air	*Dhaman*
Pumpkin	*Kaddoo, Seetaphal*
Pun	*Yamak*
Punch	*Mukka*
Punctual	*Samaynishth*
Punctuality	*Samaynishtha*
Puncture	*Pankcar*
Pungent	*Teekshn, Tikt, Jhaldar*
Pungent-cum-spicy	*Carpara*
Punishable	*Dandneey*
Punished	*Dandit*
Punishment	*Saza, Dand, Taran*
Punitive	*Dandatmak*
Punjabi folk dance	*Bhangra*
Puny	*Chatankee*
Pupil	*Shishshy*
Puppet	*Kathputlee*
Purchase	*Khareed*
(to) purchase	*Khareedna*
Purchase and sale	*Kray-vikray*
Purchasing	*Khareedaree*
Pure	*Khara, khlis*
Pure and pious	*Sattwik*
Purgation	*Recan, Virecan*
Purgative	*Viracak, Julab, Dastavar*

Purgative nut	*Jamalgota*
Purification	*Parishkriti, Shuddhikaran*
Purified	*Parishkrit*
Purify by decating	*Nitharna*
Purism	*Shuddhtavad*
Purity	*Shuddhta, Kharapan*
Purity and piety	*Sattwikta*
Purple	*Baingnee*
Purple colour	*Kakraj*
Purport	*Mana, Bhavarth, Ashay, Tatpary*
Purpose	*Prayojan, Abhipray*
Pursuer	*Pairveekar*
Pus	*Mavad, Pas, Pooy*
Push	*Dhaka, Thilna, Dhakelna*
(to) push and move	Thalna
Pushing and jostling	*Dhakka-mukkee*
Puss	*Pus*
Pussy	*Marjar*
Pustulate	*Abhidharna*
Put	*Dalna, Rakhna*
(to) put a roof (on a room or house)	*Chatna*
(to) put in a heap	*Ganjna*
(to) put off	*Tarkana*
(to) put wise through pursuation	*Samjhana bujhana*
Putrefy	*Sarna*
Putty	*Puteen*
Python	*Ajgar*

Q

Quack	*Kathvaidy, Neem-hakeem*
Quadrangle	*Catushkon*
Quadratic	*Vargatmak*
Quadrilateral	*Caturbhuj*
Quadruped	*Caua, Catushpadee*
Quaggy	*Daldala*
Quagmire	*Daldal*
Qualification	*Arhta, Kabileeyat*
Qualitative	*Gunvachak*
Quality	*Gun*
Quality of being poetic	*Kavyattv, Kavyatmakta*
Qualm	*Miclee*
Quantitative	*Mattratmak, Parimanvacak*
Quantity	*Pariman*
Quarantine	*Sangrodh*
Quarrel	*Laraeejhagra, Khatpat, Takrar*
(to) quarrel	*Larna-jhagarna*
Quarrelling	*Jhagra*
Quarrelsome	*Larakoo, Fasadee, Jhagraloo*
Quarrelsomeness	*Jhagraloopan*
Quarter	*Kwartar*
Quarter of a seer	*Paw*
Quarterly	*Timahee, Tramasik*
Quatrain	*Rubaee*
Queen	*Malika, Begam, Ranee*
Queen consort	*Pattranee*
Question	*Saval, Prashn*
Question and answer	*Prashn uttar*
Question paper	*Prashnpatr*
Questionable	*Ashankaneey*
Questionaire	*Prashnavalee*
Queue	*Katar*
Queued	*Flower-petal*

Quick	*Kshipr*
Quick ejaculation	*Sheegrapat*
Quick-temper	*Tunak-mizaj*
Quickly	*Jald*
Quickness	*Twara, Kshiprata*
Quiet	*Chup, Khamosh*
Quieten	*Cupana*
Quietly	*Cupcupata*
Quietude	*Nistabhta*
Quilt	*Lihaf, Rajaee*
Quince	*Bihee*
Quinine	*Kunain*
Quintessence	*Marm*
Quire	*Jista*
Quite	*Khasa*
Quite new	*Abhinav*
Quite often	*Bahudha*
Quite ready	*Samuddyat*
Quite right	*Theekam theek*
Quiver	*Bhatha, Nishang, Tuneer, Tarkash*
(to) quiver	*Dalakna*
Quivering	*Dalak*
Quorum	*Ganapoorti*
Quota	*Kota*
Quotation	*Uddharan*
Quoted	*Uddhrit*
Quotient	*Bhag-phal*

R

Rabbit	*Khargosh*
Rabble	*Aira-gaira*
Race	*Daur*
Racial	*Jateey*
Racial discrimination	*Vargbhad*
Racialism	*Zateeyta*
Radar	*Radar*
Radiance	*Bhas, Shubbhrta*
Radiance of the face	*Mukhkanti*
Radiant	*Bhaswar, Shubbhr*
Radiation	*Vikiransheelta*
Radiative	*Vikiransheel*
Radio	*Radiyo*
Radish	*Moolee*
Radium	*Radiam*
Radius	*Trijjya*
Rafter	*Kanree*
Rag	*Cithra*
Raid	*Chapa*
Raider	*Chapamar*
Rail	*Rel*
Rail track	*Relmarg, Rellain, Relpath*
Railing	*Reling*
Railway	*Relwai*
Railway Minister	*Rel mantree*
Railway receipt	*Biltee*
Railway signal	*Sikandara*
Railway train	*Tran, Ralgaree*
Rain	*Varsha, Barsat, Barish*
(to) rain	*Barasna*
Rain-gauge	*Varshamapak*
Rainbow	*Indrdhanush*
Raindropping	*Boondabandee*

Rainfall	*Vrishtipat*
Rainy	*Barsatee*
Rainy season	*Vrishtikal*
Raised	*Samunnat*
Raised platform	*Cabootra*
Raised structure	*Macan*
Raisin	*Kishmish*
Rakish	*Badcalan*
Rambling	*Vicaran*
Rampart	*Parkota*
Range	*Paras, Avali*
Rank	*Koti*
Rankling pain	*Cees*
Ransom	*Phirautee, Churaee*
Rape	*Balatkar*
Rapidly	*Pharphar*
Rapture	*Harshatirak*
Rare	*Viral, Durlabh,*
Rascality	*Badmashee*
Raspberry	*Rasbharee*
Rat-trap	*Coohedanee*
Rate	*Sharah, Rat, Dar*
Rather	*Balki*
Ratification	*Sattyankan*
Ratified	*Sattyankit*
Ratio	*Anupat*
Ration	*Rashan*
Rationalism	*Tarkanavad, Buddhivad*
Rationalistic	*Tarkanavadee*
Rattle	*Jhunjhuna*
(to) rattle	*Khatkana, Kharakna*
Rattle of throat	*Khur khur*
Rattling sound	*Khatka, Ghargharahat*

Rave	*Behkana*
Raven	*Domkaua, Kalakaua*
Rawness	*Kachchapan*
Razor	*Kshur*
Razor-strap	*Camota*
Re-marriage	*Punarvivah*
Re-union	*Punarmilan*
Reach	*Pahunc*
Reaction	*Abhikkriya, Pratikriya*
Reactionary	*Pratikriyakavadee, Pratikriyak*
Reactionary attitude	*Pratikriyavad*
Read	*Parhna*
(to) read aloud	*Bancna*
Readable	*Patthy, Pathneey*
Reader	*Pathak, Peshkar*
Readiness	*Asajja*
Reading	*Parhat, Vacan*
Reading and writing	*Likhana-Parhna*
Reading room	*Vacnalay*
Ready	*Taiyar*
Ready cash	*Nakad-narayan*
Ready wit	*Hazirjavabee*
Ready-made	*Banabanaya*
Ready-witted	*Hazirjawab*
Real	*Saga, Aslee*
Realism	*Yatharthvad, Yatharthvadita*
Realistic	*Yatharthvadee*
Reality	*Hakeekat, Vastvikta, Asliyat, Yatharthta*
Realization	*Vasoolee*
Really	*Vakaee*
Ream	*Rim, Reem*
Reap	*Lunna*

Reaper	*Lunara*
Reaping charges	*Lunaee*
Rear	*Picharee*
Rear part of an army	*Camdaval*
Rearing of quails	*Baterbazee*
Rearmament	*Punarastreekaran*
Reason	*Vajeh*
Reasonable	*Yuktipoorn, Yuktisangat*
Rebel	*Bagee*
Rebellion	*Vipplav, Bagavat, Rajjyviplav*
Rebirth	*Janmantar, Punarjanm*
Reborn	*Prattyutpann*
Rebounded	*Pratikshipt*
Rebuke	*Dhikkar*
Recalled	*Pratyahoot*
Recalling	*Pratyahwan*
Receining and giving	*Adan pradan*
Receipt	*Raseed, Prapti, Pavtee*
Received	*Prapt*
Receiver	*Prapak*
Receiving	*Grehan*
Reception	*Agvanee, Pashvaee*
Reception-room	*Swagat-kaksh*
Receptionist	*Swagatak*
Recess	*Maddhyavkash, Vishshrantikal*
Recital	*Uddharanee*
Recitation	*Prapathan*
Recitation of mantras	*Mantrpath*
Recitation of poetry	*Kavitapath*
Reciter of the Vedas	*Vedpath, Vedapathee*
Recluse	*Vairagee, Akantvasee, Tridandee*
Recognisable	*Abhiggyay*
Recognition	*Manyta*

Recognize	*Pehcanna*
Recommendation	*Sifarish, Sanstuti*
Reconciliation	*Punaradhan*
Recondite	*Goorh*
Reconsideration	*Punarvicar, Punarvicararth*
Reconstruction	*Punarnirman*
Record	*Abhilekh, Keertiman*
(to) record in a register etc.	*Carhana*
Record keeper	*Munsi, Lekhpal*
Recorded	*Darj*
Recorder	*Abhilekhak*
Recording machine	*Abhilekhittr*
Recovery	*Pratiprapti*
Recruitment	*Bhartee*
Rectangle	*Ayat*
Rectangular	*Ayatakar*
Rectum	*Malashay*
Recurred	*Avartit*
Recurrence	*Avartan*
Recurring	*Punaravartee, Avartak*
Red	*Lohit, Arakt, Majeethee*
Red Sea	*Lalsagar*
Red dye	*Alta*
Red face due to heat	*Tamtamahat*
Red fleshy crest of fowl	*Kalgee*
Red rape	*Lal-feeta*
Red tape	*Kagazee chakkar*
Red-beet	*Cukandar*
Red-faced	*Lalmunhan*
Red-legged patridge	*Cakor*
Red-light district	*Singarhat*
Reddish	*Lalauhan*

Reddish glow	*Arunima*
Redeem	*Ubarna*
Redeemed	*Tarit*
Redeemer	*Nistarak*
Redemption	*Taran, Khalasee*
Redistribution	*Punarvibhajan*
Redness	*Lalee*
Redress of trouble	*Kasht nivaran*
Reduced to a skeleton	*Hareela, Asthishash*
Reduced to language	*Bhashabaddh*
Reduced to writing	*Kalamband, Lekhbaddh*
Reduction	*Katautee*
Reed	*Narkat, Narkul*
Reek and smoke	*Gunguana*
Reference	*Abhidesh, Havala*
Reference book	*Sandarbh-granth*
Reference literature	*Sandarbh-sahitty*
Referendum	*Jannirdash*
Refined	*Parimarjit*
Refiner	*Shodhak*
Reflected	*Pratibimbit*
Reflection	*Aks, Paravartan*
Reflexive	*Nijvacak*
Reform	*Sudhar*
(to) reform	*Sudharna*
Reformatory	*Sudharalay*
Reformer	*Sudharak*
Refractoriness	*Tapavarodh*
Refractory	*Tapavarodhak*
Refrain of song	*Geetbhar*
Refrained	*Virat*
Refrainment	*Virati*
Refreshment	*Cabenee*

Refreshment room	*Jalpan grih*
Refuge	*Sharan, Sharnalay*
Refugee	*Sharnarthee*
Refusal	*Inkar*
Refuse	*Asweekar, Natna*
(to) refuse	*Nakarna*
Refused	*Asweekrit*
Refutable	*Khandaneey*
Refutation	*Prtivad*
Refutation and upholding	*Khandan mandan*
Region	*Pradesh*
Region-wise	*Ilakevar*
Regional	*Pradeshik, Kshatreey, Pradesheey*
Regionalism	*Pradeshikta*
Register	*Panjee, Rajistar*
Register of old type	*Bahee*
Registered	*Panjeekrit*
Registrar	*Ragistrar, Nibandhak, Prastota*
Registration	*Rajistree, Nibandhan, Panjeekaran*
Regressive	*Pratigamee*
Regret	*Khad*
Regrettable	*Khedkarak, Khedjanak*
Regular	*Niyamit*
Regularity	*Niyamitta*
Regulation	*Viniyam*
Rehabilitation	*Punarvas*
Rehearsal	*Riharsal, Poorvabhyas*
Reign	*Raj*
Reinforcement	*Kumak*
Reinstallation	*Punarsthapan*
Reinstated	*Bahal*
Reinstatement	*Bahalee*

Reject with contempt	*Thukrana*
Rejoinder	*Prattyutar*
Rejuvenation	*Kayakalp, Punarjeevan*
Related	*Sambaddh*
Related to the Vedas	*Vaidik*
Related to wing	*Paksheey*
Relating to	*Bara*
Relating to the father	*Pittry*
Relation	*Nata, Rishta, Sambandh*
Relationship	*Rishtedaree, Talluk, Natedaree*
Relative	*Rishtedar, Natedar*
Relativity	*Apekshikta, Sapekshvad*
Relaxation	*Vishranti*
Relaxed	*Vishshrant*
Release	*Vimukti, Chutkara, Rihaee*
Released	*Riha*
Relevant	*Prasangik*
Reliability	*Matbaree, Vishwasneeyta*
Reliable	*Vishshwast, Vishwasneey*
Relief	*Rahat*
Relieved	*Farig*
Religion	*Dharm*
Religious	*Dharmik, Dharmee, Dharmsheel*
Religious acts	*Dharm-karm*
Religious book	*Dharmgranth, Dharmpustak*
Religious conduct	*Dharmacaran*
Religious conscience	*Dharmbuddhi*
Religious discourse	*Katha varta*
Religious eternal	*Sanatan-dharm*
Religious faith	*Dharmnishtha*
Religious minded	*Dharmee*
Religious oblation	*Yagy*
Religious practices	*Nam-dharm*

Religiously perservering	*Sadhak*
Religiousness	*Dharmparayanta*
Relish	*Cat, Asswad*
(to) relish	*Rucna*
Relishing	*Asswadan, Rasaswadan*
Remaining	*Avshisht, Pashcardh*
Remaining part	*Shashansh*
Remains	*Avshesh*
Remark	*Ukti*
Remarkable satirical utterance	*Vakkrokti*
Remedial	*Pratividhik*
Remedy	*Pratividhi*
Remedy for all ills	*Mahaushadhi*
Remembrance	*Smaran*
Remind	*Catana*
Remorse	*Atmglani, Manastap*
Removing of a doubt	*Shanka nivaran*
Remuneration	*Mehantana, Bajvaee, Ujrat, Parishshramik*
Renaissance	*Navjagran, Punarutthan*
Rendered plane by constant use	*Silpat*
Renewal	*Naveeneekaran*
Renned	*Jaman*
Renounced	*Parityakt*
Renovation	*Naveekaran*
Renown	*Vishruti*
Renowned	*Khyat, Suprasiddh*
Rent	*Lagan, Kiraya*
Rent-deed	*Kiraanama*
Renunciation	*Vairaggy*

Reorganisation	*Punargathan*
Repairs	*Marammat*
Repayment	*Pratidan*
Repeat	*Dusrana*
(to) repeat devotedly	*Sumirna*
Repeated	*Punarukt*
Repelling	*Pratikshepan*
Repent	*Pachtana*
Repentance	*Pachtava, Pashcatap*
Repetition	*Punurukti, Avritti*
Repetition name of a diety	*Jap*
Replaceable	*Pooraneey*
Replacement	*Badlaw*
Replete with music	*Sangeetmay*
Replica	*Pratimoorti*
Report	*Riport, Rapat, Akkhya, Prativedan*
Reported	*Prativadit*
Reporter	*Riportar, Sanvadak*
Representation	*Niroopan*
Representative	*Niroopak, Pratinidhi*
Represented	*Niroopit*
Reprimand	*Mazammat, Dutkar, Dhigdand*
(to) reprimand	*Ghurakna, Tarna*
Reprisal	*Pratipeeran*
Reproach	*Dutkarna*
Reproduction	*Punarutpadan*
Reproductive	*Punarutpadak*
Reproof	*Malamat, Latar*
Republic	*Gantantr, Ganarajjy*
Republican	*Gantantrik*
Repugnant	*Jugupsit*
Repulsion	*Vitrishna, Pratikshep, Vikarshan*

Repute	*Suyash, Sukeerti, Shree, Yash, Vikhkhyati*
Request	*Nivadan, Iltija*
Requested	*Nivadit, Prarthit*
Required	*Cahia*
Requiring close consideration	*Gaurtalab*
Requiring repairs	*Marammattalab*
Requital of obligation	*Prattyupkar*
Rescue	*Uddhar, Ubar*
Rescue home	*Uddhar grih*
Rescuer	*Uddharak*
Resemble	*Julna*
Resemblance	*Anuroop, Sarooppy*
Resembling in appearance	*Hamshakl*
Reservation	*Arakshan*
Reserve fund	*Sthaee kosh*
Reserved	*Arakshit, Rizarv*
Reservoir	*Nidhan, Hauz*
Residence	*Rihaish, Vassthan, Niketan, Avas*
Resident	*Avasee, Nivasee*
Residential	*Rihaishee, Avaseey*
Residual	*Ucchisht*
Resignation	*Tyag*
Resignation Letter	*Tyag-patr*
Resile	*Lacakna*
Resin	*Ral*
Resinous wood	*Rasdaroo*
Resistance	*Pratirodhan*
Resonance	*Pratidhwani*
Resonant	*Ninadit*
Resounded	*Pratidhwanit*

Respect	*Man, Izzat*
Respect and regard	*Adab lihaz*
Respectable	*Izzatdar*
Respected	*Adarneey*
Respectful greeting	*Pranam*
Respectfully	*Sammanpoorn, Sammanpoorvak*
Respondent	*Uttarpaksh*
Responsibility	*Zimmedaree, , Uttardayittw*
Responsible	*Zimmedar, Uttardayee*
Rest	*Shash, Vishshram*
Rest house	*Dharmshala, Vishshramgrih*
Restaurant	*Rastoran, Bhojanalay*
Restive	*Ariyal*
Restivensss	*Hurdang*
Restless	*Becain, Vikal*
Restlessness	*Vikaltaa, Bachainee*
Restoration	*Punarjagaran*
Restricted	*Paband*
Restriction	*Pabandee, Pratibandh, Rok-tok*
Result	*Phal, Anjam*
Result of addition	*Yogphal*
Resultant	*Parinamee, Parinamik*
Resulted	*Phalit, Pratiphalit*
Resumption	*Punararmbh, Punargrehan*
Resurrection	*Jeernoddhar, Punaruddhar*
Resuscitator	*Punarutthapak*
Retail	*Khudra, Phutkar*
Retaliation	*Pratikar*
Retention	*Stambhan*
Retina	*Drishtipatal*
Retinue	*Parijan*
Retired	*Sevanivritt, Avkashprapt, Ritayar*
Retirement	*Avkashgrahn, Avkashprapti*

Retiring room	*Vishshramalay*
Retrenchment	*Chantnee*
Retrial	*Punarpareekshan*
Retrogression	*Pashcgaman*
Return	*Lautana*
Returnable	*Phiraoo*
Returned	*Punaragat, Pratidatt*
Revelation	*Iljam*
Revelation of a mystery	*Rehessyodghatan*
Revelry	*Maujmaza, Rangrelee*
Revenge	*Badla, Pratishodh*
Revenue	*Rajassw*
Revenue court	*Mal adalat*
Revenue stamp	*Raseedee stamp*
Revered	*Poojneey, Poojyvar, Samadrit*
Reverence	*Samadar, Adarbhav, Shraddha*
Reverend	*Sharddhay, Samadarneey*
Reverential praise	*Stuti*
Reverential service	*Caranseva*
Reverentially accepted	*Shirodhary*
Reversal	*Vyutkram, Utkram*
Reverse	*Ultana*
Reverse order	*Pratikram*
Reversed	*Bhadant, Prativartit*
Reversion	*Vilomit, Utkraman, Prativartan*
Reversion of order	*Vyat-tyay*
Review	*Sameeksha*
Reviewer	*Samalocak, Sameekshak*
Revise	*Duhrana*
Revision	*Punaravlokan, Dohrav, Nazarsanee*
Revocation	*Mansookhee*
Revoked	*Mansookh*
Revolt	*Droh*

Revolting	*Vipplavee, Drohee, Viplavkaree*
Revolution	*Inkalab, Kranti*
Revolutionary	*Krantikaree, Krantivadee*
Revolver	*Tamanca, Rivalvar*
Reward	*Puraskar, Pratiphal*
Rewarded	*Puraskrit*
Rhetorician	*Alankarshastree*
Rhetorics	*Alankarshastr*
Rheumatism	*Gathiya*
Rhinoceros	*Gainda*
Rhizome	*Kand, Kandmool*
Rhyme	*Tuk*
Rhythmic	*Talbaddh*
Ribbon	*Riban, Paranda*
Rice	*Caval, Tandul*
Rice dish	*Pulaw*
Rich	*Dhanee, Ameer, Dhanvan*
Rich and respected	*Dhanee-manee*
Rickets	*Sukhandee*
Rickshaw	*Riksha*
Rickshaw puller	*Rikshawala*
Riddance	*Nistar*
Riddle	*Pahalee, Prahalika*
Rider	*Ashshwarohee, Ghurcarha*
Ridge	*Mand, Takree, Danra*
Ridiculc	*Makhaul, Liharee, Uphas, Jaghansaee*
Ridiculous	*Uphasaspad*
Riding	*Savaree*
Riding on a horse	*Ashshvaroorh*
Rifle	*Raifal*
Right	*Hak, Adhikar*
Right angle	*Samkon*

Right move	*Sucal*
Right of preemption	*Hakshafa*
Right path	*Satpath*
Right type of attitude	*Sadvritti*
Right-wing	*Dakshin-panth*
Righteous	*Sadacaree*
Righteousness	*Sadacarita*
Rigidity of limbs	*Jakran*
Rigorous imprisonment	*Saparishshramkaravas*
Ring	*Challa, Valay*
(to) ring	*Bajna*
Ring-shaped	*Valayakar*
Ringworm	*Dad*
Riot	*Balva, Upaddrav, Danga*
Riot-ridden	*Upaddrav grast*
Rioter	*Balvaee*
Riotous	*Upaddravee, Dangebaz*
Riotousness	*Dangabazee*
Ripe age	*Poornayu*
Ripeness	*Paripakkwta*
Ripple	*Urmi, Veeci*
Rise	*Uday, Utthan*
Rise and fall	*Utarcharhav*
(to) rise and fall	*Ghatna-barhna*
Rise in price	*Moollyvriddhi*
Rise of the moon	*Candroday*
Rising	*Carhta, Udeeyman*
Rising and setting	*Udayast*
Rising of the sun	*Arunoday*
Risk	*Jokhim*
Ritual	*Sanskar, Karmkand*
Rival	*Pratiddwandwee, Spardhee, Pratispardhee*

Rivalry	*Spardha, Bada-badee, Pratispardha*
Riveer-bed	*Nadeetal*
River	*Dariya, Nadee*
River (Ganga)	*Ganga nadee*
River (Yamuna)	*Yamuna nadee*
Road	*Sarak*
Roadway	*Rathya*
Roam	*Bharmana*
Roaming	*Dayar, Vrajan*
Roaming for pleasure	*Vihar*
Roar	*Garjan, Dahar*
(to) roar	*Garjana*
Roasted	*Bhujiya*
Roasted coriander	*Gota*
Roasted meat	*Kabab*
Robber	*Chaur, Lutera, Dakoo*
Robbery	*Chaure, Dakaitee, Lutpat,*
Robe	*Jama*
Robe of honour	*Khillat*
Robot	*Yantr manav*
Rock	*Shail, Cattan, Prastar*
(to) rock	*Halrana*
Rock salt	*Saindha namak*
Rocket	*Agniban, Raket*
Rod	*Char, Dand*
Roguery	*Shathta*
Role	*Rol*
Roll	*Kharra*
(to) roll	*Balna*
(to) roll up	*Lapatna*
Roller	*Rolar*
Rolling	*Lot, Lunthan*
Rolling pin	*Belan*

Romance	*Premleela*
Roof	*Chat*
(to) roof	*Patna*
Room	*Kaksh, Kamra*
Root	*Chat*
Root meaning	*Dhattwarth*
Root of lotus	*Kamal kakree*
Rope	*Rassee, Rassa, Kasha, Rajju*
Rope tied round an animal's neck	*Garanv*
Rope-dancer	*Nat*
Rosary	*Japmala, Sumirnee*
Rose	*Gulab, Patal*
Rose-water	*Gulabjal*
Rose-water sprinkler	*Gulabpash*
Rose-wood	*Sheesham*
Rosy	*Gulabee*
Rotation	*Udbhram, Ghurnan*
Rotten	*Galip, Sariyal*
Rough	*Rookha, Khurdara*
Rough and ready	*Lihara*
Rough and rougged	*Beehar, Oobar-khabar*
Rough and uncultured	*Banjar*
Rough approximation	*Kootkat*
Roughness	*Rookhapan, Ujaddpan*
Round	*Phera, Golakar, Cakkar*
Round about twenty-five	*Gadha-pacheesi*
Round gourd	*Tinda*
Round table	*Gol mez*
Round thick dough bread	*Batee*
Round vessel	*Batloee*

Rounding pillow for cushioned seat	*Masnad*
Rounding up	*Pakar-dhakar*
Route	*Path*
Routine	*Carya*
Rover in the woods	*Vancar*
Roving	*Sair, Bhramansheel*
Roving ascetic	*Parivrajak*
Roving for joy	*Sair-sapata*
Row	*Oodham, Pant, Satar*
Row of lights	*Deepmala*
Row of trees	*Vrikshpankti*
Royal	*Rajshahee, Shahanshahee*
Royal assembly	*Rajsabha*
Royal family	*Rajkul*
Royal grandeur	*Rajshree*
Royal order	*Rajagya*
Royal palace	*Rajmahal*
Royal throne	*Rajsinhasan*
Royal treasury	*Rajkosh*
Royal umbrella	*Chatr*
Rub gently	*Sehlana*
Rub oil on some parts of the body	*Jhansna*
Rubber	*Rabar*
Rubbing	*Ragra*
Rubbing soulders in a crowd	*Ghissam-ghissa*
Rubbing stroke with the arm	*Radda*
Rubbish	*Gand, Kachra*
Rubbish-heap	*Ghoora*
Ruby	*Manik*

Rudder	*Patwar*
Ruddiness	*Runaee, Lalima*
Ruddy	*Ratnara*
Ruddy goose	*Cakva*
Rude	*Avineet, Badtameej*
Rude and impertinent	*Uddand*
Rudeness	*Badtameezee*
Ruffle	*Cunnat*
Ruffled	*Cunnatdar*
Ruin	*Ujarana*
Ruination	*Tabahee, Barbadee*
Ruined	*Barbad, Ujarna*
Ruined entirely	*Sarvswaha*
Ruinous	*Satyanashee*
Ruins	*Khandahar*
Rule	*Kayda, Niyam*
(to) rule with the hands	*Meenjna*
Ruled	*Ruldar, Shasit*
Ruler	*Shasak*
Rules and regulations	*Kayda kanoon, Vidhi-vidhan*
Ruling period	*Rajyakal*
Rumbling	*Gurgur, Gargarahat*
Ruminate (beasts)	*Jugalna*
Rumination	*Jugalee*
Rumour	*Afvah*
Rumour afloat	*Urtee khabar*
Run	*Bhagna, Daurna*
Run in cricket	*Ran*
Runner	*Dhavak*
Running	*Bhagambhag*
Rupee	*Rupaya*
Rural	*Grameen*

Rural uplift	*Gramotthan*
Ruse	*Cakma*
Rush	*Rela*
(to) rush forward	*Lapakna*
Russian	*Roosee*
Rust	*Zang*
Rusted	*Zangdar*
Rustic	*Moosalcand, Ganvaroo*
Rustication	*Nishkasan*
Rustice	*Ganvar*
Rustle	*Kharkharana*

S

Sabotage	*Tor-phor*
Sack	*Bora*
Sack cloth	*Tat*
Sacred act	*Punykarm*
Sacred ashes	*Bhabhoot*
Sacred thread	*Janeoo*
Sacred-thread ceremony	*Upnayan*
Sacrifice	*Hom, Kurbanee*
(to) sacrifice	*Varna*
Sacrificer	*Balidanee*
Sacrificial fire	*Hotagni*
Sacrificing priest	*Yajak*
Sacrosanct balance	*Dharmkanta*
Sad	*Udas*
Saddle	*Kathee*
Safe	*Tijoree*
Safeguard	*Rakshakavac*
Saffron	*Kesar*
Saffron-coloured	*Bhagwa, Kesariya*
Sagacious	*Doordarshee*
Sagacity	*Vicakshanta*
Sage	*Muneesh, Muni*
Sago	*Saboodana*
Said	*Bhanit*
Sail	*Badban*
Saint	*Sadhu, Mahatma, Jogee*
Saintly	*Sant-sulabh*
Saintly character	*Sant-caritr*
Saintly disposition	*Sadhuvritti*
Saka era	*Saka*
Salad	*Salad*
Salaried	*Vetanbhogee*
Sale	*Sel, Bikree, Vikkray*

Sale-deed	*Baynama*
Saleable	*Vikkray*
Sales tax	*Sailtax*
Salesman	*Vikkreta*
Salime	*Pank*
Saline	*Khara, Nona*
Saliva	*Lar*
Salive of a snake	*Nagphan*
Salt	*Lon, Namak, Non*
Salt-pot	*Namakdan*
Saltish	*Lona, Nunkhara*
Saltpetre	*Kalmishora, Sajjee*
Salty	*Namkeen*
Salutation	*Abhivadan*
Salutation of a flag	*Jhandabhivadan*
Salvation	*Moksh, Nirvan, Jeevan-mukti*
Same	*Aksaman, Vahee*
Sample	*Bangee, Namoona*
Sanction	*Shasti*
Sanctuary	*Sharanasthalee*
Sand	*Sikta, Rat, Baloo*
Sand-paper	*Ragmal*
Sandal	*Malyaj, Candan, Cappal*
Sandpiper	*Titihree*
Sands	*Retee*
Sandy	*Siktamay, Balua, Reteela*
Sanskrit	*Davbhasha*
Sapless	*Thanth, Rasheen*
Sapling	*Paud*
Sapodila	*Ceekoo*
Sappers and miners	*Safar-maina*
Sapphire	*Neelam, Indrneel*
Sarcastic remarks	*Bolee-tholee*

Saree	*Saree*
Sash	*Patka*
Satellite	*Upagrah*
Satiated	*Santript*
Satin	*Satan*
Satisfaction	*Santosh, Tripti*
Satisfactory	*Santoshprad, Santoshjanak*
Satisfied	*Santusht, Tusht, Tript*
Saturday	*Shaniwar*
Saturn	*Shani*
Satyug	*Dharmyug*
Sauce	*Catnee*
Savage	*Vehshee*
Savagery	*Vehsheepan*
Save	*Bacana*
Save me	*Trahimam*
Saving	*Bacat*
Saving scheme	*Bacat-yojna*
Saving some one's life	*Prandan*
Savings account	*Bacat-khata*
Savings book	*Saving book*
Saviour	*Prandata, Tarak, Paritrata*
Saw	*Ara*
(to) saw	*Ceerna*
Saw-dust	*Kunaee, Burada*
Sawyer	*Arakash*
Say something almost inaudibly	*Mirakna*
Scabby	*Papreela*
Scabies	*Khaj*
Scaffolding	*Pait*
Scale	*Roolar, Paimana, Mapnee*
(to) scale	*Dakna*

Scale of fish	*Shalak*
Scale pan	*Palra*
Scales	*Tula*
Scarce	*Dushprappy*
Scarcity	*Tora, Durlabhta*
Scare	*Hadas, Daraba, Bheeti*
(to) scare away (birds or cattle)	*Hakarna*
Scare-crow	*Bijookha, Kapat purush*
Scarf	*Gulooband*
Scatter	*Bikharna*
Scattered	*Avkeern, Vikeern*
Scattering	*Chirkaw*
Scavenger	*Halalkhor*
Scene	*Nazara, Seen*
Scenery	*Seenaree*
Scent	*Ittr*
Scented	*Suvasit*
Scented oil	*Phulal, Gandh tail*
Scented tobacco	*Zarda*
Sceptic	*Sanshayvadee*
Scepticism	*Sanshayvad*
Sceptre	*Rajdand*
Scholar	*Gyata, Vidwan*
Scholarly	*Vidushee, Pandit, Viddwattapoorn*
Scholarly people	*Buddhjan*
Scholarship	*Viddwatta, Chatrvritti*
School	*Pathshala, Viddyalay,*
Science	*Vigyan*
Science of Cooking	*Pakshastr*
Science of Health	*Swasthyvigyan*
Science of Law	*Vidhishastr*
Science of Rhetorics	*Sahittyashasttr*

Scientific	*Vaiggyanik*
Scintillation	*Timtimahat*
Scion	*Vanshaj*
Scold	*Dantna*
(to) scold	*Phatkarna*
Scolding	*Dant*
Scorched	*Dagdh*
Scorpion	*Vrishcik*
Scoundrel	*Badmash*
Scramble	*Cheena-jhaptee*
Scrape	*Khurchan*
(to) scrape	*Khurachna*
Scraper	*Khurchanee*
Scrapings	*Cheelan*
Scratch	*Kharonch, Kuredna*
(to) scratch a groove	*Khanchna*
Scratchy sensation	*Culculahat*
Scrawl	*Ghaseetna*
Scream	*Ceekh*
(to) scream	*Ceekhna*
Screaming out for help	*Ceekh-pukar*
Screen	*Cittrapat, Patal*
Screen made of reeds	*Sirkee*
Screen made of straw	*Tattee*
Screen of mind	*Smriti patal*
Screen-play	*Citr-lekh*
Screw	*Pec*
Screw-driver	*Peckas*
Screw-pine	*Ketkee*
Scrikptology	*Lipishastr*
Script	*Lipi*
Scrofula	*Kanth mala*
Scrupulous	*Dharmbheeru*

Scrupulously true in word	*Satyavadee*
Scrutiny	*Sampareekshan, Samveeksha*
Scrutiny section	*Janc-vibhag*
Scspicion	*Shankajanak*
Scuffle	*Hathapaee*
Sculptor	*Takshan*
Scuttle	*Mokha*
Sea	*Sumudr, Sagar*
Sea-beach	*Samudr-tat*
Sea-god	*Varun*
Sea-level	*Samudr-tal*
Sea-port	*Samudr-patan*
Sea-quake	*Samudr-kamp*
Sea-robber	*Samudree-daku*
Sea-word	*Samudrabhimukh*
Seal	*Seel*
Sealed	*Seelband, Muharband*
Search	*Khoj, Talash*
(to) search	*Khojna*
(to) search	*Dhoonrhna*
(to) search	*Talashna*
(to) search	*Harna*
Searcher	*Khojee*
Searchlight	*Khojbattee*
Season	*Ritu*
Season of defoliation	*Khizan*
Seasonal	*Faslee*
Seat	*Seet, Asan, Barth*
(to) seat	*Baithana*
Seat of a deity	*Dham*
Second	*Sakand, Dooa, Dwitteey*
Second class	*Doyam*

Second day of each half of a lunar month	*Dooj*
Second era of Hindu mythology	*Treta*
Second month of Hindu Calender	*Baisakh*
Second person (gram)	*Maddhypurush*
Second time	*Dobara*
Secondary	*Maddhyamik*
Secondary derivatives in Grammar	*Taddhit*
Secrecy	*Gopneeyta*
Secret	*Rahasy*
Secret Chamber	*Khufiya mehel*
Secret adultery	*Cam-coree*
Secret emissary	*Guptchar*
Secret window	*Cor khirkee*
Secretariat	*Sacivalay*
Secretary	*Saciv, Secretary*
Secretive	*Cuppa-ghunna*
Secretly	*Gup chup*
Sect	*Millat*
Section	*Anubhag*
Sector of a circle	*Vritkhand*
Secular	*Dharmnirpeksh*
Secularism	*Dharmnirpekshta*
Security	*Pratibhooti*
Security Council	*Suraksha Parishad*
Sedan chair	*Palkee*
Sediment	*Deshdroh, Talchat, Gad*
Seditionist	*Rajdrohee*
Seed	*Dana, Beej*
Seed of lotus	*Kamal gatta*

Seed of margosa tree	*Nimkauree*
Seedless	*Nirbeej*
Seedling	*Bahan*
Seeker after knowledge	*Gyan-Pipasu*
Seeker of truth	*Sattyakam*
Seeking Salvation	*Mumukshu*
Seeking favour	*Kripakankshee*
Seeking some object	*Karyarthee*
Seen	*Drisht, Vilokit*
Seer	*Trikaldarshee, Bhavishshyadarshee*
Seer of the spiritual reality	*Brahmarishi*
Seive	*Chalnee, Channee*
(to) seive	*Channa*
Seize suddenly	*Dabocna*
Seized	*Baramad*
Select	*Cunna*
Selected	*Cuninda*
Selected few	*Gina-chuna*
Selection	*Cunaw*
Self	*Khud, Swa*
Self-advancement	*Atmonnati*
Self-born	*Swayambhoo*
Selfish	*Swarthee, Matlabee*
Selfishness	*Khudgarjee, Swarthparayanta*
Selfless	*Nihsprih*
Sell	*Bacna*
Semantic change	*Arthvikar*
Semantics	*Arthvigyan*
Semblance of the face	*Mukharee*
Semen	*Veery, Shukr*
Semi-circle	*Ardhvritt*
Semi-diameter	*Ardhvyas*

Semi-final	*Upantik*
Seminary	*Gurukul*
Semitic	*Samee*
Senate	*Seenat*
Senator	*Seenator*
Send	*Pathana*
(to) send	*Bhajna*
(to) send for	*Mangana*
Sender	*Preshak*
Senile	*Burbak, Jarajeern*
Senility	*Burbhas, Vardhakky*
Senior	*Seeniyar*
Seniority	*Jyeshthta, Varishthta*
Seniormost	*Varishth*
Sensation	*Samvedan, Sansanee*
Sensational	*Sansaneekhaj*
Sensationless	*Cetnashoony*
Sense	*Hosh, Karnendriy, Gyanendriy*
Sense of duty	*Kartavy gyan*
Sense-organ of touch	*Sparshendriy*
Senseless	*Madhoshee, Besamjhee, Buddhirahit*
Sensible	*Sujan, Samavedeeny, Samajhdar*
Sensitive	*Sugrahee, Samvedansheel*
Sensitivity	*Sugrahita*
Sensory	*Sanvedik, Indriyjany*
Sensual	*Aindrik, Vishayee*
Sensual desire	*Indriy vasna*
Sensual love	*Ulfat*
Sensual pleasure	*Indriy-sukh, Vishay-sukh*
Sensuality	*Indriy-lipsa, Vishay-vasna*
Sentence	*Vakky*
Sentiment	*Manobhavna, Bhavna, Bhavnatmak*
Sentimental	*Bhavuk, Jazbatee, Bhavatmak*

Sentiments	*Jazbat*
Separable	*Viccheddy, Viyojjy*
Separate	*Juda*
(to) separate	*Algana*
(to) separate	*Bilagana*
Separated away	*Chinn*
Separation	*Viyog, Parthakky, Algaw, Judaee*
Separative	*Viyogatmak*
September	*Sitambar*
Sequence	*Parampar, Anukram, Tartamy*
Seraglio	*Antahpur*
Sergeant	*Sarjant, Havaldar*
Serial	*Dharavahik*
Serial number	*Kram sankhya*
Serially	*Nambarvar*
Series of articles	*Lakhmala*
Series of incidents	*Ghatnavalee*
Series of tinkling	*Chanchan*
Serious	*Gambheer*
Sermon	*Dharmopadesh*
Sermoniser	*Updeshak, Pravacak*
Serpent	*Ahi, Sanp*
Serpent power	*Kundalinee*
Serpentine	*Sarpil*
Servant	*Sevak, Naukar*
Serve	*Parasna*
Service	*Chakri*
Service book	*Sevapanjee*
Serving bowl	*Donga*
Serving the purpose for the time being	*Kamchalaoo*
Servitude	*Dasbhav*
Sesame	*Til*

Session	*Satr, Adhivaashan*
Set	*Kulak*
(to) set a dog after a game	*Lashkarna*
(to) set free	*Chorna*
Set in flow	*Pravahit*
Set of musical instrument	*Saz*
Set of rules	*Niyamavalee*
Set-square	*Koniya, Goniya*
Settle	*Nibarna*
(to) settle down	*Basna*
Settlement	*Nibara, Upnivesh, Niptara*
Settling down	*Jamaw*
Seven	*Sat*
Seven notes of music	*Saptswar*
Seven times	*Satguna*
Seven worlds	*Saptlok*
Seventeen	*Sattreh*
Seventh month of the Hindu calender	*Kwar*
Seventy	*Sattar*
Seventy-four	*Cauhattar*
Seventy-nine	*Unnasee*
Seventy-one	*Ikhattar*
Seventy-seven	*Sathattar*
Seventy-six	*Chihattar*
Seventy-three	*Tihattar*
Seventy-two	*Bahattar*
Several	*Anek, Kaee*
Severe	*Cilla, Darun*
Severe blow	*Vajraghat*
Severity	*Darunta*

Sew	*Tankna*
(to) sew in long stitches	*Tagna*
Sewer	*Nalee, Moree*
Sex associate	*Sahcaree*
Sex organ	*Jannendriy*
Sex psychology	*Yaun manoviggyan*
Sex-appeal	*Kam-prarna*
Sex-indulgence	*Yaunacar*
Sex-indulgent	*Yaunacree, Yaunacarik*
Sex-urging	*Kamottejak*
Sexology	*Ratishastr, Kamshastr, Kokshastr*
Sexual	*Laingik*
Sexual attraction	*Yaunakarshan*
Sexual desire	*Kamvasna*
Sexual function	*Yaundharm*
Sexual gratification	*Yauntripti*
Sexual perversion	*Yaunvikkritti*
Sexual relation	*Yaunsambandh*
Sexual urge	*Yaunbhavna*
Shabbily dress	*Phateecar*
Shade	*Rangat, Chanh, Chaya*
Shadow	*Chaya, Parchaeen*
Shadowgraph	*Chaya-citr*
Shady	*Sayadar*
Shagginess	*Jhabrapan*
Shaggy	*Jhabra*
Shake	*Siharna*
(to) shake off dust	*Jharna*
Shaky	*Danvandol*
Shallow	*Uthla, Occha*
Shallow dish	*Capnee*
Shallowness	*Halkapan, Occhapan*

Shame	*Dhat, Sharmindgee*
Shameful	*Lajjajanak, Sharmnak*
Shameless	*Lajjaheen, Besharm, Nirlajj, Begairat*
Shamelessness	*Behayaee, Nangapan, Besharmee*
Shape	*Daul*
Shape of things	*Banak*
Shape resulting from erosion	*Kataw*
Shaped	*Roop, Sakàr*
Shapely	*Sudaul*
Share	*Ansh, Shaar*
Shareholder	*Patteedar*
Sharing of crop	*Bataee*
Sharp	*Paina, Tez, Teekha,*
Sharp pain	*Cilak*
Sharp sound	*Patak*
Sharp-edged	*Kateela, Dhardar*
Sharp-tongued	*Zabandaraz*
Sharper	*Caniyan, Tanc*
Sharpness	*Tazee, Prakharta*
Shattered	*Jarjarit*
Shave	*Kshaur*
(to) shave	*Moorna*
Shave and hair-cut	*Hajamat*
Shaved	*Mundit*
Shawl	*Shal, Dushala*
She-calf of a buffalo	*Bachiya, Pariya*
She-companion	*Sathin*
She-elephant	*Hathnee*
She-goat	*Bakre*
She-hobgoblin	*Curail*
She-mule	*Khacharee*

She-peacock	*Mayooree*
She-pig	*Sookaree*
She-quail	*Bataree*
Sheath	*Myan*
Shed	*Sayban, Osara, Shad*
Shed for storing straw	*Khonpa*
Sheep	*Bhar, Mash*
Sheer obstinacy	*Hathdharmee*
Sheet	*Phalak*
Sheet of metal	*Pattar*
Sheet of water	*Jalcadar*
Shell	*Kavac*
Shell of an oyster	*Seep*
Shellac	*Capra*
Shelter	*Ashshray*
Shelterless	*Bapanah*
Shepherd	*Garariya*
Shesh Nag	*Dharneedhar*
Shield	*Jaycihn*
Shift	*Khiskana, Palee*
Shimmer	*Jilmilana*
Shine	*Camkana*
(to) shine scorchingly	*Cilcilana*
Shining	*Camakdar, Jhakajhak, Camcam*
Shiny	*Zarbark*
Ship	*Pot, Jalyan, Jahaz*
Shipwreck	*Potdhwans*
Shirker	*Kamchor*
Shirt	*Kameej*
Shiver with cold	*Thithurna*
Shivered	*Prakampit*
Shivering	*Kanpkanpi*
Shock	*Sadma, Thes, Jhatka*

Shoe	*Paijar*
Shoe-string	*Tasma*
Shoemaker	*Carmkar*
Shoes	*Juti, Joota*
Shoot	*Gabh, Pallav*
Shooting range	*Candmaree*
Shop	*Dukan, Hattee*
Shopkeeper	*Dukandar*
Short	*Kotah, Hrassw*
Short form	*Laghuroop*
Short formula	*Gur*
Short meal	*Alpahar*
Short tempered	*Badmizaj*
Short term	*Alpavadhik*
Short-lived	*Alpkalik, Kshanjeevee, Alpayu*
Short-sightedness	*Adoordarshita*
Short-statured	*Thigna*
Short-tempered	*Bigrail, Badmizaj*
Shortage	*Kamee*
Shortness	*Alpata*
Shoulder	*Kandha*
Shoulder belt	*Partala*
Shout with for sheer joy	*Kilakana*
Shovel	*Balca*
Show	*Tamasha, Dikhava*
(to) show	*Darsana, Dikhlana, Dikhana*
(to) show anger	*Khunsana*
(to) show restlessness	*Kulkulana*
Shower	*Bauchar*
Shower of fire	*Agnivarsha*
Shower of flowers	*Pushpvarsha*
Showiness	*Natakeeyta*
Showing off	*Adambar*

Showy	*Dikhaoo, Adambarpoorn, Dikhavatee*
Showy conduct	*Bahhyacar*
Shred	*Dhajjee*
Shrink	*Picakna*
Shrivel	*Cucakna*
Shrivelled	*Popla*
Shrub	*Jharee*
Shudder	*Thartharana*
Shuddering	*Thar-thar*
Shuffle (as a pack of cards)	*Phantan*
Shunted away	*Rafa*
Shunting off	*Dhata*
Shut	*Bharna, Moondna*
Shut up	*Hush*
Shy	*Sharmeela, Lajjalu*
(to) shy	*Bidakna*
Shy woman	*Lajvantee, Lajjavati*
Shylock	*Neeboo-nicor*
Shyness	*Hiyaw, Sharmeelapan, Sharmasharmee*
Sibilance	*Seetkar*
Sick	*Beemar*
Sick-bed	*Rogshayya*
Sickle	*Dantee, Hansiya*
Sickly	*Mariyal*
Side	*Or, Paksh*
Side business	*Upvyavsay*
Side sceeen of cloth	*Kanat*
Side-glance	*Kankhiyana*
Side-hero	*Upnayak*
Side-heroine	*Up nayika*
Side-long looks	*Kataksh*

Side-pillow	*Gal takiya*
Side-story	*Kathantar*
Sidereal	*Nakashattr*
Siding	*Parshw*
Sigh	*Ah*
Sight	*Deeth*
Sightly	*Rucir*
Sign	*Nishan*
Sign of discrimination	*Vibhedak-cinh*
Sign of identity	*Cinhanee*
Sign of interrogation (?)	*Prashncihn*
Sign of locative case (gram.)	*Saptmee vibhaktee*
Sign-board	*Sainbord*
Signal	*Sankat, Signal*
Signalled	*Sankatet*
Signalling	*Sankatan*
Signatory	*Hastaksharak*
Signature	*Dastkhat, Hastakshar*
Signed	*Hastaksharit*
Significance	*Ehmiyat*
Significant	*Mahatwpoorn*
Signtoken	*Nishanee*
Silence	*Maun, Khamoshee, Cuppee*
Silent	*Mook, Nishabd, Neerav*
Silent prayer	*Mansee, Maunprarthna*
Silently	*Cupcap*
Silk	*Resham, Silk*
Silken	*Kaushay, Rashmee*
Silken cloth	*Patambar, Patola*
Silver	*Roopa, Candee, Rajat*
Silver jubilee	*Rajat-jayantee*
Silver screen	*Rajatpat*

Silvery	*Rupehla*
Similar	*Samroop, Taisa*
Similarity	*Saroopta, Tadroopta, Samroopta*
Similarly	*Tathaiv*
Simile	*Upma*
Simple	*Riju, Saral*
Simple Interest	*Katvan byaj*
Simple-hearted	*Saleem, Bhola*
Simpleton	*Buddhoo, Sir-billa*
Simplicity	*Seedhapan, Sadgee, Bholapan, Saralta*
Simultaneous	*Yugpat*
Sin	*Gunah*
Since birth	*Ajanm*
Sinew	*Pattha*
Sinful	*Patkee*
Sinful act	*Adharm*
Sinful conduct	*Papacar*
Sinful deed	*Papkarm*
Sinful glance	*Kudrishti*
Sing	*Gana*
(to) sing with close lips	*Gungunana*
Singer	*Gayak, Gata, Gavaiya*
Singer of hymns	*Bhajneek*
Singing of birds	*Pihakna*
Single	*Ikka, Akehra*
Single instalment	*Akmusht*
Single-folded	*Ikehra*
Single-mindedness	*Manoyog*
Singular	*Akvacan*
Sink below	*Capna*
Sinking	*Dhansan*

Sinkling sound	*Chamacham*
Sinner	*Gunehgar*
Sinus	*Naree-vran*
Sip	*Ghoont, Chuskee*
Sir	*Janab*
Sister	*Behan, Bhaginee*
Sister hood	*Behnapa*
Sister's daughter	*Bhanjee*
Sister's husband	*Jeeja*
Sister's son	*Bhanja*
Sistrum	*Jhanjh*
Sita	*Jankee, Vaidehee*
Sitar	*Sitar*
Sitar player	*Sitarvadak*
Site of an accident	*Ghatna sthal*
Sitting	*Upasth, Upvisht*
Sitting for common dinner	*Pangat*
Sitting room	*Baithak*
Situated	*Sthit, Avasthan*
Situated at the centre	*Kandrasth*
Situated near by	*Sameepvartee*
Situated on the bank	*Tatvartee, Teerasth*
Situation	*Sthiti, Avasthan, Naubat*
Six	*Chah*
Six-monthly	*Shanmasik*
Sixer in cricket	*Chakka*
Sixteen	*Soleh*
Sixth	*Chatwan*
Sixth day after birth	*Shashthi*
Sixth day of the lunar fort-night	*Chath*

Sixth month of the Hindu Calender	*Bhadon*
Sixty	*Shashti, Sath*
Sixty-One	*Iksath*
Sixty-five	*Painsath*
Sixty-four	*Caunsath*
Sixty-nine	*Unhattar*
Sixty-seven	*Sarsath*
Sixty-six	*Chiyasath*
Sixty-three	*Tirsath*
Sixty-two	*Basath*
Size	*Akar*
Size and shape	*Akarprakar*
Skeleton	*Kankal, Asthipanjar*
Sketch	*Khaka, Rekhakriti*
Sketching	*Rekha-cittran*
Skewer	*Seekh*
Skilful	*Kushal*
Skilfulness	*Karsazee, Hunarmandee*
Skill	*Hunar, Kaushal, Jauhar*
Skilled	*Nishthant*
Skilled fighter	*Larait*
Skilled in archery	*Dhanurdharee*
Skilled in the art of talking	*Vakpatu*
Skim	*Kachna*
Skimmed milk	*Saprata*
Skin	*Khal, Twaca*
Skin Rash	*Cakatta*
Skin of deer	*Mrig-carm*
Skirt of a garment	*Daman*
Skirt worm by women	*Lehanga*
Skull	*Kapal, Khopra*

Sky	*Vyom, Asman*
Sky-blue	*Asmanee*
Sky-high	*Gagan chumbi*
Sky-scraping	*Cumbee*
Skyscraper	*Abbhrankash*
Slag	*Dhatu-mal*
Slanderer	*Pishun*
Slandering	*Pishunta*
Slanting	*Tircha*
Slap	*Jhapar, Canta, Capat, Thappar, Lappar, Dhaul*
Slapping and boxing	*Dhaul-dhappa*
Slate	*Silet*
Slate-pencil	*Silatee*
Slaughter-house	*Boocarkhana, Kasaeekhana, Vadhalay*
Slaughtered as per Muslim convention	*Halal*
Slave	*Gulam, Das*
Slave girl	*Laundee*
Slave-dealer	*Burdafarosh*
Slavery	*Dasta, Dassy*
Sledge	*Slej*
Sleep	*Nidra, Neend*
Sleep Eternal	*Mahaniddra*
Sleepiness	*Tandra, Supti*
Sleeping	*Shayan*
Sleeping berth	*Shayika*
Sleepless	*Unnidr*
Sleeplessness	*Anidra*
Sleepy	*Nidrit, Uneenda, Tandralu*
Sleeve	*Asteen*
Sleevels	*Sadree*

Sleight-of-hand	*Hastlaghav*
Slender	*Charhara, Tanvangee*
Slender twig-like stick	*Seenk*
Slice of flesh	*Botee*
Slice of melon, mango, orange, etc.	*Phank*
Slight knowledge	*Cancu-pradesh*
Sliminess	*Pankalta*
Slimy	*Pankil*
Sling	*Gophna*
Slip	*Parca, Slip*
(to) slip	*Tasakna, Tilakna, Phisalna*
(to) slip down	*Dhisarna*
Slipper	*Jootee, Sileepar*
Slipperiness	*Phislan*
Slippers	*Saleepar*
Slippery	*Rapatna*
Sliver	*Caila*
Slogan-monger	*Narabaz*
Sloganeering	*Narabazee*
Slope	*Dhalan, Nican*
Sloping	*Dhaluan*
Sloping land	*Dhakee*
Slough	*Kanchuli*
Sloven	*Phoohar*
Slovenliness	*Phooharpan*
Slow	*Dheema, Manda*
Slow and easy	*Haula-Haula*
Slow and sluggish	*Matthar*
Slowly	*Ahista, Jhirjhir*
Slowness	*Mandta*
Sluggish	*Kahil, Leecar*
Slum	*Gandee bastee*

Slump	*Mandee*
Slyness	*Makkaree*
Small	*Chota, Laghu*
Small Indian fruit	*Makoy*
Small Sword	*Tega*
Small bag	*Boree*
Small boil	*Phuriya*
Small box	*Sandookcee, Dibiya, Petee*
Small canal	*Puliya*
Small charcoal oven	*Sigree*
Small chit	*Purzee*
Small coins	*Cillar*
Small cup	*Pyalee*
Small cymbal	*Kartal*
Small dagger	*Khanjar*
Small disc	*Tava*
Small dove	*Tutroon*
Small drill	*Barmee*
Small drum	*Dholak*
Small earthen bowl	*Kullhar, Kulhiya*
Small earthen pitcher	*Matkee*
Small earthen pot used for cooking	*Handiya*
Small flag	*Jhandee*
Small flask	*Kuppee*
Small girl	*Muniyan*
Small hammer	*Hathoree*
Small hoe	*Kudalee*
Small hole	*Jhiree*
Small in quantity	*Tanmatr*
Small ladle	*Paunee*
Small lamp	*Dalee*
Small lid	*Dhaknee*

Small mark	*Cittee*
Small market	*Bajar*
Small pail	*Dolcee*
Small palanquin	*Dolee*
Small pannier	*Pitaree*
Small part	*Alpansh*
Small patch	*Cippee*
Small pebble	*Roree*
Small pestle	*Batiya, Mooslee*
Small piece	*Tukree*
Small pieces of sugarcane	*Gandari*
Small pile	*Gaddee, Dheree*
Small pincers	*Cimtee*
Small pit	*Garhaiya*
Small pitcher	*Gagri*
Small pitcher with a spout	*Jharee*
Small plank	*Takhtee*
Small receptacle for keeping vermilion	*Sindoordanee*
Small register	*Panjika*
Small room	*Kothree*
Small round lump	*Pindee*
Small shirt of a baby	*Jhangula*
Small shot	*Charra*
Small spade	*Phavree*
Small spindle	*Taklee*
Small star	*Tarika*
Small stringed instrument	*Kingiree*
Small tank with steps all around	*Bavlee*

Small tent	*Ravtee, Choldaree*
Small thick loaf baked on fire	*Tikree*
Small tract of land	*Tappa*
Small village	*Pura, Khera*
Small waterfall	*Nirjharinee*
Small-boat	*Dingee, Dongee*
Small-comb	*Kanghee*
Small-cot	*Khatola*
Smallest	*Laghutam*
Smallish	*Khurd*
Smallish cot	*Khatolee*
Smallish distillery	*Haulee*
Smallish nail	*Makh*
Smallness	*Laghuttw*
Smallpox	*Sheetla*
Smart	*Cashakna, Cilakna, Teesna*
Smarting pain	*Cinak, Tees*
Smarting sensation	*Kachot*
Smashing retort	*Munh-tor*
Smatterer	*Pallavgrahee*
Smear	*Leepna*
Smeared with oil or ghee	*Roganee*
Smell	*Mahak*
(to) smell	*Soonghna*
Smell of rawness	*Kachayandh*
Smelly	*Gandheela*
Smile	*Muskan, Smilti*
(to) smile	*Muskrana*
Smiling	*Smit, Sassmit*
Smoke	*Dhooma, Dhuna, Dhoom*
(to) smoke	*Gurgurana*

Smoke-coloured	*Dhoomil*
Smokiness	*Dhoomilta*
Smoking	*Dhoomrpan*
Smoking pipe	*Nigalee*
Smoky	*Dhuansa*
Smooth	*Cikkna, Snigdh*
Smoothen	*Ciknana*
Smoothness	*Snigdhta*
Smoulder	*Sulagna*
Smuggler	*Taskar*
Smutty	*Behooda*
Snacks	*Cooran-Catnee*
Snail	*Ghongha, Shambu*
Snake	*Bhujang, Sarp, Vyal*
Snake poisnous	*Vishdhar*
Snake-bite	*Sarpdansh*
Snake-charmer	*Sapera*
Snake-hill	*Bambee*
Snare	*Phanda*
Snares of illusions	*Bhramjal*
Snares of life	*Bhavjal*
Snatch	*Cheenna, Jhatakna*
Snatched	*Chinna*
Sneer	*Bickana*
Sneeze	*Cheenk*
(to) sneeze	*Cheenkna*
Snooze	*Oongh*
Snore	*Gharrata*
Snoring	*Kharrata*
Snout	*Thobra, Tund, Thuthna*
Snout of an animal	*Thoothan*
Snow	*Him, Tuhin, Barf*
Snow-capped	*Himavrit*

Snow-covered	*Himacchadit*
Snow-fall	*Himpat, Himvarsha*
Snow-line	*Himrekha*
Snow-man	*Himmanav*
Snow-white	*Himshvet*
Snowy	*Barfanee*
Snuff	*Sunghnee, Nas, Nasvar, Nassy*
Snuff-case	*Nasdanee*
So be it !	*Tathastu*
So that	*Taki*
So-called	*Tatha-kathit*
Soaked	*Or-prot, Tarbatar*
Soaked in sentiment	*Ras-bheena*
Soap	*Sabun*
Soap-case	*Sabun danee*
Soap-nut	*Reetha*
Soap-stone	*Gorapathar*
Sob	*Thusakna*
(to) sob	*Sisakna*
(to) sob faintly	*Subukna*
Sober	*Sanjeeda*
Sobriety	*Sanjeedgee*
Sociability	*Milansaree*
Sociable	*Milansar*
Social	*Samajee, Samajik*
Social contacts	*Rusookh*
Social dealings	*Vartan, Len-den*
Social dinner	*Preetibhoj*
Social formality	*Lokopcar*
Social reform	*Samaj-sudhar*
Social service	*Samaj-seva*
Social worker	*Samaj-sevak*
Socialistic	*Samajvadee*

Sociality	*Samajikta*
Socialization	*Samajeekaran*
Society	*Samaj*
Sociological	*Samajshastreey*
Sociologist	*Samajshastree*
Sociology	*Samajshastr*
Socks	*Moza, Jurrab*
Soda	*Soda*
Soda-water	*Sodawatar*
Sodium	*Shora*
Sodomy	*Laundabazee*
Sofa set	*Sofasat*
Soft	*Mulayam, Komal, Naram*
Soft and smooth	*Gudguda*
Soft fine wool	*Pasmina*
Soft green grass	*Doorva*
Soft hair on the body	*Rom, Roan, Rongta*
Soft-tongued	*Mridubhashee*
Softness	*Mulayamiyat, Komalta, Narmee*
Sojourn	*Kayam*
Sojourner	*Utpravasee*
Solace	*Tasallee, Santwana*
Solar	*Saur*
Solar day	*Saur divas*
Solar dynasty	*Soorryvansh*
Solar eclipse	*Soorrygrahan*
Solar month	*Saur mas*
Solar system	*Saur jagat, Saur mandal*
Solar year	*Saurvarsh*
Sold	*Farokht*
Solder	*Jhalna*
Soldering	*Jhal, Tanka*
Soldier	*Sainik*

Soldierly	*Sipahiyana*
Sole	*Padtal, Talva*
Solicitation	*Nihora*
Solid	*Thos*
Soliloquy	*Swagat-kathan*
Solitary	*Aikakee*
Solitary cell	*Kalkothree*
Solitude	*Aikant, Aikantta*
Solstice	*Ayanant*
Solubility	*Vilayta, Ghulansheelta*
Soluble	*Vilaysheel, Ghulansheel*
Solution	*Ghol, Nirakaran*
Solvency	*Shodh-kshamta*
Some	*Kucch*
Some-what	*Yatkincit*
Somehow or other	*Yan kanprakaran*
Someone	*Koee*
Somersault	*Kalabazee*
Somersaulting pigeon	*Girehbaz*
Something kept on trust	*Thatee*
Sometimes	*Gahabagaha*
Somewhere	*Kaheen*
Son	*Sut, Beta, Putr, Poot*
Son of	*Vald*
Son-inlaw	*Damad, Jamaee, Janvaee*
Song	*Geet, Tarana*
Song in urdu poetry	*Kavvalee*
Song sung on ceremonial occasions	*Mangalgan*
Soon	*Sheegghr*
Sooner or later	*Dar-sabar*
Soothed	*Pharehra*
Soothsayer	*Saguniya*

Sophistication	*Nafasat*
Sorceress	*Bhanmatee, Jadoogarnee*
Sorcery	*Jadoogaree*
Sorrow	*Shok, Dukh, Ranj*
Sorrowful	*Dukhmay, Shokmay*
Sorrowful story	*Dukhra*
Soul	*Rooh, Jeevatma*
Soul Universal	*Sarvatma*
Sound	*Niramay, Swan, Dhwani*
Sound of a big drum	*Dhamdham*
Sound like cracking	*Karkar*
Sound made by a lash	*Satak*
Sound of a conch	*Shankhdhwani*
Sound of a drum	*Dhamak*
Sound of air movement	*Sarsrahat*
Sound of bells	*Tantan*
Sound of clicking teeth	*Katkat*
Sound of cracking	*Karka*
Sound of dripping water	*Taptap*
Sound of eating	*Kachar-kachar*
Sound of hubble-bubble	*Gurgurahat*
Sound of rain drops	*Tip-Tip*
Sound of water flow	*Jharjhar*
Sound produced by a heavy blow	*Ghamaka*
Sound wave	*Dhwani-tarang*
Soup	*Rasa, Shorba*
Sour	*Khatta*
Sour and rather pungent fruit	*Kamrakh*
Source	*Srot, Udgam, Akar, Uts*

Source language	*Akarbhasha*
Source of income	*Aysrot*
Source-Book	*Akargranth*
Sourness	*Khatai*
South	*Dakkhin, Dakshin*
South Indian spiced curry	*Sanbar*
South pole	*Kumaru*
Southern	*Dakkhinee, Dakshinee*
Sovereign	*Samprabhu*
Sovereign king	*Chattrapati*
Sovereignty	*Rajsatta, Samprabhuta*
Sow	Bona
Sowing	*Vapan*
Sowing seeds	*Beejaropan*
Soyabean	*Soyabeen*
Space	*Gunjaish*
Space ship	*Antariksh yan*
Space travel	*Antariksh yatra*
Spacing	*Antaran*
Spacious sitting room	*Baithka*
Spade	*Phavra*
Span	*Pat*
Spangle affixed on the forehead	*Tikulee*
Spark	*Cingaree, Sphuling*
Sparkle	*Bhasna*
(to) sparkle with brilliance	*Jhaljhalana*
Sparrow	*Gauraiya, Ciriya*
Sparsely woven	*Jhillar*
Spastic	*Akarshee*
Speak out	*Pharmana*

(to) speak with a nasal accent	*Nakiyana*
Speaker	*Speekar, Vakta, Vartakar*
Spear	*Barcha, Bhala*
Special	*Vishash, Khas*
Special issue	*Visheshank*
Special officer	*Vishsehadhikaree*
Specialised	*Vishesheekrit*
Specialist	*Visheshaggy*
Speciality	*Vishishtta, khasiyat*
Specialization	*Vishesheekaran*
Specially	*Visheshta*
Specked	*Dageela*
Spectacles	*Ainak*
Spectator	*Darshak, Tamashaee*
Speculation	*Satta, Phatka, Phatkebazee*
Speech	*Vanee, Vaktrita, Takreer, Bhashan*
Speechless	*Avak, Nihshabd*
Speed	*Speed, Sapata, Vag, Raftar*
Speed-breaker	*Gatirodh*
Speedometer	*Vagmapee*
Speedy	*Ashu, Sheeghragamee*
Spell	*Mohinee*
Spell-down	*Mantr-mugdh*
Spelling	*Hijja, Aksharee, Vartanee*
Spend	*Kharchna, Bitana*
Spending	*Yapan*
Spending of time	*Kalyapan*
Spendthrift	*Ujaroo*
Spent	*Sarf*
Spermatozoon	*Shukkranu*
Spherical Astronomy	*Khagol vigyan*
Spice	*Chaunkna*

Spicing *Chaunkan*
Spick and span *Cak-cauband*
Spicy *Masaledar*
Spicy and delicious *Catpata*
Spider *Loota*
Spider's web *Jala, Makar-jal*
Spike *Shookee*
Spill *Chalakna*
Spin *Katna*
Spinal *Merudandeey*
Spinal cord *Merurajju*
Spindle *Takua, Takla*
Spineless *Reerhheen*
Spinning *Kataee*
Spinning and weaving *Kataee bunaee*
Spinning house *Kataee ghar*
Spinning top *Lattoo*
Spinster *Kishoree*
Spirit *Antaratma*
Spirit of renunciation *Vairaggy-bhav*
Spirit of service *Savabhav*
Spiritism *Pratviddya*
Spiritual *Atmik, Addhyatmik*
Spiritual power *Atmbal*
Spiritualism *Adhatmikee*
Spirituous liquor *Amrita*
Spit *Thookna*
Spite *Asooya*
Spitoon *Ugaldan*
Spittle *Peek, Ugal, Thook*
Spittoon *Peekdan*
Splash *Cheenta*
Splashing sound *Chap, Chapaka*

Splendid	*Bhavvy, Shobhamay*
Splendour	*Bhavvyta, Thath*
Splint	*Khapcee, Captee*
Splinter	*Kircha*
Split	*Phoot, Khandit*
Split up	*Vikhandit*
Splitting	*Vikhandan*
Spoil	*Bigarna*
Spoilage	*Bantadhar*
Spoilt	*Caupat*
Spoken	*Bhashit*
Spokesman	*Pravakta*
Sponge	*Spanj*
Spongy	*Ispanjee, Spanjee*
Spool of thread	*Anta*
Spoon	*Camca*
Sport	*Kreera*
Sportive	*Khilar*
Sportiveness	*Tabeeyatdaree*
Sports	*Khelkood*
Sportsmanship	*Khilareepan*
Spot	*Dhabba, Dag*
(to) spot out	*Lakhna*
Spotless	*Akalank*
Spotted	*Bundeedar, Citkabra, Citteedar*
Spotted antelope	*Ceetal*
Spotted panther	*Ceeta*
Sprain	*Moc*
Sprawling	*Antachit*
Spray	*Tahnee*
Spread	*Pasarna, Phailna*
(to) spread out	*Phailana, Bichana*
Spreading out	*Vispharit, Vispharan*

Spring	*Basant, Jharna, Rituraj*
Spring crop	*Rabee*
Spring festival	*Vasantotsav*
Spring in a watch	*Balkamanee*
Spring of water	*Sota*
Spring season	*Naubahar*
Spring season	*Vasant, Madhuritu*
Sprinkle	*Chirakna*
(to) sprinkle	*Burakna*
Sprituality	*Adhyatmikta*
Sprout	*Konpal*
Sprouting twig	*Kanaee*
Spun thread	*Kata*
Spy	*Bhediya*
Squabble	*Kichkich*
Squad	*Dasta*
Squaint-eyed	*Bhanga*
Squander	*Lutana*
Squanderer	*Uraookhaoo*
Square	*Caukor*
Square garden	*Carbag*
Square root	*Vargmool*
Square shape	*Vargakar*
Square-measure	*Kshettrphal*
Squared	*Vargit, Vargankit*
Squaring	*Vargkaran*
Squarred	*Pata*
Squash guord	*Kasheephal*
Squat	*Palthee*
Squatting	*Palthee*
Squeak	*Cuncunana*
Squeeze	*Garna, Nicorna*
(to) squeeze out	*Duhna*

Squint-eyed	*Tirpata*
Squirrel	*Gilehri*
Stabbing with a dagger	*Churebazee*
Stability	*Sthayittw, Tikaw, Thirta*
Stabilization	*Sthireekaran*
Stable	*Tabela, Astabal, Ghursal*
Stable for cows	*Goshala*
Stable for elephants	*Hathikhana*
Staff	*Staf*
Stag	*Barahsinga*
Stage	*Staj, Rangshala, Rangmanc, Manc, Rangkshetr*
Stage shyness	*Manc-sankoc*
Stage-manager	*Sootrdhar*
Stageability	*Abhinayta*
Stagger	*Latpatana*
Staggering gait	*Larkharahat*
Staging	*Mancan*
Stainless	*Bedag*
Staircase	*Zeena, Sopan*
Stake	*Khoonta, Danw*
Stalemate	*Zic*
Stalk	*Danthal*
Stall	*Stal, Khokha*
Stamen	*Pushpraj, Parag kesar*
Stamina	*Jeevat*
Stammer	*Haklana*
Stammering	*Haklana*
Stamp	*Stamp*
Stampede	*Bhagdar*
Standard	*Darja, Manak*
Standard of living	*Jeevan-star*
Standard bearer	*Nishanbardar*

Standardised	*parinishthit*
Standardization	*Manakeekaran*
Standarized	*Manakit*
Standing	*khara*
Standing committee	*Sthaee samiti*
Standing crop	*Kharee phasal*
Star	*Tara, Sitara*
Star-like tiny metallic objects	*Camkee*
Starch	*Shwatsar, Kalaf, Mand*
Stare	*Ghoorna*
(to) stare with anger	*Gurarna*
Starred	*Tarankit*
Stars	*Taragan*
Starvation	*Faka*
State	*Stat, Rajy, Daur, Prithakta*
State affairs	*Rajkaj*
State official	*Rajpurush*
Stated	*Kathit*
Stately	*Riyasatee*
Statement	*Bayan, Kathan*
Statesman	*Rajkarta, Rajneta*
Static	*Sthaitik, Sthitisheel*
Station	*Stashan*
Station-Master	*Stashanmaster*
Statue	*Pratima, Moorti*
Statue in stone	*Pashan-pratima*
Status	*Haisiyat, Aukat*
Statute	*Pravidhan, Samvidhi*
Statutory	*Samvidhik, Pravidhanik*
Stay (for a while)	*Tikna*
(to) stay temporarily	*Thaharna*
Stay as guest	*Mahmanee*

Staying place of a marriage party	*Janjghar*
Steady	*Sthavir, Nispand, Taktakee, Nishpad*
Steady warrior	*Randheer*
Steal	*Curana*
Stealer of the heart	*Citcor*
Stealing	*Coree*
Stealthily	*Coree-chipa*
Steam	*Steem, Bhap, Vashp*
Steamer	*Steemar*
Steel	*Ispat, Faulad*
Steep ascent	*Kharee charhaee*
Steep rise	*Uchala*
Steeped in cruelty	*Kroortapoorn*
Steeped in dust	*Dhool-dhoosarit*
Steeped in emotion	*Bhav-bheenee*
Steeple	*Lat*
Stem	*Vrint*
Stem of a flower	*Pushpdand*
Stench	*Bisayandh*
Stength	*Sabalta*
Step	*Dag, Pairee*
Step-brother	*Kathbhaee*
Step-father	*Kathbap*
Step-mother	*Upmata, Vimata*
Step-son	*Taraila*
Stepped	*Sopanit*
Sterile	*Bandhy, Vandhy*
Sterility	*Bandhyattw*
Stick	*Lakutee, Charee, Yashti*
(to) stick	*Cipakna*
Stick used for beating a drum	*Dag*

Stickiness	*Las, Laseelapan*
Stickiness viscosity	*Cipcip*
Sticking to principles	*Siddhantvad*
Sticky	*Laseela, Lesdar, Cipcipa, Lapteela*
Sticky pith	*Luab*
Stiff	*Kara*
Stiffen	*Lakrana*
Stigma	*Kalank*
Stigmatized	*Lanchit*
Still	*Cittrvat, Thir, Nistabdh*
Still more	*Mazeed*
Still-born	*Mritjat*
Stimulated	*Uddept*
Sting	*Dank, Dansh*
(to) sting	*Dasna, Danshna*
Stinking	*Badboodar*
Stipend	*Vazeefa*
Stippling	*Bindu-citran*
Stir	*Halchal*
(to) stir with fingers	*Rolna*
Stirred	*Alorit*
Stirrup	*Rakab*
Stitch	*Tankna, Tanka*
(to) stitch	*Goothna, Silna*
Stitched	*Gathna*
Stitching	*Silaee*
Stock	*Zakheera, Stak*
Stomach	*Udar, Amashay*
Stone	*Pashan, Pahan*
Stone age	*Pashan yug*
Stone bow	*Gulal*
Stone hearted	*Pashanhriday*
Stone of a fruit	*Guthlee*

Stone pestle and flat stone	*Sil-batta*
Stone pieces	*Gittee*
Stone which absorbs poison	*Zeharmohra*
Stone-bowman	*Gulalchi*
Stone-fruit	*Guthleephal*
Stone-hearted	*Sangdil, Vajrhriday*
Stone-throwing	*Patthar-bazee*
Stony	*Pathreela*
Stool	*Caukee, Stool*
Stop	*Rukna*
(to) stop	*Thamna*
(to) stop suddenly	*Thithakna*
Stop press	*Chapta-chapta*
Stopper	*Thapee, Dat*
Store	*Agar, Bhandar*
Store house	*Kothar, Bhandar ghar, Malkhana*
Store-keeper	*Bhandaree*
Storey	*Mehla, Talla, Manzil*
Storm	*Toofan, Jhanjhavat*
Stormy	*Toofanee*
Story	*Kissa, Kahanee, Katha*
Story-writer	*Kahaneekar, Kathakar*
Stout	*Patha, Sanda*
Stout and robust	*Sand-musand, Hrisht-pusht*
Stout walking stick	*Sonta*
Stove	*Stov*
Straight	*Seedha, Pranjal*
Straight forwardness	*Arjav*
Straightness	*Seedh, Pranjalta*
Straining through cloth	*Kaparchan*
Strand	*Lar*

Strange	*Vichittr, Nirala, Ajeeb*
Stranger	*Aparichit*
Stratagem	*Tikram*
Stratagem to ensnare someone	*Kapat jal*
Strategem	*Tor-jor*
Stratification	*Staran*
Straw	*Pual, Trin, Khar, Tinka*
Straw board	*Gatta*
Straw mat	*Sheetal-patee*
Stray	*Chutphut*
Strayed	*Bhoola-bhatka*
Stream	*Sarita, Jaldhar, Dhara*
Stream of tears	*Ashshrudhara*
Street	*Galee*
Strengeth	*Mazbootee, Damkham, Takat, Samarthy*
Strength and weakness	*Balabal*
Strenuousness	*Shramsaddhyta*
Stretch as a string	*Tanna*
Stretching of limbs	*Angraee*
Strictness	*Karai*
Stride	*Phal*
Strike	*Hartal*
(to) strike with the beak	*Thongna*
Striker	*Hartalee*
Striking range	*Jhapat*
String	*Dor, Doree*
String for tying garments etc.	*Tanee*
String tied to a kite	*Nakh, Kanna*
Stringed	*Taneedar*

Stringed instrument	*Tantuvaddy*
Stroll	*Ghoomna, Cehelna, Tahalna*
Stroll for pleasure	*Cehel kadmee*
Strong	*Majboot, Utkat, Balvatee*
Strong aversion	*Cirh*
Strong desire	*Ashna*
Strong desire to live	*Jijeevisha*
Strong gale	*Candvat*
Strong-headed	*Dabang*
Struck by misfortune	*Museebatzada*
Structural	*Sanracnatmak*
Structure	*Gathan, Sanracna*
Structure having twelve entrances	*Barahdaree*
Structure of body	*Deeldaul*
Struggle	*Sangharsh, Kashmakash*
Struggle for existence	*Jeevan-sangharsh*
Strumpet	*Janpad-kalyanee*
Strut	*Matak, Ithlana*
(to) strut	*Matakna*
Stubbed with jewels	*Jarit*
Stubborn	*Ardar, Ziddee*
Studded	*Jaraoo*
Student	*Shiksharthee, Chatr, Viddyarthee*
Studied	*Pathit, Swadheet*
Study	*Addhyayan*
(to) study	*Parhna-likhna*
Study room	*Addhyayan kaksh*
Studying	*Parhaee*
Stuff	*Bhara*
(to) stuff	*Thoosna*
Stunned	*Sann*
Stupefaction	*Stabdhta*

Stupefied	*Stabdh*
Stupid	*Abuddhi, Ehmak*
Stupid person	*Aundhi-khopree, Ghancakkar, Cugad*
Stupidity	*Dadhapan, Jarima, Pongapanthee*
Stupor due to illusion	*Mohniddra*
Sturdy youth	*Tandail*
Sty	*Bilnee*
Style	*Shailee, Dharra, Nihanee*
Style of singing	*Gayakee*
Sub-Soil	*Antarbhoomi*
Sub-branch	*Prashakha*
Sub-clause	*Updhara*
Sub-committee	*Upsamiti*
Sub-continent	*Upmahadweep*
Sub-department	*Upvibhag*
Sub-division	*Upbhad, Prabhag, Vibhed*
Sub-editor	*Upsampadak*
Sub-inspector (of Police)	*Thanedar*
Sub-rule	*Upniyam*
Sub-tenant	*Shikmee*
Sub-title	*Upsheershak*
Subconscious	*Avcetan, Upcetan*
Subject	*Raiyat, Mazmoon, Vishay*
Subject index	*Vishyamukramanika*
Subject matter	*Vishayvastu*
Subjection	*Parashray*
Subjective	*Atmnishth, Vyaktinishth*
Subman	*Avmanav*
Submarine	*Pandubbee*
Submerged	*Jalmagn, Pariplavit*
Submerged in water	*Jalmay*
Submissive	*Vashshy*

Submissiveness	*Vashshyta*
Subordinate	*Matehat*
Subordination	*Matehtee*
Subsantially	*Tatwatah*
Subsequent	*Parvartee*
Subservient	*Tabedar, Parvesh*
Subsidiary	*Gaun*
Subsidiary occupation	*Upjeevika*
Subsidy	*Updan*
Subsistence	*Nirvah, Guzara*
Substantial	*Tatwik, Sarvan*
Substantial derangement	*Laut-phar*
Substitute	*Avzee*
Substituted	*Pratisthapit*
Substitution	*Pratisthapan, Sthanapatti*
Subtracted	*Vyakalit*
Subtraction	*Vyavkalan*
Suburb	*Upnagar*
Suburban	*Upnagareey*
Success	*Kamyabi, Safalta*
Successful	*Safal, Kamyab*
Succession	*Uttaradhikar*
Succession of events	*Ghatna-kram*
Successive	*Anupoorvee, Uttarottar*
Successor	*Uttaradhikaree*
Such and such	*Amuk*
Such as son	*Angaj*
Suck	*Sokhna*
(to) suck	*Coosna*
Sucked	*Cooshit*
Sucking	*Adharpan*
Suckling (baby)	*Dudhmunha*

Suction	*Coosan*
Sudden	*Akasmik*
Suddenly	*Phak, Acanak, Akaek*
Suddenness	*Aikasmikta*
Suddently	*Aikbargee*
Suffer	*Bhogna*
Suffering	*Dukhbhog*
Suffering from old age	*Jaragrast*
Sufficiency	*Yathastta, Poor, Paryapta*
Sufficient	*Alam, Yathasht*
Suffix	*Pratyay*
Suffocation	*Ghutan*
Sugar	*Ceenee, Shakar*
Sugar candy	*Misree*
Sugar uprocessed	*Khandasaree*
Sugarcake in round shape	*Batasa*
Sugarcane	*Eekh, Ganna*
Suggest	*Sujhana*
Suggested meaning	*Vyanjana*
Suggestion	*Sujhav*
Suicidal	*Atmghatee, Atmghatak*
Suicide	*Atmghat, Atmhatya*
Suit	*Soot*
(to) suit nicely	*Phabna*
Suit law court	*Vad*
Suit-case	*Sootkes*
Suitability	*Phaban*
Suitable for journey	*Safree*
Suitably	*Yathayoggy*
Sulphur	*Gandhak*
Sultan	*Sultan*
Sultriness	*Umas*

Sum	*Rakam*
Summary	*Upsanhar*
Summer season	*Greeshmkal, Greeshm ritu*
Summer solstice	*Uttarayan*
Summer vacation	*Greeshmavakash*
Summit	*Shring*
Summons	*Talbee, Samman*
Sump	*Cehbacca*
Sun	*Ravi, Bhaskar, Suray*
Sun and shade	*Dhoop-chanh*
Sun-bath	*Dhoop-snan*
Sun-dial	*Dhoop- gharee, Sooraj-gharee*
Sun-flower	*Sooraj-mukhee*
Sun-glass	*Dhoop-cashma*
Sun-worship	*Soorryopasna*
Sunday	*Ravivar*
Sundry	*Cutphut*
Sunk	*Gark, Ast, Garak*
Sunlight	*Gham*
Sunrise	*Sooryoday*
Sunset	*Sooryast*
Superficiality	*Setaheepan*
Superficially	*Bala-bala*
Superfluous	*Uparphattoo*
Superfluous talk	*Cabar-cabar*
Superintendent	*Karryadhyaksh*
Superior	*Pravar*
Superlative degree	*Uttamavastha*
Superman	*Atimanav*
Supermind	*Atimanas*
Supernatural	*Alaukik, Lokottar*
Supersonic	*Atiswan*
Superstition	*Andhvishshvas*

Superstitious	*Vehmee*
Superstitious device	*Tona-totka*
Supervision	*Nigranee*
Supervisor	*Paryavakshan*
Supine	*Cit*
Supplanting	*Abhiropan*
Supplement	*Krodhpattr*
Supplementary	*Poorak, Anupooran, Paripoorak*
Suppliancy	*Yacakta*
Suppliant	*Yacak, Prarthee*
Supplicate abjectly	*Ghighiyana*
Supplication	*Minnat, Yacna*
Supplied	*Apoorit*
Supplier	*Sambharak*
Supply	*Sambharan, Praday, Apoorti, Poorti*
Support	*Sahara, Asra*
Support price	*Samarthan moolly*
Supportable	*Samarthaneey*
Supported	*Alambit, Samarthit*
Supported by law	*Vidhisammat*
Supporter	*Samarthak, Himayatee, Dhata, Pakshdhar*
Supporting	*Mandanatmak*
Suppose that	*Jano*
Supposed	*Prakkalpit*
Suppressive	*Damansheel*
Supreme	*Parbrahm*
Supreme being	*Purushottam*
Supreme consciousness	*Cidatma*
Supreme illusion	*Cidvilas*
Surely	*Nissandeh, Shartiya*
Surety	*Zamin*
Surety (person)	*Pratibhoo*

Surface	*Bhootal, Dharatal*
Surge	*Oormi*
Surgeon	*Jarrah*
Surgery	*Ceerphar, Shalycikitsa*
Surpassing	*Barha-carha*
Surprise	*Hairan, Acraj, Tajjub*
Surprising	*Ashcarryjanak*
Surrealism	*Atiyatharthvad*
Surrender	*Atmsamarpan*
Surrendering	*Ghiraw, Arpan*
Surround	*Chankna*
Survey	*Paryavalokan*
Surveying	*Sarvakshan*
Surveyor	*Sarvakshak*
Survival	*Uttarjeevan*
Surviving	*Uttarjeevee*
Survivor	*Atijeevee*
Suspended	*Nilambit, Muatal*
Suspense	*Asmanjas, Duvidha*
Suspense Account	*Uchant khata*
Suspension	*Nilamban*
Suspicion	*Sandeh*
Suspicious	*Sandehjanak*
Suspicious nature	*Shankasheel*
Sustainer	*Bharta*
Sustenance	*Udar poorti*
Swallow	*Garapna, Leelna*
(to) swallow up	*Nigalna*
Swallowed	*Udarasth*
Swallowed up by time	*Kalkavalit*
Swallowing	*Garap, Grasan*
Swan	*Maral, Hans*
Swarthiness	*Sanvlapan*

Swarthy	*Sanvla*
Swastik a sing	*Swastik*
Sway	*Dhak, Bolbala*
Sweat	*Paseena, Swed, Prasved*
Sweater	*Swatar*
Sweating	*Prasvadan*
Sweep	*Buharna*
Sweeper	*Jharoo-bardar, Bhangee, Mehtar*
Sweepings	*Batoran*
Sweet	*Misht*
Sweet baby	*Lalan, Lala*
Sweet charming	*Madhumay*
Sweet chirpings	*Kalrav*
Sweet chum	*Sajnee*
Sweet dish of milk, rice, dry fruit	*Kheer*
Sweet girl	*Lalee*
Sweet in round shap	*Laddoo*
Sweet of wheat flour	*Khurma*
Sweet potato	*Shakarkand*
Sweet prepared with sesame and sugar	*Gazak*
Sweet pumpkin	*Kumhra*
Sweet rippling sound	*Kalkal dhwani*
Sweet smell	*Saurabh*
Sweet variety of lozenge-shaped	*Sakarpara*
Sweet with a tinge of sourness	*Khattameetha*
Sweet-tongued	*Mithbola, Subhashinee*
Sweetened curry of raw mangoes	*Muramba*
Sweetened tonic	*Majoon*

Sweetheart	*Kanta*
Sweetness	*Sureelapan, Mithas, Madhuree, Madhurry*
Sweets	*Mithaee, Mishtann*
Swell	*Umarna, Soojna*
Swelling	*Soojan, Gumta, Shoth*
Swift	*Vagvan*
Swiftly	*Sarrata*
Swiftness	*Sattwarta*
Swim	*Tairna*
Swimmer	*Tairak*
Swimming	*Tairakee*
Swindler	*Thag, Anteebaz*
Swindling	*Bhagal, Ucak ka pan, Thagaee*
Swing	*Pang, Jhoola, Jhulana, Jhoonta*
(to) Swing	*Jhoolna*
Swing adorned with a seat	*Hindola*
Switch	*Swic*
Swollen gland	*Giltee*
Swoop	*Jhapatta*
(to) swoop	*Jhapatna*
Sword	*Shamsheer, Teg, Talvar, Khadg*
Swordstick	*Guptee*
Sycamore	*Goolar*
Sycophancy	*Darbardaree*
Sycophant	*Toree, Jee-huzoor*
Syllabus	*Pathman*
Symbol	*Prateek*
Symbolic	*Sanketik, Prateekatmak, Prateekvadee*
Symbolism	*Prateekvad*
Symmetrical	*Sammit*

Symmetry	*Sammiti, Pratisammy*
Sympathetic	*Dardmand*
Sympathiser	*Hamdard*
Sympathy	*Hamdardee, Sahanubhooti*
Symposium	*Goshthee, Parisamvad*
Symptom	*Lakshan*
Syndicate	*Abhishad*
Synod	*Dharmsabha*
Synonym	*Paryay*
Synonymous	*Paryayvacak*
Synonymy	*Paryaykee*
Synopsis	*Kathasar, Roop-rekha*
Synthesis	*Sanshlashan*
Synthetic	*Sanshlashik*
Syphilis	*Updansh*
Syringe	*Pickaree*
Syrup	*Sharbat*
System	*Pranalee, Kareena, Tantr*
System of education	*Shikshapranalee*
System of slavery	*Daspratha*
System of treatment	*Cikitsa paddhati*
System of ventilation	*Havadaree*
Systematized	*Niyambaddh*

T

Tabla	*Tabla*
Tabla player	*Tabla vadak*
Table	*Sarnee, Mez, Tabul*
Table cloth	*Mezposh*
Table of contents	*Vishay-soocee*
Tablet	*Tikiya, Golee, Vatika, Batee*
Tabor	*Duggee, Damroo*
Taborshaped	*Damroomddhy*
Tacit consent	*Maun-sammati*
Taciturn	*Mit-bhashee*
Tact	*Kainda*
Tactful	*Hikmatee, Jugtee, Neetikushal*
Tactfully	*Yuktipoorvak*
Tactician	*Paintrabaz*
Tactics	*Hathkanda, Chal bal, Paintra*
Tadpole	*Chuchmachlee*
Tail	*Dum, Pucch*
Tailless	*Banda, Lunda*
Tailoring shop	*Darjeekhana*
Take a bath	*Nahana*
Take across	*Tarna, Nistarna*
(to) take around	*Phirana*
(to) take care of	*Sanbhalna*
(to) take liquid through the nose	*Surakna*
(to) take upon one's shoulders	*Kandhna*
Take rest	*Sustana*
Taken	*Griheet*
Taken aback	*Hakka-bakka*
Taking of bribes	*Ghooskhoree*
Taking over by the government	*Sarkareekaran*

Tale	*Akkhyayika*
Tale of general sufferings	*Jagbeetee*
Talent	*Pratibha*
Talented	*Pratibhavan, Pratibhashalee*
Talk	*Carca, Bat*
(to) talk fretfully and loudly	*Jhauhana*
Talkative	*Vacal, Batoonee*
Talked of	*Carcit*
Tall and bulky	*Deerghkay*
Tame	*Posna*
Tamarind	*Imlee*
Tambourine	*Daphlee*
Tangent line	*Sparsh-rekha*
Tangibility	*Sparshneeyta*
Tangible	*Sparshneey*
Tank	*Vapee, Tank, Caubacca, Tankee*
Tanker	*Tankee-jahaz*
Tantalize	*Tarsana*
Tap	*Nal*
Tap-root	*Moosla*
Tape	*Feeta*
Tapping sound	*Patapat*
Target	*Nishana, Laksh*
Tarpaulin	*Tirpal*
Tassel	*Jhabba, Phundna*
Tasselled	*Jhabbadar*
Taste	*Ruci, Zayaka*
(to) taste	*Cakhna*
Tasteless	*Beswad, Feekapan*
Tasty	*Saras, Swadisht*
Tatoo	*Godna*

Tatter	*Latta*
Tattered	*Jeern-sheern*
Tattered dress	*Ceevar*
Tattooer woman	*Godanharee*
Tattooing instrument	*Godnee*
Taunt	*Tana, Mahna*
Tavern	*Kalvariya*
Tawny white	*Kapotee*
Tax	*Kar, Taiks*
Tax free	*Karmukt*
Tax-collector	*Jagatee*
Tax-payer	*Kardata*
Taxable	*Karday*
Taxation	*Karadhan*
Taxicology	*Vish-vigyan*
Taxidermist	*Carmprasadhak*
Tea	*Cay*
Tea party	*Preetigoshthee*
Tea-pot	*Caydanee*
Teach	*Parhana*
Teachable	*Shikshaneey*
Teacher	*Addhyapak, Shikshak*
Teaching	*Shikshan, Pradhyapan*
Teak-wood	*Sagaun*
Tear	*Pharna*
(to) tear to pieces	*Ceethna*
Team	*Tolee, Mandlee*
Team spirit	*Sanghbhawna*
Tear-Gas	*Ashshrugas*
Tearful	*Ashshrupoorn, Dabkaunha*
Tears	*Netrjal, Ashshru*
Tears of joy	*Harshashru, Anand ashshru*
Tears of love	*Pramashshru*

Tease	*Kalpana*
(to) tease	*Khijhana*
(to) tease	*Charna*
Technical	*Pravidhik, Takneekee*
Technicality	*Pravidhikta*
Technician	*Pravidhigy*
Technique	*Takneek, Pravidhi*
Technology	*Shilpkala, Shilpvidya*
Tedium	*Koft*
Teeth set	*Batteesee*
Tele-communication	*Doorsancar*
Telegraph	*Tar, Teligram, Telegraf*
Telegraph office	*Targhar*
Telephone	*Fon, Doorbash, Telifon*
Teleprinter	*Teliprintar*
Telescope	*Doorbeen, Doordarshak*
Tell	*Kehna*
(to) tell off	*Jancna*
Temperamental	*Manmaujee*
Temperance	*Maddytyag*
Temperate	*Samsheetoshn, Matdil, Sheetoshn*
Temperateness	*Sheetoshnata*
Temperature	*Hararat, Tapman, Tapkram*
Tempest	*Ativat*
Temple	*Devsthan, Mandir*
Temple of the ear	*Gandsthal*
Temporary	*Asthayee*
Temptation	*Pralobhan*
Ten	*Das*
Ten incarnation of Lord Vishnu	*Dashavtar*
Ten of playing cards	*Tehla*
Tenaciouslypersevering	*Dhunee*

Tenacity	*Ceemarpan*
Tenancy	*Kiraedaree*
Tenant	*Kiraedar*
Tendency of the mind	*Manogati*
Tender	*Tendar, Nivida*
Tender limbs	*Komalang*
Tender-hearted	*Dayardr*
Tending to falling	*Patansheel*
Tending to go down	*Nicauhan*
Tendon	*Kandara*
Tennis	*Tenis*
Tense	*Tanavpoorn*
Tension	*Tanav, Tanatanee*
Tent	*Khema, Tamboo*
Tent-pin	*Cob*
Tentative	*Prayogik*
Tenth	*Dasham*
Tenth constellation in Hindu Astronomy	*Magha*
Tenth day of a lunar month	*Dashmee*
Tenth month of the Hindi Calender	*Pos*
Tenure	*Padavadhi*
Tenure of Manu	*Manvantar*
Term	*Karyakal*
Term of contempt	*Dhik*
Term of salutation	*Namaste, Namaskar*
Terminal	*Avsanak*
Terminal post	*Seema-chaukee*
Termination	*Avsan*
Terminology	*Paribhashikee*
Termite	*Deemak*

Terms	*Shart*
Terrestrial	*Parthiv*
Terrible	*Bhayankar, Bhayanak*
Terrified	*Trast, Bhayakrant*
Terrifying	*Bhayavna*
Territorial waters	*Jalprangan*
Territory	*Shatr, Prant, Bhoobhag*
Terror	*Atank, Khauf*
Terror stricken	*Atankit*
Terrorism	*Atankvad*
Terrorist	*Atankvadee*
Test	*Janc, Parakh*
(to) test	*Jancna*
Testicle	*Fora*
Testimony	*Praman, Gavahee*
Testing	*Pareekshan*
Tetanus	*Dhanurvat*
Tether	*Pagha*
Tetimony	*Shahadat*
Tetrahedron	*Catushphalak*
Textile factory	*Putlee ghar*
Textual error	*Pathdosh*
Texture	*Binan, Bunavat*
Thank fully	*Sabhar*
Thanks	*Dhannyvad, Shukkriya*
That	*Vah, Ki, Dharit*
That can be	*Niyantavvy*
That is	*Yanee*
That much	*Utna*
That specified	*Falan*
That very	*Usee*
That which joins	*Yojak*
Thatch	*Chana*

Thatched roof	*Chapper, Dhaba*
The sign	*Kakpad*
Theatre	*Rangbhoomi, Thiatar, Nattyashala*
Theism	*Eeshshvarvad*
Theistic	*Astik*
Them	*Inhan, Unnhan*
Then	*To, Tada, Tab*
Theology	*Dharmshastr*
Theomania	*Dharmonmad*
Theorem	*Pramay*
Theoretically	*Siddhantatah*
Theoretician	*Siddhantavadee*
Theorist	*Siddhantagy*
Theosophist	*Thiyasofist*
Theosophy	*Thiyasofee*
There	*Udhar, Vahan*
Therefore	*Sutran, Isliye*
Thermal	*Tapeey*
These	*In*
They themselves	*Unheen*
Thick	*Garha, Ghana*
Thick sweetened milk	*Rabree*
Thicken by boiling	*Autana*
(to) thicken by boiling	*Karhna*
Thickened milk product	*Khoa*
Thickness	*Nivirta*
Thief	*Cor*
Thievish	*Cotta*
Thigh	*Uru, Jangh*
Thin	*Patla, Bareek*
Thin and bony	*Lamboo*

Thin fried saltish pan-cake	*Matthee*
Thin loaf	*Roti, Captee, Phulka*
Thin tube	*Nalika*
Thing	*Ceez, Shai*
Think	*Socna*
(to) think	*Ceetna, Vicarna*
Thinker	*Cintak, Vicarak*
Thinly	*Jheena*
Thinly woven	*Jhirjhira, Jhilmila*
Thinness	*Patla, Bareekee*
Third	*Tray, Teesra, Triteey*
Third day of each half of lunar month	*Triteeya*
Third stage of life	*Vanprasth, Triteeyashshram*
Third time	*Tibara*
Thirst	*Pyas, Trisha, Pipasa*
Thirsty	*Pyasa, Pipasu*
Thirteen	*Trayodash*
Thirteenth day after death	*Taravee*
Thirty	*Tees*
Thirty-five	*Paintees*
Thirty-four	*Cauntees*
Thirty-nine	*Untalis*
Thirty-one	*Iktees*
Thirty-seven	*Saintees*
Thirty-six	*Chattees*
Thirty-three	*Taintees*
Thirty-two	*Battees*
This	*Atad*
This much	*Itna*
This very	*Yahee*

This world	*Duniya, Ihlok*
Thorn	*Khang, Phans, Kanta*
Thorn apple	*Dhatoora*
Thorniness	*Kanteelapan*
Thornless	*Akantak*
Thorny	*Kanteela*
Thorny bush	*Nagphanee*
Thorough	*Sammyak*
Thorough beating	*Pitaee*
Thorough study	*Viloran*
Thorough test	*Janc-parakh*
Those	*Va, Un, Tin*
Though	*Halanki*
Thought	*Khayal*
Thought provoking	*Vicarotpadak*
Thoughtfully	*Vicarpoorn, Vicarpoorvak*
Thoughtfulness	*Vicarsheelta*
Thousands	*Sahastr, Hazaron*
Thrash	*Gahana*
Thread	*Soota, Dora, Taga*
(to) thread	*Pirona*
Threaded	*Cooreedar*
Threat	*Dhauns*
Three	*Teen, Trik*
Three cornered	*Tikhoonta*
Three fourth	*Paun*
Three humours of the body	*Tridosh*
Three of cards	*Tikee, Tiggee*
Three worlds	*Trilok*
Three-dimensional	*Trivim*
Three-faced	*Tinpehla*
Three-fold	*Tiguna*

Three-legged-stool	*Tipaee*
Three-storeyed	*Timanzila*
Threshing floor	*Khaliyan*
Threshold	*Dehlee*
Thrift	*Mitvyay*
Thriftiness	*Mitvyayita*
Thrifty	*Mitvyaee*
Thrill	*Sihran, Sansanahat*
Thrilled	*Pulakit, Pulakna*
Throat	*Gala, Kanth*
Throb	*Tapakna*
Throbbing	*Pharak*
Throbbing heartache	*Kasak*
Throbbing pain	*Casak, Tapak*
Thrombosis	*Shiravarodh*
Throne	*Rajgaddee, Sinhasan*
Throng	*Thatth*
Through	*Marfat*
Through the agency of	*Hasta*
Throw	*Patak*
(to) throw	*Phankna*
(to) throw down	*Patakna*
(to) throw into the blaze	*Jhonkna*
Thrown back	*Vikrisht*
Thrust in	*Ghusana*
(to) thrust into	*Ghusarna*
(to) thurst piercingly	*Hoolna*
Thud	*Dham, Phat*
Thudding	*Dhamak*
Thudding sound	*Gad, Dhardhar*
Thumb	*Angootha, Thenga*
Thumping sound	*Dhamadham*

Thunder	*Karak, Garjana*
(to) thunder	*Ghehrana*
Thunder of clouds	*Ghan-garaj*
Thundering sound	*Garjan*
Thursday	*Guruvar*
Thy	*Tera*
Thyroid gland	*Galgranthi*
Tibet	*Tibbat*
Tibetan Buddhist priest	*Lama*
Tick	*Kilnee*
Tick Parasite	*Cicra*
Ticket	*Tikat*
Ticket-checker	*Tikat parikshak, Tikat-cekar*
Ticket-window	*Tikat-khirkee*
Ticketless	*Batikat*
Tickle	*Gudgudana*
Tidiness	*Suthrapan*
Tie	*Ganthna*
(to) tie	*Bajhana*
(to) tie up	*Gathiiyana*
(to) tie with a cord	*Doriyana*
Tied	*Nibandh, Bandha*
Tied up	*Abaddh*
Tiffin	*Tifin*
Tiger	*Bagh, Vyaghr*
Tiger skin	*Baghmala, Baghambar*
Tiger-claw	*Baghnakha*
Tiger-faced	*Vyaghrmukhee*
Tight cloth	*Cust*
Tighten	*Kasna*
Tightness	*Kasavat*
Tile	*Tail, Patiya*
Till death	*Amaran*

Timber	*Kath*
Timbrel	*Toory*
Time	*Kal*
Time and again	*Bar-bar*
Time limit	*Miyad*
Time of sunset	*Pradosh*
Time-spacing	*Samayantaran*
Time-table	*Samay-Sarnee, Taim-tabul*
Timely	*Kalocit*
Timepiece	*Taim-pees*
Times	*Bar, Zamana*
Timesignal	*Samay-sankat*
Timid	*Bheeru, Boda, Kleev, Padora*
Timidity	*Bheeruta, Bodapan*
Tin	*Ranga*
Tincture	*Tincar*
Tinge of sourness	*Khatas*
Tingling sensation	*Charcharahat*
Tinkle	*Runjhun*
(to) tinkle	*Ghanghanana, Thanthanana*
(to) tinkle like bells	*Chamkana*
Tinkling	*Chanak, Ghanghanahat*
Tinkling sound	*Chamcham*
Tinned	*Dibbaband*
Tiny	*Nanha, Nikka*
Tiny block	*Gittak*
Tiny boll	*Pirkee*
Tiny whitish louse	*Leekh*
Tip	*Tip, Nok, Bakhsheesh*
Tip of the lip	*Bach*
Tip-toe	*Ujhakna*
Tired	*Thakit*
Tiredness	*Shranti*

Tireless	*Ashrant*
Tiring	*Shrantikar*
Tissue	*Ootak*
Titillation	*Gudgudee*
Title	*Khitab*
Title deed	*Kabala*
Title of honour	*Manopadhi*
Title page	*Mukhprishth*
Title-holder	*Upadhidharee*
Tittle-tattle	*Gapshap*
To	*Ko*
Tobacco	*Tambakoo*
Tobacco leaves turned into small flakes	*Surtee*
Today	*Aaj*
Toddy tree	*Tar*
Together	*Aikattr*
Toil	*Kasala, Mashakkat*
Toilsome	*Kamartor*
Token	*Pattrpushp*
Toll of a bell	*Gajar*
Toll-tax	*Margkar, Pathkar*
Tomato	*Tamatar*
Tomb	*Turbat*
Tomorrow	*Kal*
Tongue	*Jaban, Jeebh*
Tongue of gods	*Dev vanee*
Tonic	*Pushaee, Tanik, Balvardhak*
Toning up	*Balvardhan*
Tonsil	*Tansil*
Tonsure	*Coorakaran*
Too	*Ati*
Tool	*Auzar*

Tool of pesting	*Ghota*
Tooth	*Rad, Dant*
Tooth brush	*Datun*
Tooth of an elephant	*Gajdant*
Tooth-mark	*Radkshat*
Tooth-pick	*Dantkhodnee*
Tooth-powder	*Manjan*
Toothache	*Dant-peera*
Top	*Phungee*
Top position	*Sheershsthan*
Top secret of success	*Mahamantr*
Top-ranking	*Moordhanny*
Topaz	*Peetashm, Pukhraj*
Topic	*Prasang*
Topping	*Sartaj, Dhurandhar, Narpungav*
Topping person	*Shiromani*
Topsytervy	*Ulta pulta*
Torch	*Tarc, Mashal*
Torch-bearer	*Mashalcee*
Torment	*Santras*
Tormented	*Santrast*
Tormented by sex	*Kampeerit*
Torn	*Phata*
Torn and mutilated	*Kata-phata*
Torpedo	*Tarpeedo*
Torrential	*Moosaldhar*
Torrid zone	*Ushanakatibandh*
Torso	*Rund*
Tortoise	*Kacchap*
Torture	*Yantrna*
Tortures of hell	*Narak-yatna*
Toss	*Uchalna*
Total	*Yog, Jor, Total*

Total assets	*Sarmaya, Jama-poonjee*
Total eclipse	*Khagras, Sarvgras*
Total ruination	*Sattyanash*
Total war	*Samaggryuddh*
Totalitarian	*Aikdalvadee*
Totally exhausted	*Last-past*
Totally silent	*Cupka*
Totally worthless	*Nas-peeta*
Totaly unconscious	*Sangyashoony*
Touch	*Sparsh*
(to) touch	*Choona*
Touching	*Sparshee*
Touching moving	*Marmik*
Touchstone	*Nikash, Kasautee*
Tough	*Ceemar*
Tough and stout cloth	*latha*
Touring	*Paribhraman*
Touring the country	*Desh-darshan*
Tourist	*Sailanee*
Tournament	*Toornament*
Towards	*Abhi*
Towel	*Angocha, Tauliya*
Town	*Shehar, Nagar, Kasba*
Townhall	*Taunhal*
Toxicity	*Vishaktata*
Toxin	*Jaiv-vish*
Toy	*Khilauna*
Toy house	*Gharonda*
Trachoma	*Roha*
Track	*Bhookhand, Carpath, Veethee*
Tract of land	*Khita*
Traction	*Karshan*
Tractor	*Traiktar*

Trade	*Tijarat, Vyapar*
Trade union	*Mazdoor sangh*
Trade-mark	*Vyapar-cinh*
Trader	*Vanik*
Tradesman	*Vyaparee, Saudagar*
Tradesmanship	*Saudagaree*
Tradition	*Paripathee, Calava, Prampara*
Tradition of the land	*Deshacar*
Traditional	*Paramparagat, Paramparik*
Traditionalism	*Paramparavad*
Tragedy	*Hahant, Trasadee, Dukhantika*
Tragic	*Trasadik*
Tragic end	*Dukhant*
Trained	*Hunra, Prashikshit*
Trainee	*Prashikshanarthee*
Trainer	*Prashikshak*
Training	*Training, Prashikshan*
Traitorous	*Gaddar*
Traitorous conduct	*Gaddaree*
Tram car	*Tram*
Trample down	*Raundna*
Trance	*Samadhee*
Trankness in speaking	*Spashtvadita*
Tranlator	*Bhashantarkar*
Tranquil	*Prashant*
Transaction	*Sauda*
Transcript	*Anulipi*
Transcription	*Pratilakhan*
Transfer	*Tabadla, Sthanantar*
Transferability	*Hastantaraneeyta*
Transferable	*Hastantaraneey*
Transferee	*Hastantaritee*
Transference	*Sthanantaran*

Transference of power and authority	*Satantaran*
Transferred	*Sthanantarit, Hastantrit*
Transform	*Roopantar*
Transformation	*Roopantaran, Parinati*
Transformed	*Parinat*
Transfression of one's right	*Haktalfee*
Transgressor	*Atikramak*
Transient	*Anee janee*
Transit permit	*Ravana*
Transitive	*Sakarmak*
Transitiveness	*Sakarmakta*
Transitoriness	*Asthayittv*
Translation	*Anuvad, Bhashantar*
Transliteration	*Lippyantaran*
Translucence	*Parbhasakta*
Translucent	*Parbhasak*
Transmigration	*Avagaman*
Transmissibility	*Sancaransheelta*
Transmissible	*Sancaransheel, Samprashaneey*
Transmission	*Samprashan*
Transmitted	*Samprashit*
Transmitter	*Prashittr*
Transparency	*Pardarshakta*
Transparent	*Pardarshak*
Transplanting	*Ropnee*
Transport	*Parivahan*
Transportable	*Parivehneey, Vahneey*
Transposition	*Pakshantaran*
Transquillity	*Prashanti*
Transsensual	*Indriyateet*
Trap	*Phansna*

Travel	*Deshatan*
Travel-expenses	*Safar-kharc, Rah-kharc*
Traveller	*Yattree, Musafir, Paryatak*
Travelling	*Paryatan*
Traversable	*Gamneey*
Treacherous	*Kudanw*
Treacle	*Cashnee*
Treadle	*Tradil*
Treason	*Rajdroh*
Treasure	*Kosh, Khazana*
Treasurer	*Khazancee*
Treatment	*Chikitsa, Ilaj, Upcar*
Tree	*Tarvar, Taru, Vriksh, Darakht*
Tree of thick foliage	*Jhandoola*
Treeless	*Vrikshheen*
Trees of sadhus hermits	*Jata*
Trembled	*Kampit*
Tremels music	*Gitkiree*
Tremulous	*Kapayman*
Trepidation	*Dhukdhukee*
Tri-coloured	*Tiranga*
Trial	*Azmaish*
Trial of strength	*Jor-azmaee, Bal-prayog*
Triangle	*Trikon*
Triangular	*Tikona*
Tribe	*Firka, Janjati*
Tribunal	*Nyayadhikaran*
Tributary	*Sahayak nadee*
Tribute	*Khiraj*
Trick	*Kautuk*
Trickery	*Jhansa-pattee*
Trickle down	*Dhalakna*
Tricky	*Calee, Chaliya*

Trident of Lord Shiva	*Trishool*
Tried and seasoned	*Tapa-tapaya*
Triennial	*Travarshik*
Trigger	*Liblibee*
Trigonometry	*Trikonmiti*
Trio	*Tikra*
Triplicate	*Traee*
(to) triplicate	*Tehrana*
Trolley	*Thala, Tralee*
Trophy	*Vijyopahar, Vaijyantee*
Tropic of cancer	*Kark rakha*
Trot	*Dulkee*
(to) trot	*Dulakna*
Trouble	*Kasht, Takleef*
Troublesome	*Dikkat, Janjal, Jhanjhat*
Trough	*Kandal*
Trousers	*Patloon, Paint*
Trousers worn by women	*Salvar*
Truce	*Viram-sandhi*
Truck	*Trak*
True	*Satty, Sac*
True in word	*Sattyabhashee*
True to one's promise	*Akzaban*
Truly	*Sattyatah*
Trump	*Turup*
Trump card	*Vijayastr*
Trumpet	*Cingghar*
Trunk	*Trank, Dhar, Tana*
Trunk of an elephant	*Shund*
Trust	*Atbar, Bharosa, Patiyara*
(to) *Patiyana*	
Trustee	*Amanatdar, Trastee, Nyasdharee*

Trustworthy	*Vishshwasee*
Trustworthy person	*Vishshwaspatr*
Truthful	*Sacca*
Truthful by nature	*Sattyasheel*
Truthfulness	*Saccae, Saccapan, Satyasheelta*
Try	*Azmana*
Tub	*Nand, Tab*
Tube	*Tyoob, Nalee*
Tuberculosis	*Kshayrog, Tapadik*
Tubewell	*Nalkoop*
Tubular	*Nalikakar*
Tuck	*Khonsna*
Tuesday	*Mangalwar*
Tuft of hair on the crown	*Cutiya, Shikha*
Tug-of-war	*Rassakashee*
Tumbler	*Gilas*
Tummy	*Tond*
Tumour	*Rasaulee*
Tumtum	*Tamtam*
Tumult	*Kohram*
Tune	*Tarz, Tan, Lay, Rag*
Tuneful	*Sureela*
Tunnel	*Bogda, Tanel*
Turban	*Safa, Pagree*
Turbulence	*Sankshobh*
Turbulent	*Dangaee, Vikshubdh*
Turkey bird	*Tarkee*
Turmeric	*Haldee*
Turmeric species plant	*Gulbakavalee*
Turmoil	*Harbong*
Turn	*Palta, Paree, Mor, Baree*
(to) turn	*Pharna, Morna*

(to) turn about	*Palatna*
(to) turn become green	*Hariyana*
(to) turn on a lathe	*Kharadana*
(to) turn or overturn	*Ulatana palatana*
(to) turn over	*Ulatna*
Turn and twist	*Mortor*
Turn of events	*Haval*
Turned out	*Nissarit*
Turned to ashes	*Bhasmsat*
Turning bend	*Ghumaw*
Turnip	*Shaljam*
Turpentine	*Tarpeen*
Turret	*Burj, Kangoora*
Twang of a bow	*Tankar*
Twang of a bow-string	*Dhanush-tankar*
Twelve	*Barah*
Twenty	*Bees*
Twenty-eight	*Atthaees*
Twenty-five	*Pacees*
Twenty-five paisa coin	*Cavannee*
Twenty-four	*Cobees*
Twenty-nine	*Untis*
Twenty-seven	*Sattaees*
Twenty-six	*Chabbees*
Twenty-three	*Teees*
Twenty-two	*Baees*
Twig	*Kamachee*
Twilight	*Jhutputa, Sandhyalok*
Twinkling	*Jhilmil*
Twins	*Yugal, Jurvan*
Twinkle	*Timtimana*
Twist	*Ainthan, Lapat, Maror*

(to) twist	*Umathna, Ainthna, Marorna*
(to) twist a cord	*Batna*
Twisted	*Pacdar*
Two	*Do*
Two and half	*Dhaee*
Two colours	*Doranga*
Two months of the rainy season	*Savan-bhadon*
Two of cards	*Dukkee*
Two parties	*Paksh-vipaksh*
Two strings	*Dulara*
Two-dimensional	*Dvivim*
Two-faced	*Dogala, Durukha*
Two-storeyed	*Dutalla*
Type	*Bhantee, Praroop, Taip, Prakar*
Type of Indian snake	*Karait*
Typewriter	*Taipraitar*
Typhoid	*Taifayad, Motee-jhara*
Typical	*Pratiroopee*
Typist	*Taipist*
Tyrannical	*Attyacaree*
Tyranny	*Attyachar*
Tyrant	*Atatayee*

U

Udder	*Than*
Ugliness	*Kuroopta*
Ugly	*Badsoorat, Kuroop*
Ugly woman	*Dain*
Ulcer	*Phora*
Ultimate	*Antatogat*
Ultimate bliss	*Cidanand*
Ultimate good	*Parmarth*
Ultimate reality	*Cidakash*
Ultimate stage	*Carmavastha*
Ultimately	*Antatogattwa*
Ultimatum	*Altimatam*
Umarried	*Avivahit, Kwara*
Umbilical cord	*Nara*
Umbra	*Pracchaya*
Umbrella	*Chatree*
Umpire	*Nirnayak*
Unability	*Akshamta*
Unable	*Asamarth*
Unable to walk	*Pangu*
Unacceptable	*Napasand*
Unani system of medicine	*Hikmat*
Unanimity	*Mataikky*
Unanimous	*Akmat*
Unappreciative	*Bekadr*
Unarmed	*Nihattha*
Unarranged	*Atpat, Avinnyast*
Unaspirate	*Alpapran*
Unassertive	*Dabboo*
Unattached	*Alipt, Nishkarm*
Unawareness	*Bakhabree*
Unbalanced	*Asantulit*

Unbearable	*Asehneey*
Unbelievable	*Avishshwasneey*
Unbelieving	*Avishshwasee*
Unbleached cloth	*Kora, Markeen*
Unblinkingly	*Aktak*
Unborn	*Ajat, Ajanma*
Unbound	*Ajild*
Unbreakable	*Avicchaddy, Akhandneey*
Unbroken	*Atoot, Akhandit*
Unbrokenness	*Akhandta*
Uncertain	*Anishchit*
Uncertainty	*Duvidha, Sanshyatmakta*
Unchanging	*Iktan*
Uncharitable criticism	*Meen-mekh*
Unchaste woman	*Kulta, Punshcalee*
Uncivil	*Ashisht, Latthmar*
Uncivilized	*Asabbhy, Bangroo*
Uncommon	*Asadharan, Asamanny*
Uncommunicative	*Meesna*
Unconditioned	*Nirupadhi*
Unconquerable	*Ajay*
Unconquered	*Avijit*
Unconscious	*Behosh, Besudh, Acatan, Nishcasht*
Unconsciousness	*Acaitanny, Behoshee, Besudhee, Nishcashtata*
Unconstitutional	*Avaidhanik*
Uncontrollable	*Bekaboo*
Uncontrolled	*Swair, Asanyamit*
Uncovered	*Nanga, Niravaran*
Uncultivated land	*Partee*
Uncultured	*Jahil, Sanskarheen*
Undamaging	*Ahanikar*
Under compulsion	*Manbooran*

Under consideration	*Vicaradheen*
Under construction	*Nirmanadheen*
Under control	*Dabail, Vashvartee*
Under criticism	*Alochchy*
Under current	*Antardhara*
Under custody	*Hajatee*
Under inspection	*Nireekshanadheen*
Under subjection	*Paradheen*
Under-age	*Alpavyas*
Undergo	*Jhalna*
Under-mentioned	*Nimnankit*
Underground	*Bhoomigat*
Underlined	*Rakhankit*
Understand	*Samajhna Boojhna*
Undertaking	*Upakram*
Undesirable	*Avanchhaneey*
Undesirable tendency	*Dushpravritti*
Undesired	*Avanchhit*
Undeveloped	*Avikasit*
Undigested	*Anpacha*
Undisciplined	*Ucchrinkhal*
Undisturbed	*Akshubdh*
Undivided	*Avibhakt*
Undutiful Son	*Kapoot*
Uneatable	*Akhaddy*
Uneducated	*Ashikshit*
Unemotional	*Bhavheen*
Unemployed	*Berozgar*
Unequal	*Asaman*
Uneven	*Ooncha-neecha*
Unevenness	*Vishamta*
Unexpected	*Asambhavit*
Unexpectedly	*Akasmat, Baitha-baithae*

Unfailing	*Achook*
Unfailing medicine	*Ramban*
Unfair	*Dhandhlee*
Unfamiliar language	*Gitpit*
Unfamiliarity	*Ajnabipan*
Unfathomable	*Agadh*
Unfavourable	*Namuafik*
Unfit	*Nakabil*
Unforgettable	*Avismarneey*
Unfortunate	*Abhaga, Badkismat*
Unfounded	*Babuniyad*
Unfrequented	*Soona*
Unfulfilled longing	*Hirs*
Ungrateful	*Namakharam, Ehsanpharamosh*
Ungratefulness	*Akrittaggyta*
Unheard	*Ashshrut*
Unhesitatingly	*Nissankoc*
Uni-axial	*Akaksh*
Unicameral	*Aksadnee*
Unidentified	*Aceenha*
Unification	*Akeekaran*
Unified	*Akeekrit*
Uniform	*Akroop, Aksar, Vardee*
Uniformity	*Akroopta*
Unilateral	*Akanga*
Unimaginable	*Kalpanateet*
Unimagined	*Akalpit*
Unimplied	*Avivakshit*
Unimportant	*Akincit*
Unimpressive	*Prabhavheen*
Unimpressiveness	*Prabhavheenta*
Uninfatuated	*Amugdh*
Uninhabited	*Janheen*

Uninitiated	*Nigura*
Uninjured	*Akshat*
Unintelligent	*Nadan*
Uninteresting	*Neeras, Aruchikar*
Uninterrupted	*Nirvighn, Avvyahat*
Union	*Sangh, Abhisar*
Union of adjacent vowels	*Swar-sandhi*
Union of parties	*Gathbandhan*
Unionist	*Ittahadee*
Unionistic	*Aktavadee*
Unique	*Nyara, Anootha*
Uniqueness	*Addwiteeyta*
Unisexual	*Aklingee*
Unison	*Malmilap*
Unit	*Ikaee, Mattrak*
Unitary	*Matrik*
United	*Akjut, Shlisht*
United Nations	*Sanyukt rashtr*
Unity	*Akta, Ittahad*
Universal	*Sarvattrik, Vishvak, Cakkravartee*
Universality	*Sarvdashikta, Vishshwajaneenta*
Universe	*Brahmmand*
University	*Univarsitee, Vishwavidyalaya*
Unjust	*Bainsaf*
Unknowingly	*Jane anjane, Ajan, Aggeyantah*
Unlimited	*Aseemit*
Unlucky	*Badnaseeb, Amangal*
Unmannerly	*Bekayada, Bashaoor*
Unmarked	*Alakshit*
Unmarried	*Kuvara*
Unmarried girl	*Kuware*
Unmeasured	*Amapit*

Unmethodical	*Vidheeheen*
Unmethodically	*Betareh*
Unmixed	*Amishshr*
Unmoving	*Avical*
Unnatural	*Aswabhavik*
Unnecessary	*Anavashshyak*
Unobstructed	*Barok, Nishkantak*
Unoccupied	*Nikhattoo*
Unoccured	*Aghatit*
Unopened	*Munh-band*
Unopposed	*Nirvirodh*
Unorganised	*Asanghatit*
Unostentatious	*Adambarheen*
Unpaid	*Adutt*
Unparalleled	*Bemisal*
Unparliamentary	*Asansad*
Unpleasant	*Cirayandh*
Unpopular	*Alokpriy*
Unprecedented	*Abhootpoorv*
Unprincipled	*Beusool*
Unproductive	*Vandhya*
Unpunishable	*Adandneey*
Unpunished	*Adandit*
Unqualified	*Ayogy*
Unquestionable	*Ashankaneey*
Unreal	*Avastavik*
Unreal world	*Chayalok*
Unreality	*Ayatharthta*
Unrectifiable	*Amarjaneey*
Unrefined sugar	*Boora, Khand*
Unreliable	*Avishshwast*
Unrestrained	*Swairacar, Belagam, Nirankush*
Unrestricted	*Nirbaddh*

Unrhymed	*Atukant*
Unripe	*Kachcha*
Unsaid	*Akathit*
Unsalted	*Alona*
Unsatisfaction	*Atripti*
Unsatisfactory	*Asantoshjanak*
Unsatisfied	*Atript*
Unscientific	*Avaigyanik*
Unscrupulous manoeuvres	*Jor-tor*
Unseen	*Addrisht*
Unselfish	*Nihswarth*
Unsew	*Udharna*
Unskilled	*Akushal*
Unsolicited	*Ayachit*
Unstable	*Addrirh, Asthir*
Unsteadiness	*Citvikshap*
Unsteady	*Dhul mul, Capal, Cat-citta*
Unsuccessful	*Asaphal, Nakamyab*
Unsuitable	*Anupyukt*
Unsystematic	*Bedhanga*
Unsystematically	*Betareeka*
Unthinkable	*Akalpaneey, Achintaneey*
Unthinking	*Avicharee*
Unthriftiness	*Amitvyayita*
Untimely	*Asamay, Akalik, Bemauka, Bevakt*
Untimely death	*Akalmrittyu*
Untiring	*Athak*
Untouchability	*Ashrishshyta*
Untouchable	*Achoot, Asprishashy*
Untouched	*Achoota*
Untoward	*Garbar*
Untrue	*Asaty*

Untruthful	*Asattyavadee*
Unused	*Abhukt*
Unusual	*Asadharan*
Unusually tall	*Lambtarang*
Unutterable	*Nirvaccy, Akathneey*
Unveiled	*Baparda*
Unwanted	*Anchaha*
Unwavering	*Akampit*
Unwelcome	*Tok-tak*
Unwholesome	*Kupatthy*
Unworrying	*Mastana*
Unworthy	*Kupattr*
Unwritten	*Alikhit*
Up to date	*Addytan*
Upbraiding	*Phatkar*
Upheaval	*Uthal-puthal*
Uplifter	*Unnayak*
Uplifting of one-self	*Atmoddhar*
Upper class	*Uchchvarg*
Upper house	*Uchchsadan*
Upper part of the thigh	*Kach*
Upper under garment	*Baniyan*
Uppermost of a house	*Ataree*
Upraising	*Utthapan*
Uproar	*Hangama, Raula*
Uproarious	*Tumul, Oodhamee*
Uproot	*Ukharna*
(to) uproot	*Uparna*
Uprooted	*Avropit, Unmoolit*
Upto	*Tak*
Urban	*Nagar*
Urbanisation	*Nagareekaran*
Urdu poet	*Shayar*

Urdu poetry	*Shayaree*
Urgent	*Turantee*
Urge pointedly	*Tikharna*
Urinary bladder	*Moottrashay*
Urinate slowly	*Chulchulana*
Urination	*Laghushanka*
Urine	*Peshab, Mootr, Moot*
Ursa Major	*Saptarshi*
Urticaria	*Jurpittee*
Us	*Haman*
Usable	*Upyojjy*
Use	*Upyog, Istemal*
(to) use	*Baratna*
Used	*Prayukt, Vyavhrit*
Used as a suffix	*Jeevee*
Useful	*Kargar, Upyogee*
Useful for the people	*Lokopayogee*
Useful to all	*Sarvopayogee*
Useful to women	*Striyopagyogee*
Usefulness	*Upadayta*
Useless	*Bekar, Faltoo, Vyarth*
Useless talk	*Akbak, Tan-tan*
Useless thing	*Labad*
Uselessly	*Vritha*
User	*Prayokta*
Usually	*Praya, Aksar*
Usurer	*Soodkhor, Byajkhor*
Usurper all round	*Sarvhar*
Utensil-store	*Bhanrsal*
Utensils	*Basan*
Uterine	*Sahodar*
Uterine sister	*Kathbahan*
Uterus	*Bachchadani, Garbhashay*

Utility	*Upyogita*
Utter	*Uchcharnu*
Utter something inarticulately	*Gilbilana*
Utterance	*Bol, Minmin*
Utterly nervous	*Hauldil*
Uvula	*Ghantee*

V

V.P.P. (Value Payable Post)	*Vee pee*
Vacancy	*Khalee Jagah*
Vacant look	*Shoonybhav*
Vacuum	*Shoonyak*
Vagabondage	*Avargee*
Vagina	*Yoni*
Vain	*Gumanee*
Vain and false pose	*Thasak*
Vain and showy person	*Thasakdar*
Vainglorious (due to affluence)	*Mutasa*
Valiant woman	*Veerangna*
Valley	*Ghatee, Talhatee*
Valour	*Vikkram, Parakkram, Purusharth*
Valuable	*Arghy*
Valuable property	*Mal*
Valuation	*Moolyankan*
Value	*Kapatika, kaddr, Moolly*
Vampire	*Camgadar*
Vanguard	*Haraval*
Vanish away	*Urancchoo*
Vanished	*Lupt, Vilupt*
Vanishing	*Lop*
Vanity	*Garoor, Guman*
Vapour	*Bashp*
Varandah	*Baramda*
Variable	*Parivartee*
Variegated	*Rangarang, Citr-vicitra*
Variety	*Vividhta*
Variety of Indian classical dance	*Kathakalee*

Variety of Indian sweet	*Kalakand, Khaja, Gulab-jamun*
Variety of coarse grain	*Kodon*
Variety of fragrant grass	*Kapoor kachree*
Varnish	*Varnish*
Vector (Maths)	*Sadish*
Vedic hymn	*Vedmantr*
Veena	*Veena*
Vegetable	*Shak, Bhajee, Tarkaree*
Vegetable-seller	*Tarkareewala*
Vegetarian	*Niramish, Shakaharee*
Vegetarian food	*Shakahar*
Vegetation	*Vanaspati*
Vegetative	*Udbhit*
Vehicle	*Yan*
Veil	*Avgunthan, Ghoonghat, Palla, Burka*
Veiling system	*Pardadaree*
Vein	*Vahika*
Veins and muscles	*Rang-pattha*
Velvet	*Makhmal*
Venerable	*Shraddhaspad, Poojyman, Poojyvad*
Ventilation	*Sanvatan*
Ventilator	*Roshandan, Vatayan, Havakash*
Venue	*Aspad*
Venue of action	*Karmasthalee*
Verb	*Kriyapad*
Verbal	*Kriyarthak*
Verbatim	*Shabdshah*
Verbose	*Laffaz*
Verbosity	*Toomar, Lafazee*
Verification	*Sattyapan*
Verified	*Sattyapit*
Vermicelli	*Savaeen, Sivaiyan*

Vermilion	*Sindoor*
Vermilion colour	*Sindooree*
Vernal	*Vasantee*
Versatile	*Sarvatomukhee*
Versatility	*Bahuggyta*
Verse	*Paddy*
Versified	*Paddymay, Shlokbaddh*
Versifier	*Paddykar*
Versus	*Banam*
Vertical	*Udaggr, Urdhv*
Vertical swimming	*Kharee tairakee*
Vesperal evening	*Sayankaleen*
Vessel	*Bartan*
Vested	*Nihit*
Veterinary doctor	*Pashu-cikitsak*
Veterinary hospital	*Pashu Cikitsalay*
Veterinary science	*Pashu Cikitsa*
Veto	*Nishadhadhikar*
Via	*Barasta*
Vibration	*Kampan*
Vice versa	*Pratikramat*
Vice-Chairman	*Upsabhapati*
Vice-President	*Uprashtrpati*
Vice-Chancellor	*Upkulpati*
Vicinity	*Pariparshw*
Vicious	*Durgunee*
Vicious circle	*Dush cakr*
Victim of wrath	*Kopbhajan*
Victimised	*Akkshipt*
Victorious	*Vijayee, Jayant*
Victory	*Vijay, Fateh, Jay, Jeet*
Victory and defeat	*Jay-Parajay*
Victory song	*Karkha*

View	*Sammati*
View-point	*Drishtikon*
Viewed	*Drishtigat*
Vigilance	*Jagarookta*
Vigilant	*Jagarook*
Vigorous	*Ojpoorn*
Vigour	*Zora zoree*
Vile	*Dusht, Badjat*
Vilest of thieves	*Kalachor*
Village	*Dahat, Ganw, Gram*
Village industry	*Gramoddyog*
Village uplift	*Gram-sudhar*
Village-drama	*Nautankee*
Villager	*Gramvasi*
Villain	*Durjan*
Villainy	*Haramzadgee*
Vinegar	*Sirka*
Violation	*Aticar, Ullanghan*
Violation of territory	*Seemolanghan*
Violence	*Hinsa*
Violent	*Hinsak, Hinsatmak*
Violent blue gem	*Feeroza*
Violet	*Ooda, Kasnee*
Violet Blue	*Feerozee*
Violin	*Vaylin*
Viratuous	*Acharvan*
Virginity	*Kaumarry*
Virgo	*Kannyarashi*
Virile	*Veeryvan*
Virtue	*Puny*
Virtuosity	*Gunavatta*
Virtuous	*Sadgunee, Dharmatma, Punyatma*
Virtuous act	*Sukriti*

Virtuousness	*Sacarittrata*
Virus	*Anujeev, Vishanu*
Viscosity	*Shyanta, Lislisapan*
Viscous	*Cenpdar, Shyan, Lislisa*
Viscous substance	*Cenp*
Visibility	*Drishyta*
Visible	*Drishshy, Drishtigocar*
Visible irritation	*Khijlahat*
Vision	*Nigah, Beenaee*
Visitor	*Ayagaya, Abbhyagat*
Visitors' lobby	*Darshak kaksh*
Visual	*Drishyman*
Vital spot	*Marmsthal*
Vitality	*Pranvatta*
Vitamin	*Vitamin*
Vitex negundo	*Shaphalee*
Vocal music	*Kanth sangeet*
Vocation of a coolie	*Kuleegeeri*
Vocation of a shopkeeper	*Dukandaree*
Vocation of an wizard	*Ojhaee*
Vociferousness	*Mukharta*
Voice	*Avaz*
Voice of Conscience	*Antahkaran*
Voiced	*Ghosh, Mukharit*
Voiceless	*Aghosh*
Void	*Riktta*
Void of all sensation	*Sunn*
Void of sagacity	*Buddhiheen*
Volcano	*Jwalamukhee*
Volt	*Volt*
Volume	*Ayatan*

Voluntary female worker	*Sevika*
Volunteer	*Swayamsevak*
Voluptuous	*Aiyash, Vishaylolup*
Vomit	*Ugalna*
(to) vomit	*Okna, Dankna*
Vomiting	*Ultee*
Vomiting tendency	*Ubak*
Voracious writer	*Likkhar*
Voter	*Votar, Matdata*
Voting	*Matdan*
Voucher	*Pramanak*
Vow of offering	*Manautee*
Vow of silence	*Maunvrat*
Vowel	*Svar*
Vowing all-life celibacy	*Naishthik*
Voyage	*Jal yatra, Samudr-yatra*
Vulgar	*Hoosh*
Vulgarity	*Hooshpan*
Vulture	*Geedh, Giddh*
Vulva	*Bhag*

W

Wager	*Pan*
Wages	*Mazdooree*
Waggery	*Thathebazee*
Wagtail	*Khanjan*
Wail	*Bisoorna*
Waist	*Kamar, Kati*
Waist-coat	*Vaskat*
Wait	*Intzar, Prateeksha*
(to) wait	*Bilapna*
Waiting room	*Musafirkhana, Prateekshalay*
Wake up	*Jagna*
Wakefulness	*Sajagta*
Walk-out	*Bahirgaman, Sadan tyag, Sabhatyag*
Walking	*Paidal*
Wall	*Deevar, Bhitti*
Wander about	*Bhatakna*
Wandering	*Ghumakkar, Ramta*
(to) wandering	*Matargashtee*
Wandering mendicant	*Pravrajak*
Wandering yogi	*Ramta-jogee*
Want	*Tangee*
War	*Yuddh, Ran, Jang, Yuddh*
Warble	*Cehcahana*
War of words	*Vagyuddh*
War policy	*Yuddhneeti*
War-monger	*Jangbaz*
War-mongering	*Jangbazee*
War-ship	*Yuddhpot, Samar-pot*
Warapper	*Bathan*
Warbling of birds	*Ceen-ceen*
Warchariot	*Syandan*
Ward	*Vard*

Warden	*Vardan*
Warm cloth	*Garam kapra*
Warm enthusiasm	*Caw*
Warm-hearted	*Sahriday*
Warmth	*Garmahat*
Warn	*Tarajna*
Warned	*Agah*
Warning	*Catavanee*
Warp and woof	*Tana-bana*
Warrant	*Adhipatr, Parvana, Varant*
Warrior	*Yoddha, Soorma*
Was	*Tha*
Wash	*Dhona, Pakharna*
Washed	*Kshalit, Prakshalit*
Washer man	*Dhobee*
Washer woman	*Dhobin*
Washing	*Dhona*
Washing and bathing	*Nahana-dhona*
Washing place	*Dhobeeghat*
Wasp	*Bhir, Barr, Tataiya*
Wasteful	*Ganvaoo*
Wasting leprosy	*Galit kushth*
Watch	*Gharee*
Watch man	*Pehredar, Caukeedar, Rakhvala, Santaree*
Watchful	*Chaukas*
Watchmanship	*Pehradaree*
Water	*Jal, Pani*
Water of Ganga	*Gangajal*
Water pipe	*Bamba*
Water proof	*Jalseh*
Water vessel	*Lota*
Water way	*Jalmarg, Jalpath*

Water-booth	*Pyaoo*
Water-born	*Varij*
Water-carrier	*Bhishtee, Kahar, Panihar*
Water-clock	*Jalgharee*
Water-colour	*Jalrang*
Water-fall	*Jalprapat, Prapat, Nirjhar*
Water-flow	*Jalpravah*
Water-fowl	*Murgabee*
Water-hole	*Jalgart*
Water-jar	*Alinjar*
Water-lily	*Kueen, Kumudinee*
Water-lval	*Jalstar*
Water-mark	*Jalank, Jal-cihn*
Water-melon	*Tarbooj*
Water-mill	*Pancakkee*
Water-nymph	*Jalparee*
Water-pool	*Jalashay, Jalkund*
Water-snake	*Didibh*
Water-spout	*Jalstamph*
Water-spring	*Jalsrot*
Water-tax	*Jalkar*
Waterless	*Jalheen*
Watery grave	*Jalsamadhi*
Wave	*Hilor, Lahar, Kallol, Tarang*
(to) wave	*Lehrana*
Waver	*Dagmagana*
Wavering	*Dagmagahat*
Wavy	*Tarangit, Lahardar*
Wavy border	*Katvan*
Wavy line	*Lahariya*
Wax	*Mom*
Way	*Panth, Taur*
Way of dealing	*Ravaiya*

Way of twing	*Jeevan-kram*
Wayfarer	*Rahee, Rahgeer, Rahcalta*
Waylaying	*Batmaree*
Ways	*Cal-dhal*
We	*Ham*
Weak	*Kamzor, Durbal, Lacar, Nirbal*
Weak-hearted	*Kachdila*
Weakness	*Nirbalta, Kamzoree*
Wealth	*Dhan, Sampada, Daulat, Sampatti*
Wealthiness	*Ameeree*
Wealthy	*Daulatmand, Maldar, Raees, Sampattivan*
Wealthy person	*Sahookar, Sath, Dhannasath, Sahoo*
Weapon	*Hathiyar, Astr*
Wear and tear	*Ghisan*
Wearied	*Shrant*
Weariness	*klanti*
Weary and exhausted	*Thaka-manda*
Weaver	*Julaha, Bunkar*
Weave	*Binna, Bunna*
Weaver's shuttle	*Dharkee*
Weaver's tool	*Rach*
Weaver-bird	*Baya*
Web of worldly attachment	*Mayajal*
Wed	*Byahna*
Wedge	*Saila*
Wedged chip	*Pancar*
Wednesday	*Budhwar*
Weed our	*Cikhurna*
Weeding hook	*Khurpa*
Week	*Saptah, Hafta*
Week-end	*Saptahant*

Weekly *Saptahik, Haftavar*
Weep *Rona*
Weep bitterly *Phaphakna*
Weeping *Rudan, Rulaee*
Weigh *Jokhna, Tolna, Taulna*
Weigh the pro and cons *Socna-samajhna*
Weighed *Tulit*
Weighing scale *Tarazoo*
Weighment *Nap-taul*
Weight *Vajan, Tol, Taul, Bat*
Weight substitute *Dhara*
Weighty *Vajandar*
Welcome address *Abhinandanpatr*
Welcome effect *Suprabhav*
Welcome stranger *Samagat*
Welcomed *Abhinandit*
Welfare *Kushal mangal, Kushal-ksham*
Welfare tidings *Kushal samachar*
Well *Koop, Kuan*
Well done *Khoob, Shabash*
Well of life *Bhavkoop*
Well wishing *Khairkhah*
Well-advised *Sumantrit*
Well-arranged *Suvvyavasthit*
Well-behaved *Susheel*
Well-being *Ksham, Shivattw*
Well-built *Paripusht, Sughar, Sugathit*
Well-considered *Suvicarit*
Well-cultured *Susanskrit*
Well-decorated *Susajjit*
Well-deserving person *Supatr*
Well-instructed *Seekha-para*
Well-known *Suvidit, Neknamee, Vikhyat*

Well-meaning	*Sadashayee*
Well-mentioned	*Sadashay*
Well-off	*Khushhal*
Well-poised	*Susthir*
Well-protected	*Surakshit*
Well-reputed	*Suvikhyat, Supratishthit*
Well-said	*Subhashit*
Well-situated	*Susthit*
Well-trimmed	*Mukatta*
Well-versed	*Seekha sikhaya, Vatta, Parangat*
Well-wisher	*Hitaishee, Hitcintak, Shubhcintak*
Well-wishing	*Hitcintan*
West	*Pashcim*
Westernization	*Pashcattyeekaran*
Wet	*Geela, Tar*
Wet-nurse	*Dhay, Dhattree*
Wetness	*Geelapan*
What	*Kya*
What a shame	*Toba toba*
What sort	*Kaisa*
Wheat	*Kanak, Gehoon*
Wheatish	*Gehuna*
Wheedle	*Phuslana*
Wheel	*Pahiya, Cakka, Cakr*
Wheel of repression	*Damancakr*
Wheel of time	*Kalchakr*
Wheeze	*Ghargharana*
When	*Kab, Jab*
Where	*Jidhar*
Where abouts	*Gharghat, Thaur-thikana*
Whetstone	*San, Sillee*
Which	*Tis, Kim, Jis*
While	*Jabki*

Whim	*Sanak*
Whimper	*Thunakna*
Whimsical	*Aujhar, Lehree*
Whip	*Hantar, Kora, Sacetak*
Whirlpool	*Jalavart*
Whirlwind	*Vatcakr, Baboola*
Whisk	*Canvar*
Whiskered	*Mucchal, Muchandar*
Whiskers	*Galmuccha*
Whisper	*Phusphus*
(to) whisper	*Phusphusana*
Whispering	*Kanaphoosee*
Whispering rumour	*Sungun*
Whispering sound	*Phusphuṣahat*
Whistle	*Seetee*
White	*Shwet, Citta, Ujla*
White antelope	*Gavay*
White paper	*Shwetpattr*
White wash	*Potna*
White washer	*Kalaeegar*
White-complexioned damsel	*Goree*
Whiteness	*Safedee, Ujlapan*
Whitewashing	*Putaee*
Whitish soil for cleansing purposes	*Rakh*
Whitlow	*Galka*
Who	*Kaun, Jo*
Who holds	*Dharee*
Who interferes	*Dastandaz*
Who retaliates	*Pratihinsak*
Who seeks forgiveness	*Kshamaprarthee*
Who seeks interview	*Sakshatkaree*

Who speaks bitterly	*Katubhashee*
Who supports the poor	*Gareebparvar*
Whole	*Samooca, Sara, Sabut*
Whole-time	*Poornkalik*
Wholesale	*Thok*
Wholesale market	*Dareeba*
Wholesale mess	*Garbar ghotala*
Wholesaler	*Thok-vikkrata*
Wholly	*Sarasar, Sangopang*
Whom	*Kinhan*
(to) whom	*Kisa*
Whooping cough	*Dhansee, Kalee khansee*
Whose husband is alive	*Sadhwa, Saubhaggyavatee*
Why	*Kyon*
Wick	*Batee*
Wicked	*Duratma, Kubuddhi*
Wicked person	*Lucca*
Wicked son	*Kuputr*
Wickedness	*Pajeepan, Durjanta, Khotapan*
Wicker-basket	*Daliya*
Wicker-box	*Pitara*
Wide	*Caura, Prithu*
Wide tumbler	*Tamlot*
Widely informed	*Bahushrut*
Widow	*Vidhwa, Beva*
Widow hood	*Vaidhavvy, Vidhwapan*
Widow since childhood	*Balvidhva*
Widower	*Randua*
Widows home	*Vidhvashshram*
Width of a cloth	*Pana*
Wife	*Joroo, Lugaee, Beevee, Patnee, Gharvalee*

Wife of Lord Shiva	*Gauree*
Wife of a Brahman	*Brahmmanee, Panditanee*
Wife of a deity or celestial damsel	*Devangana*
Wife of a dom.	*Domnee*
Wife of a gardener	*Malin*
Wife of an oilman	*Talin*
Wife of father's elder brother	*Taee*
Wife of husband's elder brother	*Jeethanee*
Wife of husband's younger brother	*Devranee*
Wife of perceptor	*Guruanee*
Wife of wife's brother	*Salhaj*
Wife's brother	*Sala*
Wife's sister	*Salee*
Wighing	*Jokh*
Wighty	*Jandar*
Wild	*Sehraee, Banaila*
Wild beast	*Bancar*
Wild boar	*Varah*
Wild buffalo	*Arna*
Wild plum	*Jharbaree*
Wild with emotion	*Bhavonmatt*
Wilderness	*Biyaban*
Wildly	*Batahasha*
Wilful conduct	*Swacchakar*
Wilfully	*Kasdan, Iradatan*
Wilfulness	*Swacchakarita*
Will	*Vaseeyat, Iccha patr*
Will power	*Atmshakti*
Win	*Jeetna*

Wind	*Hava, Pavan*
Wind furnace	*Pavan bhattee*
Wind mill	*Pavan cakkee, Havaee-cakkee*
Winding	*Ghumawdar*
Window	*Khirkee, Jharokha*
Window or door shade	*Jhanp*
Windstorm	*Andhee*
Wine	*Asav, Daroo, Madira, Sura*
Wine drinking house	*Madhushala*
Wine-cup	*Zam*
Wine-maid	*Madhubala*
Wing of a bird	*Daina*
Winged	*Dainadar*
Wink	*Jhapakna, Jhapna*
Wink the eyes over and again	*Mickana*
Winking	*Nimeelan*
Winking of the eyes	*Micakna*
Winnow	*Osana, Pachorna, Phatakna*
Winnowing basket	*Chaj*
Winter	*Jara*
Winter solstice	*Dakshinayan*
Wintry	*Sheetkaleen*
Wire	*Tar*
Wire gauze	*Tarjalee*
Wireless	*Batar*
Wisdom	*Buddhimata, Akl, Sujanta, Buddhimani*
Wise	*Aklmand, Buddhiman*
Wise man	*Maneeshee, Vibuddh*
Wish	*Marzee, Iccha*
Wishful thinking	*Manmodak*
Wit and humour	*Hansee dillagee*

Witch	*Dakini*
With	*Poorvak, Samat*
With a happy ending	*Sukhant*
With a liberal yield of milk	*Dudhail*
With a lingling sound	*Chanachan*
With a purpose	*Sabhipray*
With alliteration	*Sanupras*
With animates and inanimates	*Sacaracar*
With attendents	*Saparikar*
With clipped moustache	*Muchkata*
With due care	*Yatnpoorvak*
With due insistence	*Aggrahpoorvak*
With due observance of the conjugal tie	*Gathjora*
With family	*Saparivar*
With love	*Sasnah*
With pride	*Sabhiman*
With respect	*Sadar*
Withered	*Jhurkut*
Within the reach of senses	*Gochar*
Without	*Bgair, Nir, Bila, Viheen*
Without any desire	*Nirabhilash*
Without any merits	*Vigun*
Without any obstruction	*Berok-tok*
Without any reason	*Khamakhah, Jhooth mooth, Bevajeh*
Without any substance	*Phokat*
Without attributes	*Nirgun*
Without blinking	*Nirnimash*

Without cause	*Nishkaran*
Without collyrium	*Niranjan, Besabab*
Without delay	*Avilamb*
Without dispute	*Nirdwandw*
Without doubt	*Zaroor-Zaroor*
Without enthusiasm	*Nirutsah*
Without exception	*Nirapvad*
Without feathers	*Bapar*
Without fee	*Nihshulk*
Without gap	*Benaga, Niravkash*
Without hair	*Vikac*
Without leaves	*Viparn, Nipattr*
Without love	*Nissnah*
Without name	*Benam*
Without order	*Kramheen*
Without precedent	*Benazeer*
Without pride	*Nirbhiman*
Without purpose	*Bematlab*
Without seeds	*Bedana*
Without shelter	*Ashshrayheen*
Without sorrow	*Ashok*
Without support	*Niralamb*
Witness	*Sakshee, Gavah*
Witness box	*Katghara*
Witticism	*Lateefa*
Witty	*Vyutpannmati*
Wizard	*Ojha*
Wolf	*Harha, Bhariya*
Woman	*Aurat, Naree*
Woman attendant	*Kaneez*
Woman dancer	*Nacnee*
Woman having a graceful gait	*Gazgamini*

Woman having eyes like lotus	*Kamalnaynee*
Woman having no issue	*Nipootee*
Woman in her menstrual period	*Rajasswala*
Woman leader	*Nettree*
Woman of good fortune	*Saubhaggyashalinee*
Woman of loosing morals	*Swacchandcarinee*
Woman sharper	*Chappan churi*
Woman social worker	*Samaj-savika*
Woman swindler	*Thagnee*
Woman who practises black magic	*Tonhee*
Woman who sells grass	*Ghasiyarin*
Woman writer	*Lakhika*
Woman's shawl	*Orhnee*
Womanhood	*Streetv*
Womanishness	*Jananapan*
Womanising	*Lugaeebazee*
Womanizer	*Lugaeebaz*
Womb	*Kukshi, Garbh*
Women's world	*Naree jagat*
Wonder	*Aashcary, Ajooba*
Wonderful	*Adbhut, Ashcarykarak*
Wonderment	*Hairat, Camatkriti*
Wonderstruc	*Camatkrit*
Wonderstruck	*Ashcarycakit*
Wont	*Tav*
Wood	*Lakree*
Wood Industry	*Kashth uddyog*
Wood of apple tree	*Vilw*

Wood-craft	*Kashthkala*
Wood-like	*Katha*
Wood-pecker	*Kathphora, Lakar-phora*
Wooden board	*Pattee*
Wooden hammer	*Mungra*
Wooden ladle	*Doee*
Wooden plank	*Pata*
Wooden pot	*Ookhal*
Wooden sandal	*Kharaoon*
Wooden slippers	*Cattee*
Wooden tub	*Kathauta*
Woodlands	*Vanasthalee*
Woodman	*Lakarhara*
Woods	*Vipin*
Woolen	*Oonee*
Woollen shawl	*Loee*
Woprdy quarrel	*Jhanw-jhanw*
Word	*Lafj*
Word meaning	*Shabdarth*
Word power	*Shabdshakti*
Word-trap	*Shabdjal*
Wordly	*Sansarik, Sansaree*
Wordly affairs	*Prapanc*
Wordly wisdom	*Duniyasazee*
Wordy altercation	*Kaha-sunee*
Wordy duel	*Jharap*
Wordy encounter	*Nok-jhonk*
Wordy etiquette	*Shishtacaree*
Wordy play	*Shabdadambar*
Work	*Kaj, Kriti*
Worker	*Karyakarta, Karinda*
Working	*Kajee*
Working committee	*Kary samiti*

Working day	*Karydivas*
Working plan	*Davarh*
Workshop	*Kary shala, Karm shala*
World	*Vishw, Lok, Duniya, Jahan, Jagat, Sansar*
World of Imagination	*Kalpanalok*
World of living beings	*Jeevlok*
World of manes	*Pitrilok*
World of reality	*Vastujagat*
Worldliness	*Duniyadaree, Sansarikta*
Worldly	*Jagatik, Duniyadar*
Worldly wise	*Duniyasaz*
Worm	*Keera, Pilloo, Kansalaee*
Worn out	*Jeern, Shikasta*
Worn-out vehicle	*Chakra*
Worried	*Cintagrast*
Worry	*Cinta*
Worship	*Bhajan poojan, Pooja, Upasana, Aradhana*
Worship of beauty	*Husnparastee*
Worship of gods	*Davopasana*
Worship of Shakti	*Shakti-pooja*
Worshipped	*Poojit*
Worshipper	*Poojak, Aradhak*
Worth being published	*Prakashneey*
Worth communicating	*Soocaneey*
Worth consideration	*Vicarneey*
Worth exploiting	*Shoshaneey*
Worth knowing	*Vigyay, Gyatavy*
Worth seeing	*Vilokneey, Drashtavy*
Worthless	*Nikamma, Nalayak, Nakara*
Worthless object	*Theekree*
Worthlessness	*Nalayakee*

Worthy preceptor	*Sadguru*
Worthy son	*Sapoot*
Wound	*Vran, Ghaw, Jakhm*
Wounded	*Zakhmee, Kshat*
Wounded and dismembered	*Kshat-vikshat*
Wrapped	*Vashtit*
Wrath	*Amarsh, Taish*
Wreathe	*Gumphna*
Wreath of bones	*Haraval*
Wreath of green leaves	*Vandanvar*
Wreathed	*Gumphit*
Wrench	*Rinc*
Wrestler	*Pehalvan, Kushteebaz*
Wrestling	*Pehalvanee*
Wrestling bout	*Dangal, Kushtee, Mallyuddh*
Wrestling ground	*Akhara, Mallbhoomi, Mallshal*
Wrigging	*Kulbulahat*
Wriggle	*Bilbilana*
Wrinkle	*Sikuran, Jhurree*
Wrist	*Kalaee, Pahunca*
Wrist-watch	*Kalaee gharee*
Writ of mandamus	*Parmadesh*
Writ petition	*Samadesh-yacika*
Write	Likhna
Writer	*Lekhek*
Writer of a book	*Pustakkar, Granthkar*
Writing	*Likhat*
Writing pad	*Pattrikavlee*
Written	*Likhit, Likha, Annkit*
Written agreement	*Sarkhat, Karar nama*
Written award	*Pancnama*
Written deed	*Likhat-parhat*

Written order	*Hukmnama, Aggyapti*
Written passage	*Ibarat*
Written pledge	*Pratigyapatr*
Written preliminary sketch	*Masauda*
Written proof	*Kagazee sabut*
Wrong	*Galat*
Wrong motive	*Kubhav*
Wrong path	*Vipath*
Wrong spot	*Kuthanw*
Wrong way	*Kupath*
Wrongful effort	*Kucash*

X

Xylophone	*Jaltarang*

Y

Yak	*Suragay, Neelgay*
Yam	*Zameekand*
Yamuna river	*Tarnija*
Yardstick	*Gaz*
Yarn spindle	*Khukhree*
Yawn	*Ubasi, Jambhaee*
(to) yawn	*Jambakoo*
Yawning	*Garappa*
Year	*Sal, Baras, Varsh*
Year before last	*Pariyar sal*
Yearly	*Salana*
Yellow	*Peela, Basantee*
Yellow clay	*Peelee-mittee*
Yellow cloth	*Peetambar*
Yellow ochre	*Ramraj*
Yellowness	*Peelapan*
Yes	*Han*
Yet	*Tathapi*
Yog	*Padmasan*
Yogi	*Yogee*
You	*Tujhe, Tum*
Young	*Balee*
Young age	*Alpavastha*
Young boy	*Yuvak*
Young girl	*Yuvtee*
Young man	*Yuva*

Young of a snake	*Sapola*
Young shootlet	*Gopha*
Young woman	*Tarunee*
Younger brother	*Anuj*
Your excellency	*Maha Mahim*
Your honour	*Mahasya*
Yours	*Tumhara*
Yours faithfully	*Bhavdeey*
Yourself	*Swayam*
Youth	*Gabroo, Yauvan, Javanee, Yuvavastha*
Youthfully brave	*Javanmard*

Z

Zeal	*Zom*
Zeal and enthusiasm	*Sargarmee*
Zealous	*Josheela*
Zenith	*Urdhvbindu*
Zero	*Sifar, Sunya*
Zinc	*Jasta*
Zodiac	*Rashicakkr*
Zonal Officer	*Mandal adhikaree*
Zone	*Mandal*
Zoo	*Ciriyaghar*